MY BOOKY WOOK

MY BOOKY WOOK

Russell Brand

HODDER &
STOUGHTON

First published in Great Britain in 2007 by Hodder & Stoughton
An Hachette Livre UK company

1

Copyright © Russell Brand 2007

The right of Russell Brand to be identified as the Author
of the Work has been asserted by him in accordance
with the Copyright, Designs and Patents Act 1988.

Some names and identities have been changed to protect the privacy of the individuals involved.

A CIP catalogue record for this title is available from the British Library.

Hardback ISBN 978 0 340 93615 3
Trade Paperback ISBN 978 0340 93616 0

Typeset in Jenson by Hewer Text UK Ltd, Edinburgh
Printed and bound by Clays Ltd, St Ives plc

Hodder & Stoughton policy is to use papers that are natural,
renewable and recyclable products and made from wood grown in
sustainable forests. The logging and manufacturing processes are expected
to conform to the environmental regulations of the country of origin.

Hodder & Stoughton Ltd
338 Euston Road
London NW1 3BH

www.hodder.co.uk

For my mum,
the most important woman in my life,
this book is dedicated to you.
Now for God's sake don't read it.

'The line between good and evil runs not through states, nor between classes, nor between political parties either, but through every human heart'

Alexander Solzhenitsyn, *The Gulag Archipelago*

'Mary: Tell me, Edmund: Do you have someone special in your life?
Edmund: Well, yes, as a matter of fact, I do.
Mary: Who?
Edmund: Me.
Mary: No, I mean someone you love, cherish and want to keep safe from all the horror and the hurt.
Edmund: Erm . . . Still me, really'

Richard Curtis and Ben Elton,
Blackadder Goes Forth

Contents

Part III

Part IV

Part I

'And that I walk thus proudly crowned withal
Is that 'tis my distinction; if I fall,
I shall not weep out of the vital day,
To-morrow dust, nor wear a dull decay'

Percy Bysshe Shelley,
'And That I Walk Thus
Proudly Crowned Withal'

'When I was small and five
I found a pencil sharpener alive!
He lay in lonely grasses
Looking for work.
I bought a pencil for him.
He ate and ate until all that was
Left was a pile of wood dust.
It was the happiest pencil sharpener
I ever had'

Spike Milligan, '2B or not 2B'

1

April Fool

On the morning of April Fools' Day, 2005, I woke up in a sexual addiction treatment centre in a suburb of Philadelphia. As I limped out of the drab dog's bed in which I was expected to sleep for the next thirty wankless nights, I observed the previous incumbent had left a thread of unravelled dental floss by the pillow – most likely as a noose for his poor, famished dinkle.

When I'd arrived the day before, the counsellors had taken away my copy of the *Guardian*, as there was a depiction of the Venus de Milo on the front page of the Culture section, but let me keep the *Sun*, which obviously had a page 3 lovely. What kind of pervert police force censors a truncated sculpture but lets Keeley Hazell pass without question? 'Blimey, this devious swine's got a picture of a concrete bird with no arms – hanging's too good for him, to the incinerator! Keep that picture of stunner Keeley though.' If they were to censor London Town they would ignore Soho but think that the statue of Alison Lapper in Trafalgar Square had been commissioned by Caligula.

Being all holed up in the aptly named KeyStone clinic (while the facility did not have its own uniformed police force, the suggestion of bungling silent film cops is appropriate) was an all too familiar drag. Not that I'd ever been incarcerated in sex chokey before, lord no, but it was the umpteenth time that I'd been confronted with the galling reality that there are things over which I have no control and people who can force their will upon you. Teachers, sex police, actual police, drug counsellors; people who can make you sit in a drugless, sexless cell either real or metaphorical and ponder the actuality of life's solitary essence. In the end it's just you. Alone.

Who needs that grim reality stuffed into their noggin of a morning? Not me. I couldn't even distract myself with a wank over that gorgeous slag Venus de Milo; well, she's asking for it, going out all nude, not even wearing any arms.

The necessity for harsh self-assessment and acceptance of death's inevitability wasn't the only thing I hated about that KeyStone place. No, those two troubling factors vied for supremacy with multitudinous bastard truths. I hated my fucking bed: the mattress was sponge, and you had to stretch your own sheet over this miserable little single divan in the corner of the room. And I hated the fucking room itself where the strangled urges of onanism clung to the walls like mildew. I particularly hated the American grey squirrels that were running around outside – just free, like idiots, giggling and touching each other in the early spring sunshine. The triumph of these little divs over our indigenous, noble, red, British squirrel had become a searing metaphor for my own subjugation at the hands of the anti-fuck-Yanks. To make my surrender to conformity more official I was obliged to sign this thing (opposite).

I wish I'd been photographed signing it like when a footballer joins a new team grinning and holding a pen. Or that I'd got an attorney to go through it with a fine-tooth comb: 'You're gonna have to remove that no bumming clause,' I imagine him saying. Most likely you're right curious as to why a fella who plainly enjoys how's yer father as much as I do would go on a special holiday to 'sex camp' (which is a misleading title as the main

Extended Care Unit
The Center for Healing from
Sexual Compulsivity and Trauma

UHS KeyStone Recovery Center-Extended Care Unit

Celibacy Contract

In admitting myself to the ECU, I have admitted to the staff and myself that I have become powerless over my sexual behavior.

In order to start recovery and maximize my treatment program, I agree to abide by the conditions of this contract.

CONDITIONS:
- NO MASTURBATION
- NO SEDUCTIVE BEHAVIOR
- NO PORNOGRAPHIC MATERIAL
- NO SEXUAL CONTACT WITH ANOTHER PERSON
- REPORT SEXUAL FANTASIZING TO APPROPRIATE STAFF AND PEERS

The purpose of this contract is to help remove sexually-dependent behaviors, cope with fantasy and help me back to future healthy sexuality.

Adherence to this contract may result in a recall of many childhood memories. Anxiety will probably increase, as I will be unable to use sexual behavior as a coping mechanism. The staff is here to assist me, and is aware of reactions to celibacy; they are here for my support.

With this contract, for the benefit of my recovery, I am choosing to not allow myself the legal and human right to conjugal visitation.

The contract is in effect for 12 weeks for addicts and length of program stay for co-addicts.

_____   31/03/05
Resident Signature   Date

_____   3·31·05
Staff Witness Signature   Date

****

I have read the above Celibacy Contract. I agree to the above for my loved one, and I will provide support.

_____   _____
Significant Other Signature   Date

2000 Providence Avenue
Chester, PA 19013
(610)876-8448 · (800)733-6840
fax (610)876-2217

thrust of their creed is 'no fucking'). The short answer is I was forced. The long answer is this . . .

Many people are sceptical about the idea of what I like to call 'sexy addiction', thinking it a spurious notion, invented primarily to help Hollywood film stars evade responsibility for their unrestrained priapic excesses. But I reckon there is such a thing.

Addiction, by definition, is a compulsive behaviour that you cannot control or relinquish, in spite of its destructive consequences. And if the story I am about to recount proves nothing else, it demonstrates that this formula can be applied to sex just as easily as it can be to drugs or alcohol.

Having successfully rid myself, one day at a time, in my twenties, of parallel addictions to the ol' drugs and drinks – if you pluralise drink to drinks and then discuss it with the trembling reverence that alcoholics tend to, it's funny, e.g. 'My life was destroyed by drinks', 'I valued drinks over my wife and kids'. Drinks! I imagine them all lined up in bottles and glasses with malevolent intent, the bastards – I was now, at this time, doing a lot of monkey business.

I have always accrued status and validation through my indiscretions (even before I attained the unique accolade of 'Shagger of the Year' from the *Sun* – not perhaps the greatest testimonial to the good work they do at KeyStone), but sex is also recreational for me. We all need something to help us unwind at the end of the day. You might have a glass of wine, or a joint, or a big delicious blob of heroin to silence your silly brainbox of its witterings, but there has to be some form of punctuation, or life just seems utterly relentless.

And this is what sex provides for me – a breathing space, when you're outside of yourself and your own head. Especially in the actual moment of climax, where you literally go, 'Ah, there's that, then. I've unwound. I've let go.' Not without good reason do the French describe an orgasm as a 'little death'. That's exactly what it is for me (in a good way though, obviously) – a little moment away, a holiday from my head. I hope death is like a big French orgasm, although meeting Saint

Peter will be embarrassing, all smothered in grog and shrouded in post-orgasmic guilt.

Part of my problem was that these holidays – incessant as they were – no longer seemed to have the required calming effect. I suppose if you kept frantically scuttling off to Pontin's every half-hour and ejaculating in the swimming pool then it'd become depressing after a while. At the time, I was on the brink of becoming sufficiently well known for my carnal overindulgences to cause me professional difficulties. My manager, John Noel, of whom you'll learn more later but for now think of as a big, kind, lovely, vicious bastard, like a Darth Vader from Manchester running a school for disadvantaged children; John, who had previously successfully forced me into drug rehabilitation, thought a little stretch in winky-nick would do me the power of good, and used threats, bullying, love and blackmail to make me go.

They don't go in for the pampering of clients at John Noel Management. Even now, with my own TV production company, radio show, parts in films, DVD and stand-up tour, I still don't have 'yes' men surrounding me, I have 'fuck off' men. I suppose I ought to be grateful to have such close relationships with the people I work with – John, Nik, who's John's son and brilliant in his own right, and Matt and Gee from the Radio 2 show. They all seem to be dedicated not only to the fulfilment of professional objectives, but also to anchoring me to a terrain where my ego is manageable.

And so it was spitefully decided not to send me to some sort of celebrity treatment centre, like the world-renowned Meadows Clinic in Arizona, because that's not the style of John Noel and the other stewards of my wellbeing. Instead, they insisted I should go to a facility where not all the places were private, where a certain proportion of people were there on judicial programmes

– 'jail-swerves' they call them, when you're a drug addict and you're offered a choice of prison or rehab. The same option exists for the terminally saucy – get treatment or go to prison; in prison there'll be much more sex but it could err on the side of coercive.

The nature of my early sexual encounters, which will be outlined in the pages to follow, had unravelled any mystique or sentimentality around my sexuality, and made it something quite raw and rude. But I'm fortunate in that there's nothing especially peculiar or odd about my erotic predilections. It's the scale of my sexual endeavours that causes the problems, not the nature of them.

I just like girls, all different ones, in an unsophisticated, unevolved way, like a *Sun* reader or a yobbo at a bus stop in Basildon, perhaps because, at my core, that's what I am. I'm a bloke from Grays with a good job and a terrific haircut who's been given a Wonka ticket to a lovely sex factory 'cos of the ol' fame, and while Augustus Gloop drowns and Veruca Salt goes blue, I'm cleaning up, I'm rinsin' it baby!

To this day, I feel a fierce warmth for women that have the same disregard for the social conventions of sexual protocol as I do. I love it when I meet a woman and her sexuality is dancing across her face, so it's apparent that all we need to do is nod and find a cupboard.

So anyway, I didn't want to go to that sexual treatment centre, but all the do-gooders – and I mean that literally, as they did generally do good (I've never really understood why people employ that term pejoratively) – they all insisted, and I sort of, kind of agreed. Just to shut everyone up, really, and for the same reason that I finally gave up drink and drugs – because my ambition is the most powerful force within me, so once people convinced me that my sexual behaviour might become damaging to my career, I found it easier to think of it as a flaw that needed to be remedied.

I wasn't properly famous at this point. But I'd done a couple of *Big Brothers*, and was starting to become a more recognisable figure. It was just before I started to dress cool (Collins defines cool as 'Worzel Gummidge dressed for a bondage party') – at this stage I was still kitting myself out in tight jeans and t-shirts, like a kind of urban beach-bum. And it was in just such casual, relaxed attire that I made my way – on my own – first to Heathrow airport, then to Philadelphia, and then to the KeyStone Center.

The physical process of getting there was one of the most ridicu-*larse* journeys of my life. It felt strange to be chatting up the air hostesses on the American Airlines flight, knowing that I was on my way to a residential treatment centre for sexual addiction. I got off the plane at Philadelphia airport, looked around at all the girls in the terminus and thought, 'Well, this is weird,' and then got in the back of the cab. They took me to the general hospital first – this terrifying all-American institution (which I was all too soon to revisit under circumstances that'll bend your bones and shrivel your baby-makers) – before realising it was this KeyStone place I was meant to be going to.

I had no idea of what to expect when I arrived. I'd spoken to one of the counsellors – the reassuringly named Travis Flowers (counsellors, in my experience, seem to be named using the Charles Dickens method, where the character's name gives a very obvious clue to their nature: Bill Sykes, psycho, Mr Bumble, bumbling, Fagin, an unforgivable anti-Semitic stereotype). The gentleman who saved me from the brown fangs of smack addiction was preposterously called Chip Somers, chipper summers, like an upbeat holiday. I spoke to Travis – whose name indicates trust and growth – several times on the phone before setting out. I told him about the lack of control I was exercising over who I was having sex with. It was a right lot of nonsense going on. I was pursuing hanky-panky like it was a job, like there was a league table that I had to be at the summit of. And as I explained how I toiled each day with the diligence of Bobby Moore and the grit of Julian Dicks, humming slave songs to keep my spirits up, Travis reassured me that I was just the sort of person who needed KeyStone's help.

The clinic, when we found it, was in the middle of this square in some quiet Philadelphia suburb. The house looked like a normal American family home does – you know, where they've got the sloping roof to the porch bit and gardens around it, a bit like where the Waltons lived, all pastoral and sweet, but with John-Boy chained up in the mop cupboard scrabbling around trying to fiddle with his goolies through a mask of tears. Over the road there was a church: a modern grey building, which constantly played a recording of church bells. Strange it was. Why no proper bells? I never went in but I bet it was a robot church for androids, where the Bible was in binary and their Jesus had laser eyes and metal claws.

I was greeted on the steps of the clinic by one of the counsellors. I can't remember her name, but she was wearing a t-shirt with frogs on. It turned out she was obsessed with 'em, and when I asked her why she said, 'When I was a kid, there was a pond near my house which all the frogs would try to get back to, and they'd get killed crossing over the road, so I used to try and help them across.'

'Fucking hell,' I thought. 'D'ya wanna have a clearer analogy etched on your t-shirt? How troublingly apposite that your mission in life should now be to save people from destruction as they pursue their natural instinct to spawn.'

At this point, the frog-lady introduced me to a subdued and pinch-faced individual. 'Arthur will show you around,' she said cheerfully. 'He's gonna be your roommate.' (In the film, Arthur would be played by Rick Moranis or William H. Macy.) Arthur showed me round the kitchen with its horrible meaty American meals. Meals which I, as a vegetarian, couldn't eat, so I would have to live on fruit for the whole month, like a little ape.

One by one, I began to meet more of my fellow clients, or patients, or inmates, or perverts – whatever you want to call them, including an intimidating Puerto Rican cove who looked like a hybrid of Colin Farrell's 'Bullseye' character from the film *Daredevil* and Bill Sykes's dog in *Oliver Twist* (whose name was also 'Bullseye', strangely enough), who kept calling me 'London' – 'Hey, London!'

I resented being called 'London'. There are eight million people living in London, and my identity, I hope, is quite specific. He addressed me the same way he would've Ken Livingstone or Danny Baker – God knows what they'd be doing there. I'm not even from London; I'm from Essex. (Though I suppose 'Essex' would have been even less appropriate – it has, after all, got the three letters 's-e-x' in it and that's what caused all this bother.)

This demeaning and geographically inaccurate mode of address was just one aspect of what soon began to seem like a concerted campaign to dismantle every element of my persona. It was not just my copy of the *Guardian* that had been confiscated on my arrival, but also my Richard Pryor CDs and my William Burroughs novel. And I'd not been at KeyStone long before my attire began to attract complaints. Apparently, the way my excess belt hung in front of my crotch was confusing and enticing to the pervert fraternity as it suggested a phallus. So they censored me. I was like Elvis 'the Pelvis' Presley on Ed Sullivan, I tells ya, punished for the crime of being sexy. (Him on the telly, me in a dingy sex centre . . . any analogy will break down under scrutiny.)

As the days went on, I started to learn why other people were in there. I quickly found out that Arthur was a paedophile who had eloped with his thirteen-year-old foster daughter. If he went back to Arizona to face the charges, he'd be in line for either lifetime imprisonment or execution. This revelation came as a bit of a blow and made me question the rationale of the whole dashed trip. 'Okay,' I thought, 'I've a bit of an eye for the ladies, now as a kind of punishment I'm rooming with a paedophile, is that gonna be helpful?' Like them lads that get sent down for nicking a car radio and end up sharing a cell with a diligent, bank robber mentor who schools them in criminality. I went down to the office and started making frantic phone-calls home, saying, 'Get me out of this place.' If I'd been less terrified I might've paused to dream up a new reality show format, 'I'm a celebrity get me out of this demented sex centre', where minor faces off the box are forced to doss down with, say, Peter Sutcliffe for the amusement of an apathetic nation.

John was on holiday – he'd gone skiing or something – so I was trying in vain to get through to other people and tell them I was reluctant to share a room with this paedophile chap. No one I spoke to was prepared to sanction my departure so, out of fear, desperation and a kind of morbid curiosity, I decided to stay.

It's extraordinary how quickly you get institutionalised in that kind of environment. You start wearing, not pyjamas exactly, as you do get dressed, but certainly indoorsy sorts of clothes. They have meetings every morning and afternoon. The rituals are astonishing. You have to go round the room introducing yourself – 'Hello, I'm Russell' – and then admitting to your recent transgressions. These aren't really wrongdoings as we would normally understand them, more everyday actions which have developed a sexual component.

'I had an erotic thought.' Or 'I did some eroticised humour earlier today.' (I liked the phrase 'eroticised humour' very much – it seemed like such a perfect description of what I do for a living, that a few months later I made it the title of a live show which I took to the Edinburgh Festival.) Or 'I experienced eroticised rage.' Then you'd round the whole thing off by saying, 'My goal for today is to get through the KeyStone experience and just live it as best I can.'

People began to customise this closing declaration, I suppose as a way of emphasising their own particular characters. But far from lessening the institutional feel of the whole proceedings, it kind of exacerbated it. Soon enough, each person seemed to have their own slogan: 'Hello, I'm Stuart, and I'm gonna swim like a KeyStone dolphin.' These customised slogans would often be drawn from the totemic cuddly toy that we were each obliged to select from the mantelpiece. I had a camel. He was forced upon me and I loathed and resented him. Or someone else would say, 'I'm gonna ride the KeyStone Express,' and all the others would make supportive train-noises – 'Wooh! Wooh!' And I'd be sat there in the middle thinking, 'Oh great, I'm in a nuthouse.'

I've never felt more English in my life than when I was sat in that American cliché swap shop. They'd say, 'I hear your pain, it's good that you shared.' And I'd be thinking 'Oh do fuck off. For Christ's sake, someone put *EastEnders* on the fucking telly and get me a glass of Beefeater gin and a toasted crumpet.'

In that situation, alienated from my normal surroundings, I realised that the outer surface of what I thought was my unique, individual identity was just a set of routines. We all have an essential self, but if you spend every day chopping up meat on a slab, and selling it by the pound, soon you'll find you've become a butcher. And if you don't want to become a butcher (and why would you?), you're going to have to cut right through to the bare bones of your own character in the hope of finding out who you really are. Which bloody hurts. ☞

2

Umbilical Noose

Now for the old formative years, which traditionally in auto-biographies are a bit boring – not in this one, however. My childhood is so jam-packed with melodrama and sentimentality (described as 'the unearned emotion') that you'll doubtless use these very pages to mop up your abundant tears.

Once, for a TV programme – which has been my motivation and justification for a good many personal atrocities – I had regression therapy, where a therapist hypno-regresses you back to past lives you didn't have. In the car there my mate Matt Morgan (writing partner, Radio 2 co-host, companion and creative soul-mate) kept murmuring facts about Anne Frank at a subtle, almost subliminal volume in the vain hope that I'd spend my session complaining about Nazis in the stairwell. As it transpired, my past lives all coincided with historical periods covered by *Blackadder*. 'I'm in a medieval courtyard, I'm beating up that idiot Baldrick, I can hear the theme tune from *Blackadder* . . .' 'I'm in Regency London at the court of the glutinous Prince George – played by Hugh Laurie – and I can hear the theme tune to . . . *Blackadder* . . . Christ, I'd better run, I think that's the SS at the door!'

Before the past lives were accessed, I had to be regressed through my childhood. As I rendered the bleak, joyless depiction of my infancy, the therapist remarked, 'Can you not see anything positive?' 'No,' was my response. 'This is depressing – let's just fast-forward to *Blackadder Goes Forth*, not the last episode though.'

So that's what you've let yourself in for. Fortunately, both for you and me, I grew up to become a comedian and will make it as jolly as possible. In the words of Morrissey – I can smile about it now, but at the time it was terrible.

I suppose you want to know how it was that I came to be on this dirty little circle we call 'world'? Well, I was born at midnight on the 4 June 1975. My parents, Barbara and Ron, had fought fiercely throughout the pregnancy. There was one incident which Alf Garnett creator Johnny Speight would have rejected as absurdly chauvinistic – 'People will lose sympathy for Alf,' he might have told himself, 'don't put that in' – where my father, in a bizarre reversal of the dynamic one would expect, made my heavily pregnant mother push his broken-down van, while he steered and swore.

It was a rapid yet complicated birth. I was born with my mouth open, and my umbilical cord wrapped around my throat, as if I was thinking, 'Well, if this is all there is, I'm off. Cheque please.'

My parents separated when I was about six months old. My mother, who had been told she could never have children, adored me and was doting and protective. My father, himself fatherless (his own dad had died when he was seven) was a sporadic presence, affording me cyclonic visits at the weekends. He would invariably arrive late, to find me ready and waiting for him, all dressed up and mummified in my duffel coat – toddlers can't move properly in winter coats, they're like little trussed-up Hannibal Lecters scanning the world with their eyes . . . Then a huge argument would ensue, which would generally end with both my mother and myself in tears.

Some of my earliest recollections are of seeing Dad on Saturdays – him leaving me watching the TV at his flat in Brentwood, while he read the papers or diddled birds in the room next door. I would mainly watch comedy videos, Elvis films and porn. Another very early memory is of our dog Sam being put down. I was only about two or three at the time, but I loved that dog. I remember him not wanting to get into the car to be taken to the vet's, and me saying through a mist of tears, 'Come on, Mum, let's go down the pub.'

My very first utterance in life was not a single word, but a sentence. It was, 'Don't do that.' Why is that the first thing I said? What kind of infancy was I having that before I learnt 'mum', or 'dad', I learnt, 'Could you stop? Whatever it is that's going on, just pack it in . . .' On reflection, it was probably because I'd just been told not to do something that I made this my debut proclamation, rather than because I had the pressing need to bring some unpleasant incident to a conclusion. More normal words like 'bird', 'clock' and 'mum' did follow fairly soon after, and 'tis good that I've got a mum who remembers all them things. In fact, my childhood can't have been that bad if someone loved me enough to document my first words.

That person – my mum – still lives in the house I grew up in, in the small town of Grays in Essex, on the northern side of the Thames estuary. The street is called Grays End Close – a name apparently designed to emphasise that no one who lives there is likely to be going anywhere else. Grays. End. Close.

I trained, as I suppose all children do, to practise seduction and manipulation on my mother, but the particular nature of our circumstances inclined me to focus on this strand of my development to the exclusion of all others – to the extent that I simply didn't feel equipped for other activities or human relationships. First I hated playschool, then I hated infant school – just as I've subsequently hated every institution that I've ever been forced to try and fit into.

The outside world was fearsome. But I was safe with my mum, and at least once – when I was really young – raised the possibility of matrimony. I remember saying to her, 'Why don't we just get married? That seems like a sensible solution to all this fuss and bother.' I hadn't foreseen the difficulties that could subsequently arise with such an arrangement. Although it's not that long ago, there was much more stigma attached to being a single-parent family when I was growing up than there is now. My friends' parents were all still married, and I remember the fact that my mum and dad were divorced being regarded quite sympathetically at school.

My mum had lots of female friends, so I had a kind of matriarchal upbringing – surrounded by women. As well as my dad's sisters, Janet and Joan, who gave me picture books which I would later get extra use out of by changing the words to make them offensive and rude, there were lots of other aunties who were not actually blood relations. There was Auntie Brenda – who drove my mum to the hospital to have me (because my mum was out walking the dog when I decided to get all nice and born) – and Auntie Pat. She used to give me books as well.

Then there was Auntie Josie, the woman from over the way. My mum's still friends with her now. In my early childhood Josie loomed large. She was 'brassy'. There was one occasion as a small child when I heard my mum on the phone to her. Josie's hot water had stopped working and she asked if she could come and have a bath at our house. Knowing that Josie was on her way over, I quickly decamped to the bathroom, taking with me as many of my toys as I could get my hands on. 'Oh, Russell's in there,' my mum warned her. 'Don't worry, I don't mind,' she replied, 'he's only a little boy.'

'Ha, ha, ha, you fools!' I exulted privately. I knew exactly what I was doing. As a result of my subterfuge, Josie was there in the bath, naked, and I was on the floor, innocently playing with cars (and other things I weren't even that interested in), all the time watching her wash her glorious breasts. 'That's it,' I thought, 'keep washing; after all, I'm only a little boy. What do I know of the pleasures of the flesh?' I really was quite manipulative, even at that early age. I was already a weary connoisseur of my dad's pornography and had begun to develop my almost supernatural ability for guessing women's bra sizes. Just the statistics alone turn me on a bit. 34G. Cor. 36F. Blimey. It's only a number and a letter but it thrills me. That's why I could never play the game Battleships. 'Thirty-two C – I've sunk your battleship.' You may have sunk my battleship but you've also decorated my pants.

As a result of this matriarchal upbringing, I have been bequeathed a kind of hotline to capable, working-class women of a certain age. I am truly comfortable in their company. That's probably why all the women I have surrounded myself with in recent years – Lynne, my housekeeper, Sharon who buys my clothes, and Nicola who does my make-up – all have the same accent. The only exception is Leila, my yoga teacher, who is American, but she's like the others in that she's a very strong woman – warm and spiritual.

My relationship with conventional masculinity has always been much more problematic. I didn't have a lot of friends when I was growing up, but I did still encounter a few of my friends' dads. When I did, I didn't much care for these 'Dad' chaps. Great, oafish, hairy boors they were – working nights and belching. 'Quiet! My dad's on nights,' people would say, interrupting one of my eloquently bellowed soliloquies. 'Dad? Nights?' I'd enquire. Then the beast would awaken from a musty, darkened cave and come Fee-Fi-Fo-ing out, sniffing the air. 'Perhaps we ought to play at mine,' I'd suggest, 'your house seems to be inhabited by refugees from Roald Dahl's jotter.' Then off we'd scramble back to the comfort of my doting mum.

My own father was only discussed in hushed tones. 'You don't want to grow up like him,' people would say, all grave. But whenever I saw him he seemed to me a kind of Essex Cavalier – every week a different woman and a new scheme for riches. 'I would like to grow up like him,' I'd think.

Even though there were times when he had loads of money, he never met the £25-a-week maintenance payments that he was required to make, and this exacerbated the impoverishment of the household I grew up in. I remember Mum showing me the agreement which said how much he was meant to send, and when I saw him, it was my duty to try to get it off him.

My mum did numerous jobs – taking me with her until I began playschool, where I was frequently in trouble, having daily tantrums when she left me behind. Ridicu-larse to get in trouble at playschool really. How bad could it be? 'We must talk to you about Russell. There's been another stabbing in the sandpit.' I do remember inspecting the spittle-flecked faces of senselessly en-raged adults, looming like ogres, thinking, 'Well, this all seems like a bit of a storm in a teacup.' I was awake as a child. I knew it was nonsense. I don't regard my childhood as some foreign country. I still feel myself within the same vessel – my flesh a rocket of which I am the captain and chief cosmo-naughty.

Is this something to be proud of? That I've not grown up? I don't wanna get all Holden Caulfield about it, but I do see the passage into adulthood as a betrayal of the innocent values of childhood. Even the most savage monsters that history or red-top tabloids can parade were once just soppy tots, and before that snug lil' foetuses – and I've never met a foetus that I didn't like yet.

My mum sustained us through a variety of dead-end jobs: she sold dishwashers to pubs; she was a cocktail waitress in a London club for a bit; and she'd drive up to the Commercial Road in east London, buy black sacks of wholesale clothes, and then sell them at 'Clothes Parties'. What I recall of this is the Asian folks I'd meet in the shops and the attention I'd get. Then all the women coming round to the parties at ours, trying on clothes and smoking Silk Cuts but smelling all nice. I liked women.

My dad had been a brilliant footballer in his youth. When he was sixteen or seventeen, he was invited to go for a trial at West Ham. He didn't actually end up going, because he was too nervous and afraid of rejection. But my nan kept clippings from the local paper of games he'd played for Dagenham Boys, which was a team people like Terry Venables had turned out for. I remember he'd played against 'Chopper' Harris once.

My dad was an angry man, yet he had an amazing energy about him too. I always wanted to emulate his enthusiasm and effervescence.

These were the kind of capers he made money from: he had a market stall in Romford selling these prints – laser prints, they were called – which were just vivid photographs. Double-glazing, that was another one. Then it was water-filters. And when I was a small child, he worked as a photographer. He wasn't trained in any way, but he still used to do people's wedding photos; some lad at my school complained that the photos of his mum's wedding had been done in an alarmingly shoddy fashion and that his aunt's legs had been retrospectively added in pencil.

I think that largely because of growing up just with my mum for the first seven years of my life, and thinking of my dad as sort of heroic, but absent (and maybe even abstract), I found it very difficult to consort with other children. I would often behave flamboyantly – jumping around and hurting myself, or doing disgusting things just to get attention. I did a lovely line in ant-eating, for example. 'Wanna see me eat some ants?' I'd ask some nittish prig of a kid. They'd, of course, be well into the scheme – this was well before Xboxes and people were glad of any entertainment. My mum seems to have spent her entire childhood playing with something called a 'Button Box', which alarmingly is not a euphemism but simply a stinking, lousy box of buttons – what a lot of tosh. So in the early '80s to see live ant-eating was pretty much akin to some of the more ostentatious hoopla peddled by that goon David Copperfield (magician, not eponymous Dickens hero). But I only did it for the amusement of others – I never, ever ate ants alone. I was a social ant-eater, never an ant-wanker.

I ain't never really had much fun. I particularly dislike pre-ordained happy occasions. I don't mind Christmas so much, because everyone's involved, as long as they're Christians or lazy atheists, or Muslim but into tinsel. But I've never had a good New Year's Eve, and I don't like birthdays, or any other time when you're meant to be happy. I'm against the prescription of, say, 'Ooh, it's Christmas o'clock. Smile everyone!' For me happiness occurs arbitrarily: a moment of eye contact on a bus, where all at once you fall in love; or a frozen second in a park where it's enough that there are trees in the world. I don't like New Year's Eve. I don't think bliss could ever be preceded by a countdown and the chiming of a pompous clock, unless that's what death's like. My mum worked hard to make my birthdays jolly but they were always a right stomach-churning drag.

I'd been kicking around for exactly five years when the occasion were inappropriately marked by an act of festive arson. My mum had made me a big teddy-bear cake with a ribbon round its neck. The ribbon caught fire off the candles. All the other children thought it was really exciting that this had happened, but

I saw it for what it was – a grim portent for the forthcoming year. While them other twits grinned out merry drips of piss, I thought, 'Well, if this happened in a Ted Hughes poem, the protagonist wouldn't see six.'

Then my dad burst in all silly string and cheap charisma. He'd always turn up on birthdays – in archetypal bad-parent fashion – with things you shouldn't give kids; stuff you could set fire to. 'Wa-hey! I've bought you this big thing. It's a gun.' 'Thanks Dad . . . Bye.' My mum would be all upset, there'd be silly string on the settee, excited children and their wee everywhere and my father gone, just a little cloud of smoke left behind in the place where he'd been.

The cake was horribly maimed. It was during the Falklands War and images of Simon Weston were abundant, so this lent the fire-ravaged teddy another potent layer. 'Would you like a piece of *Belgrano* gateau, young man?' People could still eat it, but the damage had been done.

It was also in relatively early childhood that the first stirrings of the wild man junkie persona, which would later occupy my life for a decade or more, can retrospectively be divined. It was at this lad Ben Nicholson's birthday party. I remember going round there and being all crazy and off the hook – jumping in his paddling pool and knocking things over and being all mental. If it had been an office party, I'd have photocopied my arse or effed some temp in the stock cupboard but, as it wasn't, I simply did the childish equivalent. Which meant, I think, I stood on the edge of a plastic paddling pool making it haemorrhage into the lawn, and taunted the children's entertainer with a balloon sausage dog that I held between my legs as a humorously misshapen phallus.

When I saw Ben at school the next Monday, I was expecting him to say, 'Hey, Russell, great party man. You're wild! Listen,

I'm thinking of going to Vegas next week – wanna come?' But instead he sobbed, 'You're the bad boy who ruined my birthday,' and ran off crying. 'Jeez, what a downer – that kid totally killed my buzz. I was the life and soul of that poxy little shindig – man what a square.' Thus another friendship was dashed on the cruel rocks amid the storm of my self-destruction.

You'll see later that I made no great leaps forward in the ensuing decades, either with regards to my conduct at parties or my perception of my own conduct. Many's the time I'd strut off stage at some dingy comedy pit thinking, 'There! Feel the magic!' as the audience queued for refunds.

From quite early on, I had this idea of compartmentalised identities – 'This is how you are with your mum, and this is how you are with your dad' – so it seemed like I could never absolutely be myself. And this image of myself as compromised and inconsistent made me want to withdraw from the world even further. I had a sense of formulating a papier-mâché version of myself to send out in the world, while I sat controlling it remotely from some snug suburban barracks. When I used to watch TV as a tot, I'd sit really close to the screen: just trying to get into that box. ☞

3

Shame Innit?

Over the road from where I grew up there was a disused chalkpit and an overgrown and abandoned army barracks. I would go there – losing days at a time – to retrieve newts: these quick, sharp, darting slivers of energy. I'd liberate them from the slavery of nature – trees and ponds and that – knowing that they craved the freedom of a tiny death in my bedroom opposite.

It was amazing, that bit of wasteground. Obviously now, through the nostalgic haze of my adult perspective, it seems impossible that this place could ever have existed. There were these concrete bunkers – utterly featureless, like Stonehenge, but all overgrown with brambles and moss. They were linked together by underground tunnels, in which you'd have to completely trust yourself – walking into absolute, terrifying darkness, within which anything could lurk.

I remember the stink of damp, the occasional crisp-packet, discarded solvents, and evidence of sexual congress. There was a burnt-out car, and a pervasive sense that tramps might have been there. The whole place had a mythical air about it and – informed as I was by reading C.S. Lewis and Enid Blyton at a very early age – it felt like a fantastic kingdom. I was lucky to have a place where my fantasy life could manifest itself.

There was one bit that was all red sands, like Luke Skywalker's home planet. And, with all the lakes and chalk mountains, it wouldn't have surprised me to look up and see two moons. It just seemed extraordinary that you could be in grey, desolate, sub-urban Essex, and there would be something so exotic so nearby.

Apart from the wilderness over the road, the psycho-geography of Grays was basically irrelevant to me. There's not a particular cultural identity to growing up in industrial Essex, and southern suburbia in general: it's just very banal. And I didn't really feel safe in that place. I didn't really like it. It felt closed to me.

As a child, the idea of class would obviously not have been a reference point that I would have had (even now, I don't feel like I am enmeshed in any particular identity in that area. Whenever I'm in any kind of social group, I always tend to think I won't fit in, and gravitate towards an identity that will stand out). But, looking back, by the late '70s and early '80s, that old-fashioned sense of a monolithic working-class community had largely broken down. Where my nan on my dad's side lived, at Lillechurch Road in Dagenham, everyone still worked at Ford's. But there was no sense of cultural identity other than that. My grandad Bert had worked there too (my nan had remarried, some years after my dad's father's early death). But there was no cohesion. Nothing felt right. Everything seemed broken and ugly, boring and vacant.

My paternal grandmother was fantastic, though. In terms of how she spoke, the obvious comparison would be Catherine Tate's 'Nan' character, but not hard. My nan was kind and gentle, yet also very strong, and even dominant, in a non-aggressive way. I spent a lot of time in that house in Dagenham, growing up. My nan was an utterly benign presence in my life. And throughout my early years – until her death, when I was in my mid-twenties

– my nan would fix me with a sympathetic stare, cock her head and say, 'Aaah, shame, innit?', as if my whole existence was vaguely regrettable. This was a sentiment with which I often concurred.

One of the first facilities I developed to keep some distance between me and adversity was showing off. I remember, when I was quite young, doing a Frank Spencer impression to my maternal grandmother – the one I didn't much get on with. (My friend Matt Morgan says it's wrong to have Nan league tables, but I think that element of competition brings out the best in them.) My mum – who was my first audience, and an indulgent one at that – said, 'He does a really good Frank Spencer – go on, do it.' So I did it, and everyone really laughed.

'Do it again, do it again,' they cried. So I did. And they all agreed it wasn't as good the second time. 'No, you've lost it. You've lost that uncanny knack of impersonating Michael Crawford' – this precious window of opportunity had slammed shut almost as soon as it had opened.

While the thrill of receiving consistent acclaim for my hilarious impressions was to be denied me for a little while longer, an additional source of dangerous nourishment was my dad's reservoir of porn. I think I always had a premature awareness of sexuality, but Ron Brand's penchant for leaving me to occupy my infant mind with his cache of girlie magazines certainly did nothing to stem the erotic tide.

I adored the cartoons in *Playboy*. Either they'd be one page, or sometimes a story drifting towards a climax where someone got their boobs out. There was something quite eerie and perverted about them. I suppose because they were cartoons and porn at the same time, and these are not two things you expect to see together. You kind of feel – especially as a four-year-old child – that cartoons should just be of rabbits, but even the rabbits had erotic connotations in that beloved filthy rag. All these magazines were always clear about the market they were catering for. They were called things like *Jugs* and *Big Ones*.

'And what exactly is our target demographic? What were you hoping to capture at *Jugs* magazine?' 'Well, if we had to put our manifesto into one word, it would be "Jugs"; if it were three it would be "Great Big Tits".' Brilliant, those magazines were. I don't know whether I was already genetically predestined to like women with massive boobs, but, as it turns out, I do.

My dad can't have had much money then, because when we went on holiday, he took me to Pontin's. I don't know exactly where, but I suppose the beauty of Pontin's lies in its uniformity. (They've found a winning formula and they're sticking to it – the same as McDonald's: you'll never turn up at a Pontin's and discover it's been hijacked by a Colonel Kurtz-type figure who dresses the Bluecoats as wizards and insist that the Lovely Legs competition is replaced by necromancy.)

We went to Pontin's a few times. I didn't like that 'Crocodile Club' much, though. It was too much pressure, the demands too great; it was like being in the Hitler Youth. The children were co-opted off and coerced into being in a gang, with this abominable crocodile mascot as their leader. Well, I didn't share any of his beliefs. In fact, I felt that he was a despot. 'Do you think we could usurp this crocodile guy? I mean what are his policies exactly? I think it would be easy enough to overthrow him – I'll just say he tried to wank me off in the Punch & Judy booth. Surely that would be grounds for dismissal?' I remember feeling all unpopular, lurching about doing some supposedly upbeat holiday activity. I was probably in the adventure playground. I don't know how adventurous a few metal poles roped together with a pallet on top can really be – scaffolding that's been painted red ain't my idea of adventure. Amid the banality a little girl approached me and said, 'Your dad's in bed with my mum – do you want to come and have a look?' I paused. 'Yeah, alright.'

The chalet window was open, and there was a net curtain being delicately teased by the summer breeze. It were like a French film noir, but set in Pontin's. Actually, my dad wasn't in bed with the woman at that point – he was in the bed on his own, and she was in the bathroom. I said, 'Alright dad, can I have fifty pee for the arcade?' At that point, the woman walked out of the bathroom naked, and shrieked. She tried to cover herself up – all knockers and skin everywhere almost independently trying to escape her – like she was a vet's assistant bungling her way through her first day, mishandling a litter of recalcitrant piglets. I watched her and pressed record on the ol' brain box. 'Intriguing,' I thought.

My dad gave me the money through the window. He didn't seem bothered or embarrassed by the whole thing at all. He was just muddling through life, was dear Ron Brand. He did his best, as we all do, groping his way through fatherhood without a template. The little girl's dad never found out. He was just playing crazy golf while the real craziness took place in his wife's knickers.

Less bizarre but equally impacting were the early trips to Upton Park to enjoy our other shared passion, The Hammers. I didn't do badly on the West Ham front: he took me a fair bit, probably three or four times a season, starting when I was really young. I loved everything about it – the intensity, the proximity, the noise, the journey there. There's a very good description, I think it's in the play *When Saturday Comes*, of how when you leave your house to go to the match you're on your own. Then you see another person in a football scarf. Then one or two of you become the trickle. Then the trickle becomes the river. Then the river becomes the flood. Then you get the sense of, '*Oh my god, we're all heading towards Shangri-la.'* Every time I stroll down Green Street I involuntarily recall feeling all anxious, nervous and small, the stench of shit food and belched booze, but most of all the numinous thrill on ascending the stairs within the ground and seeing anew the improbably bright, livid, lurid green pitch. Sometimes by happy chance you'll see the pitch as the Irons run out and the crowd's roar will greet you as it does them and you know that you're everything and nothing. I felt this too when I entered Saint Peter's Basilica in Rome. Regarding the ceiling, I understood why people believe in God. Because God appears to be present. 'This could be it, it could literally, physically be God: not just some abstract idea.'

Leaving the ground and seeing everyone depart onto Green Street, I once asked, 'Is that all the people in the world, Dad?' It was so exhilarating – the singing, and the violence, because even when it's not enacted, the violence is still there, there's a kind of hum, constantly present in the language used towards the players, the referee, and the opposing fans. Malevolence lurks unseen within us all; even when all tiny and webbed in snot and sweeties I felt it in me. A need to be naughty or bad – and even this innocuous, forthcoming tale seems to me to indicate an innate malady . . .

In the film *Citizen Kane*, there's that scene where Kane is dying, clutching a snowstorm globe. As he dies, he drops it on the floor and utters the word 'Rosebud'. Because when he was a kid he had that sledge, 'Rosebud', that he used to bomb down hills on, and he really loved it. In spite of the fact that in later life he became a millionaire and built a business empire and had all that power and all that success, when it came to the moment of his death, it was being a child on that sledge that he remembered. Perhaps for all of us there is a moment that epitomises our lives – a moment when you're more yourself than at any other time, an instant of absolute self-realisation. Well, that was Kane's, and this is mine . . .

It all began with a nice old man who lived on our street, talking to me about some flowers that he'd grown in his garden. I think over time I have perhaps, if not sanitised this old man, at least Disney-fied him. For now, in my mind's eye, when I cast my thoughts back, I see a twinkle-eyed Geppetto character, smoking a pipe and wearing lederhosen as he tends to his nasturtiums. They beam back at him and grin – perhaps even jigging about like the battery-operated dancing flowers that were to become popular a decade or so later. The passage of time has also allowed me to lacquer the memory with the old man's unexpressed suspicion that I were in need of a patriarch, a father-figure, and him being all kind and guiding me towards an understanding of nature.

As I recall it now, he put a fatherly arm around me, and what he said next could almost be a song from *The Lion King* about the cycle of life. 'And these flowers grow, and one day they die, but they'll grow again. These flowers are perennial. Their seed is eternal. Flower begets flower and on we must go – from now until the end of time. Always it were thus, like a line of human bellybuttons stretching back to Adam and Eve.'

Then, the old man paused. 'Oh well,' he said, 'I'll just pop into the toilet for a wee . . . Don't stamp on those flowers, will you?'

'Don't stamp on those flowers . . .' Why say that? Had he not parted with the words, 'Don't stamp on those flowers', I wouldn't have. It just wouldn't've occurred to me. I might have stamped on one to make an example of it. But in the sentence, 'Don't stamp on those flowers', the word 'don't' is feeble, impotent and easy to ignore. Whereas 'STAMP ON THOSE FLOWERS' has a real linguistic verve; 'stamp on those flowers' could be a slogan, a catchphrase, a banner under which nations could unite. So the moment he shuffled out of view, all old and friendly, I stamped on them flowers. I stamped 'em till there was naught but mush, till they were but a memory of flowers; I stamped with a ferocity that meant that flowers everywhere would never again feel safe. It was a floral 9/11. I knew it was bad but I couldn't deny the urge; I know why them medieval loons were so keen to believe in demonic possession because I gave vent in that moment to a timeless darkness, the parameters of which extend beyond my being and transgress the very borders of evil itself.

I was angry towards them flowers – just growing there, thinking they were better than us. It was a bit like in Stanley Holloway's rendition of 'Albert and the Lion'. My dad was obsessed with that poem – he made me recite it with him, verse for verse, at one of his ill-advised weddings. There's a line where the little boy, Albert, takes umbrage at the lion's lack of gusto: 'Now Albert had heard about lions,/How they was ferocious and wild – /To see Wallace lying so peaceful,/Well, it didn't seem right to the child.' Well, it didn't seem right to me that the flowers should be there, all peaceful and beautiful. The poem continues: 'So straight'way the brave little fella,/Not showing a morsel of fear,/Took his stick with its 'orse's 'ead 'andle/And pushed it in Wallace's ear.' My memory of the poem has spanned decades in which the marriage it was learned to serve could've played out a dozen times.

I took my cue from the brave young protagonist of this famous tale and stamped down on that beauty: stamped it into the soil. Them smug, up-reaching flowers, greedily sucking up sun. 'I don't know what photosynthesis is, and I don't know what's in it for me, because I've never felt any of its advantages. I think it's a cruel trick . . .' So I were satisfied to stamp them down, and then waited with a churning gut for the old man's return.

He came back, beaming and benevolent, still with his leathery face and furrowed brow and them sort of thick, dirty fingers and leathery palms that old men often go in for; it seems somehow satisfying to smell their jumpers and fall asleep on their laps. He trundled back down the path, all warm, avuncular and glowing. He glanced first at me, and then at his devastated flowerbed; all ploughed up and butchered, like a Ripper victim – like Pearly Poll, lying gutted in Hanway Street, Spitalfields. And his anger grew the same way he'd explained to me that flowers grew. First there was a tiny seed of rage – 'Oh Russell, what did you do that for? I thought you were a good boy – a nice little boy.' Swiftly came the spring and his anger bloomed into raging triffids. And suddenly this warm man, this gentle man, was shouting and screaming at me, incandescent with fury. I can still remember his roar – this visceral sound booming up from his guts – 'GET *HOME!*'

I raced home, a refugee from the botanical carnage, to sanctuary; only the pathologically mischievous know the relief of closing the door behind them, locking out the world and its tight angry fist clutching dockets and penalties for parental perusal. I was excited by what had happened, but also sort of sad.

I never spoke to that old man again. I closed down that account which could have been quite rewarding. Time has bleached away my memories of the period immediately prior to the beginning of this narrative, but it feels as if the old man's kindly overture was not an isolated incident. He seems, retrospectively, to have had a tendency to take me under his wing and witter away encouragingly. Having the knowledge that I'm being destructive and then doing it anyway: I'm still trapped in that pattern. In fact, I made myself a victim of it again as recently as the night before I wrote this very paragraph.

I was at a do and thought, 'Russell, why don't you just go home? Tomorrow morning will still be tomorrow morning, whatever you do now. Why not forgo the opportunity for a sexy adventure and wake up on clean sheets with a clean mind?' Alas the demons were unwilling to negotiate and more flowers were damned. This is why I currently find myself turning to celebrity hypnotist Paul McKenna to brain-ma-tise me into change. But if celebrity hypnotist Paul McKenna can't help me, who else is there to turn to? ☞

4

Fledgling Hospice

I like animals very much – lovable, dumb chums, loyal, decent and lovely – and if I'd had my way I'd've been reared in a menagerie. In my childhood there always seemed to be massive obstacles between me and any simple pleasure; as if I were unwittingly a character in a peculiarly trivial Greek tragedy. For instance, I really wanted to get another dog, but my mum was always opposed to this idea. Until one day, my dad, in typically irresponsible fashion, purchased this huge, dopey German shepherd, unwittingly starting an inter-parent canine arms race where my approval and love were sought through dog acquisition.

Toby was the name of my dad's pre-emptive strike – a really lovely, big-footed, lumbering, daft dog. When my dad cleared off to live in Düsseldorf with the woman who later became his third wife, he left Toby with my tiny nan, this huge great beast filling her mid-terrace house, as if it were a pebble-dashed waistcoat he were wearing to the dog Oscars.

I remember him sitting on her lap, while she peeped round to join the chatter or watch the telly. My nan'd never mutter a word against him, as if to do so would be sacrilege. She knew that it was the manifestation of my dad's id, Toby being more dogma than dog. Off they'd go for bone-crunching walks round the estate, awaiting the appearance of an inevitable cat who'd send them both off on a ridiculous, sledless husky ride down the concrete slopes of Dagenham. Her busted hands belatedly evolved into a twisted glove fit only for clasping a constantly taut leather lead; if this painful development troubled her, it was a burden she endured silently. As with many women of her generation and class, this unspectacular martyrdom was never remarked upon, as it was simply her duty to give and be a mother.

My mum struck back at the Toby purchase by acquiring us a four-legged financial drain of our own. Alas, she got it from a refuge for delinquent hounds. I was not involved in the selection process. I was disappointed that it weren't little enough: I wanted it to be more of a puppy, so I could share in the joy of its infancy and mould it into a bespoke companion adhering to some rather unique requirements; the mutt was due to be my only friend and salvation, you can't just get them off the rack. I'm sure when God was selecting Jesus for his mission to redeem the people of Earth he didn't just hurl a potato out of his office window shouting, 'Whomever this spud may strike, boy, have I got a job for you!' I imagine there was a rigorous selection process, a kind of celestial X Factor, although, given the story's dénouement, perhaps † Factor would be more fitting.

Life's never a postcard of life, is it? It never feels like how you'd want it to look. I suppose my very specific canine preferences would probably have been formed by reading Enid Blyton. I really enjoyed her as a child – even books like *The Naughtiest Girl in the School*, which were only meant for girls. I was a cross-reader, feasting on the forbidden fruit of girl fiction: what a turn-on. So I wanted a well-balanced, cheerful, mongrel, Enid Blyton-type dog along the lines of her immortal 'Timmy', that I could have grown up with – not the Looney-bitch that turned up. Topsy was a mixed blessing. As a result of coming from dog borstal, she was a bit troubled and would take any opportunity to tear things up. She tore up a koala bear that was stuffed with polystyrene balls, once. I remember looking through the letterbox and seeing the stairs and the hallway all covered in white plastic, like a suburban Narnia.

Also, Topsy ate money. Not in the metaphorical sense of having to go to the vet's and have a lot of operations or anything. She just liked eating money.

My mum would leave cash on the kitchen work surface after those 'Clothes Parties', and once Topsy ate it. I like to think that Topsy was a vehement anticapitalist and that this money-guzzling was a statement of some kind, but I only like to think that 'cos I'm a twit.

I was seven years old when my mother got cancer for the first time; she had to have a hysterectomy, which was difficult for her and cemented me forever as an only child. If you have no brothers and sisters it defines you for life; even when you're thirty you refer to yourself as an only child.

While she was in hospital, I found myself uprooted from the security of Grays. End. Close. and forced to go and live with her family. They're good people, but I'd never felt part of the family; I watched Christmases and birthdays through patio doors in my mind. The first night at my maternal grandmother's house in Brentwood I wet the bed. She humiliated me while we changed the sheets, saying I was 'too old for that sort of business', and that I was bad and responsible for my mother's illness. I've found that difficult to forget. She was a much-loved woman, my grand-mother, Dusty Miller, and meant the world to her children and my cousins. I took that exchange as further evidence that there was something wrong with me.

The hospital my Mum was in (the same one where I was born, in Orsett in Essex) was all decaying and falling apart: it's been made into flats now. Everything's been made into flats now: schools, churches, hospitals. What are we to do when the occupants of these flats have children, get married, get ill and die? Bury them in the scarce earth only to learn their coffins have been made into flats now.

The hospital became the bleak venue of a courtship between my mum and her new boyfriend Colin. I fucking hated Colin.

Before she was ill, she used to have these parties – of which I would be quite disapproving – at which loads of people would gather downstairs, making adult noises, not sexy noises, just the adult rumble, punctured with Sid James laughs and the clinking of glass. I think Colin had first crossed our threshold to attend one of these gatherings, and then visited her when she was in hospital.

My mum eventually recovered, and I went back home to live with her again. She told me that she had only survived because she loved me so much. For the first seven years of my life, the house in Grays had been a kind of extension of my mother's womb – a comfortable environment in which I felt safe. In later life I wrote a poem about mum's illness called 'Hysterectomy Angel', which ended with the somewhat troubling (at least in terms of conventional Freudian psychoanalysis) line: 'When I fall in love, it will be with Mother.'

But now my incestuous bubble was about to be punctured by the arrival of this swarthy yet utterly humdrum man. Colin was a good-looking individual – somewhere between David Hasselhoff and George Best. He, like my dad, had been a brilliant footballer in his youth. He was handsome but utterly lacked glamour. Not that lacking glamour is necessarily a terrible thing; Alan Bennett lacks glamour and is perhaps the greatest living Englishman.

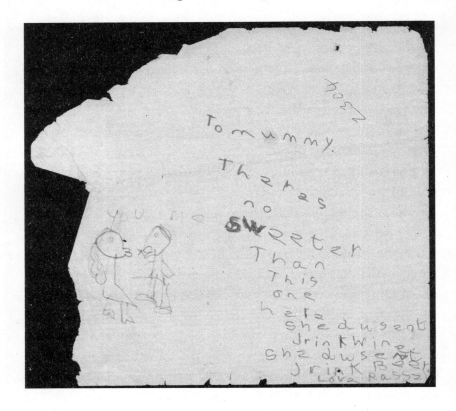

Colin was, I suppose, part of the paradigm where dead beautiful women sometimes neglect to develop a personality, because they'll be invited to functions regardless: 'Just pop a frock on, and I'll take you wherever you want to go.' A personality for the incredibly beautiful can be a pointless cargo, regardless of gender. Colin moved into the house that we already inhabited, and never really recovered from the sense that he lived in a home that my mum and dad had occupied together.

Because Colin had a job (he initially worked nights in a factory, checking breeze blocks, and then later became a van driver), there was a flush of new income into the household. Whenever a new consumer item was bought – a sofa, or a washing machine – it would be worshipped like a Dyson Deity entering the home: as dear Morrissey said, 'Each household appliance is like a new science in my town.' Colin would extract a tiresome price for these exciting new material idols.

I remember these pointless, hateful drills he had, like rotating the sofa cushions at night – lest the sofa should show some sign of the passing of time, or experience, or joy. And him sat forever in reluctant pants in the corner of the room, clutching a can of Tennent's Super, or some other homeless lager, the faithful TV remote forever resting on his naked thighs like Blofeld's cat.

I was unable to categorise or understand the flow of Colin's moods. All I knew was that he were perpetually displeased with something, and fundamentally disapproved of me. I was the antithesis of all that he stood for – this simple, working-class man, a humble individual with low expectations of life, whose only dream of becoming a successful footballer had long ago been packed away. And while in retrospect I can understand his resentment of my Quentin Crisp quirkiness – flitting around, all self-absorbed and vain and unusual – for me, he was a toxic interloper in my home. Colin: this essentially misanthropic man, not having enough vitality to be actively hateful, but constantly down on all life.

I had a growing sense that I was a disappointment to people: not only that I wasn't the kind of person my dad would have wanted me to be, but also that I wasn't able to look after my mum; either to prevent her from getting ill, or to stop Colin from moving in. All that seemed to be left to me were my own limited resources, and an intensifying thirst for animal friendships.

I really craved the company of animals – the wordless simplicity of it. Even now, with my cat Morrissey, I cherish the moments that I'm absolutely alone with him, and the unrecorded tenderness that no one will ever know of – the simplicity of 'Oh, I'm just here, with this cat.' I don't even feed him that much any more, 'cos Lynne, the housekeeper, does that now. But he seems to want something from me that isn't food, and perhaps that thing is love.

My relationship with Topsy quickly grew very intense. Perhaps because she was a problem dog, we had more in common that I'd initially realised. I remember sometimes cuddling her too hard so that she would yelp. 'Here, have some of my painful love,' my febrile embrace would tell her. 'It is constrictive and controlling and painful, like all love should be.' In later life, I have come to realise that any expression of love which ends in a yelp probably requires modification.

When we first got Topsy, she would be allowed to sleep in the bed with me: I hope it is not necessary for me to stress the platonic nature of that relationship – not platonic in the purist sense, there was no philosophical discourse, but we certainly didn't fuck, which is usually what people mean by platonic; which I bet would really piss Plato off, that for all his thinking and chatting his name has become an adjective for describing sexless trysts. But, when Colin came, an absurd edict was introduced whereby she was no longer allowed upstairs.

I evidently had a lot of anger and hate in me about this, because I would perch at the top of the stairs and lure her to come up – 'Topsy! Topsy! Topsy!' Then, when she would slink nervously upwards to the forbidden terrain of the upper floor, I would suddenly become Mr Hyde. 'Oh dear, Topsy,' I would declaim, in a rather arch manner, 'you know perfectly well you're not allowed upstairs' before cruelly kicking her back down to the bottom again, where I would rejoin her and give her a sympathetic cuddle, regretfully muttering, 'Oh Christ! Were you kicked down the stairs? This is terrible.'

That's quite fucked-up, isn't it? My friend Matt Morgan says Topsy must've thought she lived in a house with twins – an evil one who lived on the landing, and a good one who dwelt downstairs. I feel very guilty about this conduct and try to offer amends by treating animals with respect at all times. (In fact, while writing this, a gnat, which has been biting me all evening, rested momentarily on my keyboard and, though I'm quite cross about its blood-sucking, I gently requested that it dine on me no further rather than dashing out its wicked brain onto the space bar. It ignored my attempts at a civil solution, suggesting that perhaps our leaders are right and you can't negotiate with terrorists. Or gnats.)

With Topsy at my side, I'd head over the road to rescue the innocent creatures of the chalky wilderness from the tyranny of free will. How I rejoiced in rescuing those nestlings. 'My God! I've got this thing. Now I can take it to my house, I can have this innocent, terrified bird, staring up at me and exuding this strange, sweaty smell.'

I would make a new home for them in my AT-AT Walker – a *Star Wars* toy with legs from *The Empire Strikes Back*: it struck back very hard at Essex's wildlife, with me as the Emperor's well-intentioned idiot apprentice. All my other *Star Wars* figures lived in there too, so if you opened it up you'd see Lando Calrissian, a storm-trooper and a baby sparrow – an unlikely trio, yes, the three'v' em've all got their foibles, sure, but they've got each other, and they'll all learn something on this journey they're taking together.

The problem with rescuing baby birds is that it's very hard to get them to eat properly. You have to chop 'em up worms, which they don't want to eat. Which I quite understand because they look and smell awful, writhing on a spoon like spastic spaghetti (spazghetti?); I wasn't prepared to pop it in my gob like their real mum would've done. 'My real mum chews my food up and regurgitates it,' one might've said. 'I don't care what your real mum does, while you're under my roof, in my AT-AT Walker, you'll live by my rules.' Sadly, my avian nursery had a one hundred per cent failure rate. If I was a rehabilitation centre for fledglings, the AT-AT Walker would have been sold off to pay for counselling for the grief-stricken parents.

For me it seemed like an opportunity to have something of my own. I really loved those little pricks. I kept having to get rid of their bodies, like Bill Oddie as a hit man, and they looked all dead. In Enid Blyton, the animals would always survive. But even now, I don't think I'd be able to get a little baby bird to live – how does anyone do it? I suppose it takes a lot of devotion. You've got to be doing it all the time, like when Terry Nutkins has those otters in his bath. I think one of them otters scoffed down his finger by way of thanks. So in a way I was just unknowingly avenging Nutkin's lost digit; you send one of ours to the hospital, we'll send one of yours to a *Star Wars* merchandise morgue. In fact loads of yours.

This bit of my childhood might be a bit of a downer to read; it was a bit of a downer to live an' all. The period around my seventh birthday has been studied by so many analysts and counsellors that it's little wonder that I was such a show-off, as if I could feel the eyes of future do-gooders peering at me through the decades. I had an insular yet somehow idyllic early childhood – which was okay, so long as I wasn't forced to leave the house or do anything with other people – that was suddenly brought to an end by a sequence of dramatic shocks. My mum getting ill, Colin turning up, then my dad, with the best of intentions and a pocket full of transitory cash, deciding to send me to a posh, private school called Gidea Park. Academically, I would inevitably lag behind the privileged elite of Gidea Park College, so my dad arranged for me to have private tuition with the bloke next door to him, who looked a bit like the former Labour Party leader Michael Foot (it wasn't actually him, he was a beautiful and idealistic man, they just looked similar).

Once, when I got a question right, this chap – by way of congratulation – stuck his finger up my arse and felt my balls. 'This is unusual,' I thought. I wondered if perhaps I might've encouraged him, because I'd said something I'd heard on *Only Fools and Horses*. To describe my bafflement at a mathematical problem, I'd employed a phrase which Del Boy used – 'Rodney, I've been looking for you like a tit in a trance' – only changing 'tit', which I knew was rude, to 'clown'.

'But it's not "clown" in a trance, is it?' he responded, lasciviously. By referring to this lewd colloquialism, it seemed I'd signalled my complicity in the world of adult sexuality. Just a few moments later, he was copping a feel, and besmirching the purity of what would later become popularly known as my ball-bags. As a currency for rewarding academic achievement, I think it's unlikely to supersede the gold star. Although I thought it odd, I wasn't particularly cheesed off. What most aggrieved me about the whole sorry business was that soon after it happened, I told my mum, she in turn told my dad who didn't go to the police, because he said he'd deal with it. But he never did anything. Later in life, when he would sometimes drunkenly allude to parenting errors in a 'Sorry I wasn't a good dad' kind of way, I often felt this was what he was referring to. And if he'd beaten the poor old sod up or something, I would have seen that as an act of heroism. I didn't see that tutor again, one hopes on account of his bizarre antics.

My brief foray into the world of private tuition was not, however, entirely disastrous. I should say at this point that, when

I think about what tribe I belong to, where my loyalties lie and what my affiliations are, stories about going to see a tutor on a Saturday seem very much out of sync, both with how I regard myself, and how I want to be regarded by others. That aside, there was something about this new tutor woman I went to see which was far from compromising to my identity. In fact, it's something I still crave in women now.

I remember being taken round to her house, and she said, 'Okay Russell, what are we gonna do today?' I replied that I didn't want to do anything and had a big tantrum, insisting, 'I can't be bothered: all I'm going to do is scribble on this bit of paper.'

Instead of being upset by this, she just said, 'Oh, alright.' So I got on with that for a while, until it got boring. And then she asked if I wanted to do any more of that or would I prefer to do something else. And I said, 'I'll do something else.' Retrospectively, I realise that this must've been a rare encounter with someone who knew how to deal with me. The form of parenting I was used to was very much damage limitation. I'd have got myself into some awful situation and my mum would arrive all flustered – 'Russell's done this thing!' – then I would be mollycoddled and assuaged.

In this woman's house, I remember there being a conservatory area with a lot of light in it. It seemed a very comfortable place, and she made me feel really at ease. She had one of those little organ things where, when you press the key, a little toy will open its mouth. I still feel a sense of technicolour comfort when thinking about that. Sitting in her house was a kind of sanctuary. I never went back there again.

5

'Diddle-Di-Diddle-Di'

I went to that Gidea Park College in the end. I remember I had to get a new uniform for it – a cap and stuff like that. I tolerated it, even though I'd naturally been opposed to all institutions, from playschool onwards.

I used to travel to school with these kids whose parents ran a pub called The Old Shant, which my mum always said looked like a public toilet, because its exterior was decorated with ceramics. Some days their parents used to take us and other days my mum would. One of the kids was a girl called Maxine. Her name stuck in my mind because my mum's car – a capacious vehicle – was an Austin Maxi. Maxine told me the first joke that I can still remember. 'There's two men who were going to go to a pub, so they met outside The King's Head, but it was shut, so they went to The King's Arms, and that was shut as well. They went to The Queen's Legs and that was shut, but they decided to wait outside. Then their mate walks past and says, "What are you doing here?" And one of them replies, "Oh, we're waiting for The Queen's Legs to open, so we can have a drink."'

'Well that's just brilliant,' I thought. 'It sounds like they're going to drink the queen's wee, these men. That's what's implicit in their response. God bless'em, these two – I'm right behind them.'

It did seem a posh sort of school to me, though my dad insisted that all the other pupils were children of stallholders from Romford market, but it still felt really alien. I disliked the teachers. One really stern, vicious spinster – I can't recall her real name, but if she turned up in Dickens, she would be called Miss Snickersnatch – was what I can only describe as a lady-bastard.

Maybe I adapted this story in childhood to get sympathy from my mother, but as I remember it, she took this pencil sharpener thing that I had, with a rubber attached, and threw it in the bin, then tore up my work. Why would a teacher do such a thing? That, surely, must be a lie. But it feels like t'were true. Chief among my accomplishments at Gidea Park was the ant-eating. It seemed a very small investment of discomfort for the amount of attention you received. Ants don't really taste of anything. I mean, there's the indignity of picking them up off the floor, of course, but once an ant's in your mouth, it's very much like any other bit of detritus you might pick from between your teeth. It has no specifically ant-like qualities. You can't feel it serve its queen or lay eggs.

Another dubious attention-seeking device that I invented at this school was the game 'genital-grabbing', which is very simple and easy to play but fraught with dreadful connotations for its participants and severe vilification for its unwitting inventor. Still, it really caught on among my fellow students, rapidly becoming a deviant craze. This act of violation would be accompanied by a comedic noise, a tinkling bell sound – 'diddle-di-diddle-di' – which one would now liken to a mobile-phone ringtone. At that time, I didn't think of this activity as sexual, but it does seem a little odd that this would be the kind of social tool that I would manufacture – going up to people and grabbing their winkies or vaginas (it is disgrace that in these enlightened times we still haven't reached consensus on an inoffensive word to describe prepubescent female sex organs. Male is a synonym Mardi Gras – 'willy', 'winky', 'dinkle', 'tassel'? Female – 'moo moo' and 'noony' and all sorts of crap I've heard; damn it, what are we afraid of?) It was only through their clothes, though – I wasn't a pervert.

There was a girl called Lucy who I quite liked and had expressed my affection towards through the left-field ritual of the ol' 'diddle-di-diddle-di' game. My mum had to go up the school about that. I've always been a 'your parents have got to come up the school' type of person. Even now, when I do something wrong – if I say something inappropriate on a live TV show, for example – I half expect to have to deliver a note to Barbara Brand: 'Please come up to Channel 4 head office, Russell's done something despicable.' The teachers had to tell my mum all about my embarrassing exploits: 'He's been grabbing children's genitals. Of course, he is a child himself, and that makes it just about bearable. If he were doing this in a decade's time, crikey! That really would be a problem.' The problem may have been worse but for the fact that it only took my dad a term to squander his nouveaux riches, so he didn't pay the school fees, and so I had to leave and go back to the normal state primary school I'd been at twelve weeks previously. But by then, of course, everything had moved on and it was all different – like how your house looks when you come back off your holiday.

What mattered at Little Thurrock primary school was being good at football (and I weren't good at football). If you weren't good at either football or, failing that, fighting (or ideally, both), you might just as well have come to school wearing a pair of your mum's tights, with your balls and cock looking like disgruntled, tiny burglars on a dreadful bank raid. 'You're on a hiding to nothing – you'll end up serving ten to twenty down the front of your mum's tights with no chance of a reprieve, I tells ya!'

I think it berserk that I still feel embarrassed about things I did when I was a child. Decades have now passed; I should be able to remember a faux pas from when I was eight without feeling ashamed. There was this teacher at that school, Miss Savage, not in a Dickens way, younger than I am now, probably, fizzing with the enthusiasm of a recently graduated teacher. She started a school cricket team in addition to her dinosaur and painting lessons; she said that I was good at bowling. I thought, 'Oh my God! I might be in that team.' When she announced the team, in the traditional and casually cruel way they do in schools, seemingly designed to exact as much tension as possible, very much akin to the reality shows of today, throughout the list, I thought 'the next one will be me', but it never was. 'Oh right,' I thought, 'the cricket team is not going to be the thing I can cling onto.'

It would not have long served as a raft of salvation; I'm not designed for sport. Since Colin's coup, I could no longer find solace at home. After school had finished for the day I just used to hang around the buildings of Little Thurrock; I didn't have anything to do or anywhere else to go where I felt comfortable. I once cornered Miss Savage and another young teacher, Miss Marris; they were all giggly and embarrassed, leafing through a teaching manual in their minds and saying, 'Russell, you're just going to have to go home – school is finished.' I simply remained, doing the odd voices and catchphrases that I had. 'I demand an explanation'; that was one of my favourites – clearly enunciated, and with the same kind of camp twang I'd use now. 'That's unkind!' was another. I know these don't sound especially hilarious now, but the humour was very much in the delivery.

Both these catchphrases could've had practical application in another episode of inappropriate muckiness that occurred at this grubby juncture. I had a babysitter – he was somewhere between fifteen and seventeen. I still feel odd about this event. It didn't seem that bad or horrible at the time, just macabre: a hot, prickly, awkward affair, with me stood, fully clothed, in an empty bath, and the familiar room interrupted by strange smells, pubic hair and an erection.

What I recall of it is giddy and vaguely exhilarating, like the vacuous, vapid thrill of Las Vegas: 'This doesn't seem right. This is why Bin Laden hates America – it's gone wrong.' There shouldn't be all this light and oxygen and no clocks and tigers prowling above my head in a Perspex cage. There shouldn't be this man beating out a solipsistic rhythm of onanism. The rhythm concluded with the lash of his sperm hitting the plastic on the back of the toilet, where the mechanism is, the cistern, the bit you have to lift up when you break the toilet at someone else's house and have to peer into its innards like a junior house doctor. 'There's that ball thing. Oh no, it's not working.' I'd like never again to conduct open-bog surgery in a stranger's lavvy.

It's an incredibly intimate thing, the primal state you go into, just before you ejaculate. Then, afterwards, there's a fug of guilt which descends. I'd imagine that vague sense of regret must be enhanced by the presence of a child: 'I would ruffle your hair, you little scamp, but I've got cum on my fingers.' I felt complicit once more as I'd been inquisitive earlier in the evening, asking, 'What is spunk? What is it like?' He goes, 'I'll show you, if you like' – an improper suggestion that were met with a woozy, vertiginous 'Okay.' The next thing I knew he was saying, 'You mustn't tell anyone', and then closing the bathroom door. He looked over at me from within his pink-cheeked frenzy and said, 'It'd be quicker if you helped.' 'Oh I bet it would,' I thought, like a world-weary hooker but, unlike a world-weary hooker, I also thought, 'Fuck that for a laugh' and declined. 'No, you're alright mate, I'll give the ol' wanking off a man in a toilet a bit of a swerve for a couple of decades.' When I did eventually get round to wanking off a man (for a TV programme, obviously), it transpired it didn't get any easier with age.

I did have at this unusual and challenging time a friend, a human friend called Sam. I loved Sam. He was my best friend growing up – a lovely, lovely boy. We went to Hampton Court in 1985, when my mum and Colin had decided to try and adopt the pose of normalcy. In our household, mundanity were regularly achieved, banality flourished unchecked, but normalcy were seldom seen. We went into that maze. It was a joy to be lost in there – thinking of Henry VIII with his stockings round his knees, chasing after some scullery maid with a hard-on and an axe.

Towards the end of the day a game of 'It' was played with my mum, Colin and Sam, with me feeling resentful that Colin was more affable towards Sam than me; and when he tagged me and slapped me round the head in one conveniently vindictive action, I saw it as a manifestation of repressed hatred rather than an accident. 'Fuck off!' I shouted. As is often the case when a child swears at an adult, it had incredible resonance and rang out like a gunshot; a flock of pigeons took off from a nearby tree, a twitchy stag looked over its shoulder and I stormed off impotently as I realised 'I can't actually go anywhere, because I'm only fucking ten years old. Right, I'll start adult life now: let's get a CV done.' In the car on the way home – another idyllic day out spoiled, my 'fuck off' hanging in the air – I remember hearing the first reports of the Heysel tragedy. It was strangely comforting to me that the world should be so fucked.

How Christmas Should Feel

When I was eleven, I got a gerbil, Barney. It was not a popular purchase, nor was it easily achieved. I was like a dogged Greenpeace campaigner – dedicatedly fighting for what I believed in against equally resolute opposition. In a way, having to lobby so relentlessly to secure a pet set me in good stead in later life when seducing pious women. 'Please take your bra off! Please?' 'Can I see your bottom? Oh go on?' By puberty I had learned that nothing worth having could be easily attained and to succeed one must be single-minded. By my twenties I would relish the challenge of chaste maids and the search for the correct combination of words required to decode their moral resistance. Jumping through hoops, ducking questions, feigning indifference to sex. 'I'm not bothered about sex, we can just cuddle.' The nobstacle course, I call it. Perhaps worryingly there was a corollary between getting my hands on rodents as a boy and boobies as a man.

How I adored that hard-won gerbil. Barney. A good solid, blokey name for the new totem of my happiness. I worshipped Barney the way primitive people worshipped the animals they hunted, seeing in the creature a connection to the natural and the divine. My devotion was swiftly rewarded when Barney, with scant regard for his gender, quite brilliantly had a litter of babies. I treasure the memory of these tiny, pink, squirming chipolatas. It was miraculous – like how Christmas should feel.

Six of them there were, just squeaking, blind little nitwits, foetal and helpless at first, but with their diligent, ever-watchful man-mum constantly nurturing them they all survived, passing through several adorable stages on their journey to maturity. They develop fur before they can see; there were two black ones, two gold ones and two brown ones – an incredible gerbil spectrum. Who knew rodents were capable of such an array of colours? They would bumble about with their little eyes shut, mewing at the world. I wasn't meant to touch them in case their mum didn't like it, but I did, all the time, and Barney didn't mind. I let them run about all over my bedroom and Barney would scuttle about, collecting them up and popping them back in their nest. Ah! Aaaaah! They were so beautiful. They were like people, living their little lives, growing day by day. Their eyes opened and they'd frolic and play and communicate by stamping their little feet like Thumper in *Bambi*. It was truly beautiful. A gerbil utopia: we were all equal and treated each other with respect; egalitarianism wasn't an issue, it was a self-regulating society founded on love.

Then, the second they were old enough, the little perverts started fucking each other. 'Oh well,' I thought, ever the liberal, 'who cares if they're related, as long as they're taking precautions.' They weren't. 'Well, that doesn't matter. We'll soon have a mighty army of gerbils and we can begin a crusade to spread our values across the globe.' Weeks passed, gerbils germinated. I awoke one morning, lifted my bleary head from the pillow and glanced over towards the colony to see Sandy, one of the females, with a little pink baby in her paws, eating it. Just chewing into its head she was, as if infanticide was as natural a way to begin the day as a croissant. 'Shake dreams from your hair,/My pretty child, my sweet one', as Jim Morrison said, '. . . choose the sign of your day'. For me the sign of that day was a baby gerbil being eaten by its auntie. 'Good portent for the coming day, d'ya think?' The second generation stuck rigidly to the Old Testament model and ballsed Eden right up. I had to impose apartheids, work out whose babies were whose, because they were all popping out nippers. I think Barney disgraced himself by getting pregnant with one of his son's children; I despaired of them. I did consider a Sodom and Gomorrah-style smiting, preserving only Barney, but when I looked at their little faces my wrath was assuaged: 'How can I stay mad at you? You incestuous, cannibal little slags.'

Time now for a bit more of the ol' cancer, my poor mother only four years into remission from the previous encounter fell ill once more. On this occasion, it was breast cancer, and she had to go back to that same grim, run-down Orsett medical facility in order to have a mastectomy. But Brenda (one of them numerous aunties who had been with my mum when I was born) really fought for her to get into the Royal Marsden in West London – the Manchester United of cancer hospitals – so she ended up going in there to have radiotherapy instead. I had to go and stay at my nan's. My mum's mother. So I was a little apprehensive.

My mum used to send me these postcards from hospital. They were of chimpanzees dressed in a series of notable London costumes – beefeater, policeman, judge. On the other side it would say, 'Hello Russell – hope you're being a good boy.' There'd always be some encoded 'Try and be a good boy' message stitched into it. Well, I wish I'd been naughtier, if anything.

When I look back, it's not those misdeeds that I regret – I'd do them again, I tells ya – but the times when I conformed. I regret that I didn't realise that actually they've got no power over you at school – it's all just a trick to indoctrinate you into being a conditioned, tame, placid citizen. Rebel, children, I urge you, fight the turgid slick of conformity with which they seek to smother your glory.

As respite from the starchy gloom of my nan's house, I'd sometimes get to stay at my dad's. This was quite funny really, as he was an incapable sort of man – it was a bit like a John Hughes comedy, *Uncle Buck*, or Daddy Fuck, him trying to look after me in his bachelor pad in Brentwood, as if the man–child dynamic had never before occurred and we were pioneers, trying to work out this peculiar situation together.

'What time do you go to bed?' he once asked me. Well, bedtime to children is a remarkable currency and a powerful playground status symbol: 'What time's your bedtime?' some schoolyard wag'd enquire. I'd be too nervous to respond. 'You look like an eight o'clock kind of guy to me, you're missing the best part of the day.'

In this moment my father was naively handing me the keys to the Promised Land, he was allowing me to set my own bedtime. 'Oh, about ten o'clock,' I responded, nonchalantly studying my nails while my heart beat at gerbil speed. As a junkie I would revive this 'Oh my God, I'm getting away with it' sensation when travelling through airport customs with a bottom full of heroin, but for now I was smuggling my way to a late-night opiate heaven. My dear dad didn't realise that children don't go to bed when they like till my mum came out of hospital; by then it was too late, I'd tasted the sweet elixir of late-night telly.

With his pinewood bathroom and impractical, deep-pile carpets, and all these faintly pornographic things hanging around, like the poster of that tennis player scratching her arse, it was not a tastefully decorated apartment. There were brass lions either side of the fireplace, and an old camera – which was actually quite nice – in the middle of the front room, and a lot of pornography.

The contrast between the two households was stark. My dad's family were theoretically Catholic, but not in practice very religious at all – after his dad died there was no time for any of that rhubarb. My mum's side, on the other hand, were prim and proper Protestants. So one night I'd be stuck in this really stuffy, controlling, 'Look at this L.S. Lowry book and be enthused by a fireplace' type of atmosphere, and the next I'd be at my dad's. He'd drift off and I'd settle down to watch hardcore porn – black men with huge cocks fucking white women up the arse. Good it was. I was more content there, with the hands-off parenting, than in the throttling, restrictive kind my nan practised.

I thought Ron Brand was great and in lots of ways he is: he taught me that you can get what you want if you refuse to let circumstances defeat you, and perhaps there is no more valuable lesson. I only wish I'd felt he liked me more. 'They still make you play in goal, son?' he once asked me, in reference to my low status as a school footballer; in the question, for me, was confirmation of my inadequacy. I shouldn't be made to play in goal by them, I should be out there, in the middle of the park, making surging runs and delivering intelligent balls, controlling the game and rallying the team. I'm just not any good at football, daft that it seems so important; my mate Ade's legs don't work and he has responded to that problem by becoming one of the world's best wheelchair basketball players. I still almost daily lament my inability to trap a ball. Occasionally, I get phone-calls from former West Ham striker and legend Tony Cottee – which, incidentally, is as bonkers and exciting as Robin Hood popping round for dinner or Dick Whittington offering to feed your fish while you're on holiday – asking me to participate in celebrity football matches and part of me wants to, so much, but I'm scared and embarrassed. 'Don't worry,' he once said, 'we can stick you in goal.'

How I viewed my dad at that point was as this magnificent bloke who was either reading newspapers, picking his nose, farting, or making an incredible fuss of women. Sometimes he would turn the light of his attention on me and it would be brilliant. He'd tease me and wind me up and be very funny, but he'd get bored really quickly, and then I'd just be there again – all tubby and useless. Tubby because I sought solace in chocolate consumption, the foil wrappers of the delicious P-p-p-Penguin bars I'd scoff, a perspicacious trailer for the tin-foil tapestry I would later weave with smack and crack. I was a connoisseur of the Penguin, which came in yellow, green, blue and red wrappers. I was a particular devotee of the blue variety, even though all penguins are the same below the surface, which I think is as perfect an analogy as we're likely to get for the futility of racism. Once the blues were devoured I'd feast upon their inferior cousins the greens, then the reds, and finally those filthy heathens the yellows.

When my mum recovered I was happy to return home. She again said she'd pulled through because she loved me so much. I felt proud and responsible for her improved health. 'Better be grateful, 'cos your mum's not died,' adults intoned. Auntie Brenda said, 'If your mum tells you to go down the end of the garden and jump up and down, you'd better do it.' I thought such an eventuality would be a sign that she'd gone loopy and if she said anything of the sort I'd write to Dr Barnardo myself and demand refuge. Before I had chance to put pen to paper it was disconcertingly decreed that I should go to boarding school to make me less clingy; Hockerill, a state-run boarding school in Bishop's Stortford. Now what I should've done is at the audition or interview or whatever it was that took place in that musty room full of swivel-eyed skeleton folk, is carried on like a nut, gurning, swearing and talking about Satan so they'd've thought –

BISHOP'S STORTFORD HOCKERHILL COLLEGE   C 1502

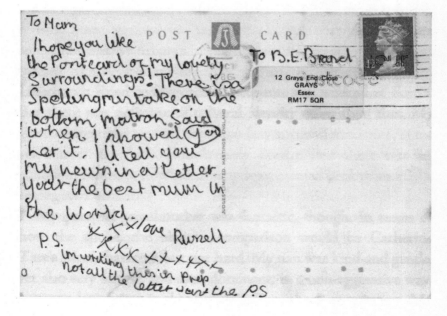

POST   CARD

To Mom
I hope you like
the Pontcard of my lovely
Surroundings! There is a
Spelling mistake on the
bottom matron said
when I showed you
her it. I'll tell you
my news in a letter
Your the best mum in
the World.
         x x x love Russell
P.S. x x x x x x x x
    im writing this in prep
    not all the letter just the P.S

To B.E. Brand
12 Grays End Close
GRAYS
Essex
RM17 5QR

'Uh oh, this boy'll be a drain on resources' but I'm such a vain nit that I charmed them and tried my best. They took on a few troubled kids a year, in the hope of setting them straight, and they concurred that I'd benefit under that remit.

Visiting my nan the day before departure, I smashed up the bathroom in an impotent prison protest. That night, my dog Topsy died. She opted to spend her last evening behind the sofa alone to prepare for the hereafter. The next morning she lay with her dry, pink tongue lolling out – undignified in death. I tried to put it back in her mouth; a squeamish, teary mortician, I couldn't make her passing palatable. I was taken to Hockerill drained of defiance and broken. As she left me, my mum sobbed with a grief so profound it was hard to imagine that the tears would ever stop. That night in the dormitory I wet the bed. I was on the top bunk, so the piss drizzled through the mattress. The boy below, deposed by the acrid shower, remained magnanimous and sweet. My pyjamas were all sticky-legged. Strip lighting graffitied over the protective darkness and a cliché of a matron made me change the sheets. Even Tony Cottee and Frank McAvennie, the hastily Blu-tacked saints upon the wall, could do nothing to alleviate my fluorescently lit nocturnal shame. ☞

7

One McAvennie

Hockerill allowed pets, so I had my filthy clan of murderous, sex-crazed gerbils and a General Woundwort-style rabbit (that arsehole from *Watership Down*) that I picked up at a rural auction I had attended with one of my aunts. The rabbit was being sold by the pound for meat but I saw in the still live creature the possibility for a better outcome for both of us and bought him off a farmer, saving him from the pot, dragging out his life long enough for him to bite me on the arm, delivering a scar that remains to this day along with the self-harming scars that I angrily etched a few years later. Being gored by a rabbit is embarrassing; if someone survives a shark attack you think them a hero, people strain to marvel at their scars. If you bear the mark of a brutal encounter with a rabbit, people assume you're somehow to blame. They still have teeth, it still hurts – perhaps more, because a shark attack would necessarily take place in salt water which is an anaesthetic; there you have it, rabbit bites are worse than a shark's. Peter Cook disliked rabbits solely on the basis that they have no pads on their paws, their claws reach uninterrupted right up their dirty little wrists.

I spent all my spare time at Hockerill playing Subbuteo – against myself. First I'd be the attackers and then the defence. I would compete against me in a complex series of leagues, while a new poster of Alan Devonshire cut out from *Shoot* peered down, befuddled by all the pointless cheating. Subbuteo is more manageable than actual football. You can play it while lying on your stomach, and you can control all twenty-two players. The position of footballing deity – hovering astride the table like a mighty colossus, deciding the outcomes of all the games in a world where West Ham topped every league and won every cup – was one I felt myself quite well suited to. By now I'd taken residence in my imagination, preferring it to the real world. I used to make my own match-day programmes, and I painted Frank McAvennie's head blond. Georgie Parris, West Ham's number three, he were a black lad, so I painted up his face and hands all nice. There weren't so many black players in them days, but them that there were – Tony Daley of Villa, John Barnes at Liverpool, Viv Anderson at United – were just some of the players keenly represented by me. It's quite difficult not to get paint on the kit and as I was quite obsessive I didn't like to field players in tarnished shirts, so this initially 'right on' attitude often led to black players being left on the bench, which seems a bit racist. Actually so was the blond Chelsea striker Kerry Dixon because the yellow paint ran down the back of his neck like a punctured soft-boiled egg. Plus Frank McAvennie felt undermined by the presence of another blond and I had to placate him.

My interaction with small plastic replica sports figures went much better than my interaction with living things. The pets at school were kept in a stable. When I was cleaning the gerbils' cage, I'd balance it precariously on the edge of a workbench and they'd do a bit of scurrying around and sniffing the air while I was changing their bedding. Eventually, one stupid day, the cage toppled over. As it fell, the world slowed down and I watched in horror as it landed across two of their twitching little bodies. One of them was Barney, the originator – my gerbil Adam and Eve.

She lay on the floor, kicking and dying her trivial vermin death, and my world became naught but a huge, shrill noise like a sharp red line through a Kandinsky painting. How ghastly it was – looking at Barney's pointless corpse thinking, 'Fuck! She's dead.' But after some silence and staring I thought, 'It's dead, and that's that.'

Perhaps due to the feelings of impotence which beset me in all other areas of my life at Hockerill, I was glad to discover that I was able to make people laugh. 'Make people laugh': I even love the idiom – there's no choice. The person making them do it has the power. And while I'd always seemed to have that capacity to an extent, it became much more pronounced in that boarding-school environment.

As we all lay abed at night, I would conjure up pornographic stories from the depths of my own dirty brainbox, and prattle them out to my disciples, an eroticised Christ or a teen Larry Flynt or a chubby, lonely Marquis de Sade. *Jugs* magazine informed the style of my sexy gospels; all that tireless wanking was finally paying off. There was a chorus of appreciative fiddling, pounding beneath the sheets – a requiem of masturbation for our fast-departing innocence.

One day, for a laugh – which has been the chief motivating factor in many of my worst decisions – I drew a face on my penis. It was on what would technically be termed the bell-end. I'm not circumcised, so the whole mechanism of the joke is that you show someone your penis, then pull back your foreskin to reveal the punchline – a grinning face.

At first, everyone thought it was very funny, and they were correct. But, some grass ratted me out for this breakthrough, a breakthrough for which I ought to have been given some kind of rosette. Instead I was subjected to a corrupt investigation. This teacher who didn't really like me found out about 'Helmet Harry', as it had by then been dubbed. I can't remember the exact language he used to describe what I'd done. It can't have been 'defaced your penis' because, rather than removing its face, I had innovatively given it one. He found some euphemistic way of asking me if he could see my cockleberry – which was rather a grand term for the half-developed nub I had to offer him. It could be argued, by me, that there was something quite heroic about my determination to give this region of my body such a widespread public airing, what with it being such a lovable titch. I was a showman, even before I knew it; the theatre was in my blood. But I didn't much fancy giving this teacher a butcher's as he struck me as being a wrong 'un. He looked to me like a talcy Simon Bates; that's to say a regular Simon Bates all covered in talcum powder. So I just said, 'No, it's alright, I'll be fine.'

He confirmed himself to have not had the most legitimate of motives by the rapidity with which he acquiesced to my demurral. A genuinely concerned teacher who wasn't out on the nonce would say, 'Now come on, boy, this is an important medical matter,' but he just went, 'Oh, alright.' And shuffled off looking a bit disappointed. Clearly he was chancing his arm for a glimpse of Helmet Harry, and who can blame him? It were the talk of the school: 'If you only see one cock this year, make sure it's Russell Brand's "Helmet Harry" – buy a ticket, steal a ticket, pose as a concerned teacher, but don't miss this personified prepubescent penis – it's got a face.'

News of Helmet Harry quickly got around the school, but it did not bring me the kind of celebrity I would have wished for. Instead I was ridiculed in corridors, bullied and victimised. My notoriety followed me everywhere – 'Russell Brand? Are you that kid who drew the face on his helmet?' 'Yes, I'm afraid I am. Would you like an autograph, and if so, where would you like it?' This was an ignominious affair that I would be glad to see the back of.

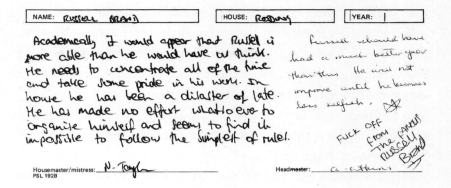

NAME: RUSSELL BRAND HOUSE: RODDING YEAR: 1

Academically, I would appear that Russel is more able than he would have us think. He needs to concentrate all of the time and take some pride in his work. In house he has been a disaster of late. He has made no effort whatsoever to organise himself and seems to find it impossible to follow the simplest of rules.

Russell should have had a much better year than this. He will not improve until he becomes less selfish. ✗

FUCK OFF FROM RUSSELL BRAND

Housemaster/mistress: N. Taylor
PSL 192B

Headmaster: C. Atkins

I really hated that place from then on and got in a lot of trouble, getting in bother by spitting and being all rebellious on the ghost train on a trip to Thorpe Park. This bloke emerged with a torch – which is a nice touch on a ghost train – and said, 'We don't like gobbers.' I thought, 'There is more to me than this. I'm not a full-time gobber, I have other abilities. Have you not seen Helmet Harry? The kids love it – it's the new Rubik's Cube.'

When they eventually expelled me it was for piffle. Me and this lad went to the girls' dorm. I think he was fucking a thirteen-year-old girl when he was eleven, which sounds awfully rude but they seemed to enjoy it and no one got hurt. Far from being a swashbuckling love rat I was terrified and begged the conjugal kids to accompany me back to the boys' dorm. Because I was so scared, the girls came back with us. The pre-teen sex machine leapt back into bed with his older bird, and her friend got into bed with me for a saucy bout of nothing at all, while I planned out how I'd turn the episode into a pornographic story with which to regale my friends. But then a prefect came along. The other girl hid under the bedclothes of her schoolboy sweetheart, but me and the girl I was with tried – in vain – to hide under the bed.

'Brand!' the prefect shouted, very formally, 'get out from under your bed'; proving that children shouldn't be given SS-style powers or they'll play up, without the need for the Stanford Experiment. And the girl dramatically emerged from beneath the bed. Hoopla ensued. My mum had to come up the school – with an aunt, of course, not Colin. The expulsion was a joy, despite my mum crying and my Auntie Janet, Sam's mum, looking disappointed. The headmistress trotted out an irrelevant send-off. 'You've never tried at this school – you've constantly been in trouble.' I tuned out and stared. 'Fuck you! I've won. I'm free. There's nothing you can do. Just spluttering language. Say things at me. Go on, say what you want – I'm out of here. I'm gone!'

When I got back home in my demob suit, Colin made me get rid of my pets as a punishment. I was only allowed to keep one gerbil. I swallowed this predictable piece of petty cruelty down into the ol' hate factory. Somehow those boffins at Hockerill, who I'd so fastidiously despised, had managed to give me quite a good education. I suppose I was trapped there and forced to learn. From then on, I could define myself as being cleverer than everyone else. When I went back to Grays School – which was just the normal comprehensive that most of the kids I'd known at primary school had gone to – no one seemed to know what the fuck was going on with anything. I thought: 'Hang on, these people are idiots.' And this instinctive humility would stand me in good stead throughout the years of academic underachievement that stretched ahead of me. ☞

8

I've Got a Bone to Pick with You

For about three years in my early teens, people were always mistaking me for a girl, because I had long hair and quite a sort of pretty face and was a bit chubby and went through puberty late. I'd be talking to a young lad for twenty minutes, and then he'd say, 'Wanna come down the pictures?' and I'd have to try and indicate that I was male with the limited tools at my disposal. 'Grrr, aren't girls terrific? Fancy a fight? Isn't Julian Dicks the absolute limit?'

One of the consequences of this was to make me very aware of my appearance. But however much I tried to adapt how I looked – by getting a new haircut, or changing the kind of clothes I wore – it didn't really seem to make any difference.

As a way of coping with this, I developed a trait that I have maintained to this day when I'm around very masculine men, which is that I go all camp. 'Oh hello,' I say, like a cross between Dot Cotton and Frankie Howerd. 'You're a big handsome beefcake, int'cha?' ''Ere – would you like me to dab your nut-sack with a lolly-stick, or lift your balls up with a spoon?'

I was really nervous about my sexuality in my early teens. I always felt kind of outside of things – always getting notes from my mum to get me off games (I hated them showers and that cold thigh-slap bonhomie, me trudging about all pudgy and unloved on some hard pitch, while other kids excelled, brilliantly occupying their newly masculine bodies) – but I never thought I was gay. I just didn't have that impulse.

In a worrying template for later sexual activity, my first and second kisses occurred within seconds of each other, with different girls. It was in a classroom at Grays School. The teacher had gone off to do something and I got off with this girl called Louise first, and then another one called Leigh. I was thirteen or fourteen at the time. And although those were my first two proper kisses, no one would have known it at the time, 'cos I paraded around like I were a Vegas pimp – some kind of gun-toting cock-merchant.

I told all them people at Grays School that the reason I was expelled from boarding school was because of getting caught with girls in my dorm – which was, of course, true. But I repackaged it brilliantly to make myself come across as some kind of George Best/Jimmy Page character, rather than a porcine nit, nervously skittering about in a dressing gown.

My first proper girlfriend was Tracey Boatman, who lived opposite me in Grays End Close. I used to hold notes up at my bedroom window to her. Her dad Jim was a milkman. I can't remember what her mum did, but she was dead into religion. She liked it. Jesus, Catholicism: any part of that belief system she was wholeheartedly into.

I was aware of Tracey all of my life, but I didn't go out with her till I was thirteen. She was lovely, actually. She's still alright as well. I saw her recently when I was back in Grays for the weekend – with her husband and two daughters – and it was sort of sad but gratifying to go back to their kitchen while her mum Sue knocked up Sunday lunch, with her dad trundling around in the background.

At school, I once inadvertently wrote a poem about a milkman called Jim. It weren't meant to be about Tracey's dad, but this Jim in the poem didn't come off at all well. And when I read it out in an English lesson, she erupted into tears. I had to explain that the connection hadn't occurred to me – 'A lot of my art comes from an unconscious place, Tracey. I go into a kind of trance: I'm like Jackson Pollock when I sling them words on the page.'

It was nice going out with her. She was one of them girls that matured early and went out with a few boys in our year. I remember my first sexual fumblings with Tracey very clearly. I was terrified of revealing my genitals after the Helmet Harry fiasco – I considered him more of a hindrance than an ally, that little fellow. I thought it might be better if he remained within the confines of my novelty Christmas pants with a tartan pattern and a Tasmanian devil on them.

From the minute I clattered – belatedly – into puberty, I was on a spree of hopeless, doomed romances. I fell in love with Nikki. She was a year older than me, and I think she fancied me at first. I remember her perhaps gently proposing the idea of a liaison, and me responding with such overstated ebullience that her pipsqueak affections were smashed into mush.

'Perhaps you'd like to go out somewhere?' she might have suggested. 'Yes, and perhaps you'd like to save my fucking soul, 'cos I'm suicidal. Please look after me.'

Nikki only lived in the next street, and I used to get on her nerves because I would go round to her house so much. I went round there on Christmas Day – Christmas Day! My dad and mum had clubbed together to buy me these Reebok Pump Classics – great big ridiculous trainers that pumped right up, with a basketball on the tongue. There was no reason for me to have trainers that pumped up. It was unnecessary. It were a gimmick.

But I was still round Nikki's house wearing them as soon as I'd got them out of the box. She was there with another lad from her year at school, sat in her bedroom, and I remember this bloke

GRAYS SCHOOL

PUPIL REPORT FORM

Pupil's Name: ..... RUSSELL BRAND .... Form ..... 4Ky ....

Please comment below on this pupil and return as soon as possible.

To: ...... MR SEAL .... Date .26.4.1990 ....

Thankyou.

Attendance

     O.K.

Conduct

     Juvenile - not rude but constantly winding up the
     other pupils and acting the fool.

Attitude to work

     Treats it all as a big joke.

Progress

     None

     General Comments: Class much better without him.

Reporting Teacher: ...... MRS ANSELL ....
Subject :   P.S.E.
            ....

<u>GRAYS SCHOOL</u>

<u>PUPIL REPORT FORM</u>

Pupil's Name: ...<u>RUSSELL BRAND</u>............. Form ....<u>4Ky</u>......

Please comment below on this pupil and return as soon as possible.

To: ..<u>MR SEAL</u>....................... Date .<u>26.4.1990</u>....

Thankyou.

<u>Attendance</u>

Erratic!

<u>Conduct</u>

Improved of late!

However has a very high opinion of himself.
Sometimes gives the impression that rules do not
apply to him.

<u>Attitude to work</u>

Very poor - more interested in friends and projecting
the right image.

<u>Progress</u>

NIL!

General Comment: Generally speaking a 'waste of space' has
no interest in subject, but does not make any effort to change
his approach.

Reporting Teacher: ......MR RIDER.....................

Subject : ......P.E.........................

RUSSELL BRAND

going – very sarcastically – 'So, what did you get for Christmas?' And I was just standing there, in these two gleaming white igloos. Ah, the sweet embarrassment. I've learned now that when I'm in a situation where my first impulse is to hide the shame I feel forever, that when rendered as a yarn the scenario will probably be funny, so my second impulse is, 'That's probably material.'

My second experience with *that* babysitter was a good example of this kind of situation. When I was twelve or thirteen, my mum and Colin were going out and decided that I would have a babysitter – even though I was too sophisticated to require a chaperone. When I found out that the person entrusted with this responsibility was to be the same upstanding young citizen who had masturbated in front of me five years before, I was even less keen on the idea.

'I don't want a babysitter – I'm too old,' was my initial plea. When this was dismissed I swiftly segued into the more controversial, 'When I was a child, he wanked himself off, and asked me to help him.' Of course, they thought I was lying. Having sung like a bird to no avail after getting fingered by that tutor, I hadn't told either of my parents about the thing with the babysitter when it first happened.

'Don't tell anyone,' he'd said, conspiratorially, 'they'll think I'm weird.'

And initially he got his way, but later on I did discuss the episode with a few people who lived on our street, and someone came up with the phrase 'gay phase'. This had obviously got back to him, as when he eventually came round – my anguished protests having been to no avail – I remember him saying, in an inquisitive way, 'What is a gay phase?' Like he thought that might be a possible explanation.

Apparently, some adolescents go through a 'gay phase' where

they want children to wank them off. That was a bit of a misunderstanding on the part of the people of Grays End Close – about the difference between homosexuality and asking a child to wank you off. 'Both of these activities belong in a box of things we think are disgusting: put them in with animal abuse and racial tolerance.'

Cross about my loose lips, the moment we were reunited he uttered the ominous words, 'I've got a bone to pick with you.'

'I remember that bone,' I might have replied, had I been feeling a little more sure of myself in this tricky social situation. 'I remember you picking it till it sprayed cum on the back of the toilet with a plastic splat.'

Nothing bad happened on his second babysitting assignment, evidently it was a phase and aside from the wanking incident he were a lovely lad, but a pattern of me taking extreme action in a quest to be heard was beginning to emerge. When I eventually started cutting myself – aged thirteen or fourteen – it was frustration and anger that led to it. My response to being trapped or thwarted was to slash myself with a knife or some broken glass – a mode of sanguinary melodrama to which I would periodically return, right up into my twenties.

I also began to dabble with bulimia. It seemed a very practical procedure at the time. I'd got all fat; when I started to get bullied at school as a result, I thought there must be a simple solution, and it turned out there was – eat loads and then puke it out. I'd always been a really fussy child, growing up. As a kid, I only liked to eat beefburgers, sausages, fish fingers, waffles – lumps of things, food that had been in the *Beano*. 'This is from Birds Eye, we can trust those guys – look at that smiling old Captain, he's just like Uncle Albert.'

In an ideal world, I preferred food that was sealed individually – Weetabix, Penguins, Wagon Wheels – and

I was very suspicious of anything that'd been mixed. Sausages stuck in a mound of mash was about as sophisticated as my tastes got. (Even now, when I find something I like eating, I'll eat it all the time. In my twenties, I spent years living on Weetabix in the morning, with SuperNoodles and a can of tuna later on.) Colin was annoyed by the bulimia fad. 'Did you puke up in the sink again? Don't. It's clogging the drain up.'

I became a vegetarian at fourteen. There was a lad at our school called Daniel Zahl, whose father was a socialist with a beard, like the 'Modern Parents' in *Viz*. Daniel took me and Sam Crooks to a Vegetarian Society meeting, where they showed us videos of factory farming. I made a commitment in that room that would one day lead to me becoming crowned the World's Sexiest Vegetarian, a title you're ineligible for, no matter how sexy you are, unless you don't eat meat. Morrissey perpetually steeled my resolve, and the probability that my principled dietary stand would annoy Colin was the deciding factor.

'Vindictive vegetarianism', I like to call it. I've never regretted it. I'm incredibly sentimental about animals. It's the only opportunity I get to occupy the moral high ground: when I got clean, after chatting to some Krishna conscious devotees, I gave up fish as well. They said if you put death into your body you will emit death, but I'm in it mostly for the high ground. 'You're vegetarian?' comes the enquiry. 'Yes.' Then the inevitable, 'Do you eat fish?' This is where they catch a lot of people out: the inquisitor is already at this stage anticipating a 'Yes' and loading up with, 'Ah, well, you're not a proper vegetarian then are you because fish are incredibly sensitive and some of them write haikus.' That's why I have to stifle a smug grin when I reply, 'No. No, I don't eat fish because it's cruel to them, the lovely little things.' And on particularly smarmy days, 'If you put death into your body you emit death.' Even as a junkie I stayed true – 'I shall have heroin, but I shan't have a hamburger.' What a sexy little paradox. ☞

9

Teacher's Whisky

The first time I'd ever tasted alcohol had been in the staff-room at Little Thurrock primary school, when I was probably nine or ten years old. There was a rota of jobs you had to do at that school, and one of them was cleaning the staff-room. This seems nuts. Why on earth were children entrusted with the task of cleaning the staff-room? Especially as the place was awash with booze. This incident seems so daft and unlikely that my better judgement is trying to insist that it didn't occur – but it did; they got the pupils to work at the school like it was a nineteenth-century Lancashire mill. It wasn't hard graft – they never made me tarmac the playground for example – but this isn't something for which I feel I ought to express gratitude; I should've just been listening to stories about ducks and colouring in. And while we're on the subject of ducks, which we plainly are, the story 'The Ugly Duckling' ought be banned as the central character wasn't a duckling or he wouldn't have grown up into a swan. He was a cygnet. He shouldn't have been allowed to hang round with them other little ducks either; the whole thing is a filthy, corrupt mess. Nonetheless I'd rather sit pie-eyed and agog being brainwashed by that stinking propaganda than apply Mr Sheen to the staff-room cupboard.

It was Martin Phillips and me toiling that day; he was a funny little character, tightly curled hair and NHS specs. Him and me had to clean the staff-room, and in the cupboard we found a little half-bottle of Teacher's whisky, which seemed an appropriate brand, for it was, after all, teachers' whisky.

I sipped a little bit of the naughty water and treacherously reassured my reluctant accomplice – 'Martin, this is delicious' – and passed the bottle. He really committed to it, and drank with such beautiful, unblinking faith. With an almighty glug he tipped the bottle upright into his own little Martin Phillips face, and the liquid filled his cheeks with this foul, medicinal, despicable taste, and the surging heat poured into him. It was a lovely thing to watch, and the whole episode was happily consequence-free.

The first time I got drunk was at my auntie's house one Christmas. On this occasion, I got really pissed, and gave an early indication of the seemingly infinite capacity I have to adapt instantly to new circumstances. This was the first time I'd ever got properly inebriated, and yet I straight away became a pitiful, lachrymose drunk, saying to my younger cousin Sam – who was about three years old – 'Don't you ever get like this, son.' But I'd only just got like it, that day, for a half-hour. It wasn't like alcohol had been the ruin of me – my whole empire in ruins, and all the fault of the demon drink.

I was fourteen or fifteen and it was six glasses of white wine that did the trick. As I was drinking them, I thought, 'I wonder what'll happen if I just keep on doing this?' The need to find out what will happen if I don't relent or moderate my actions has been a constant source of difficulty and discomfort in my life.

It was the same with prepubescent masturbation. I remember being on the bathroom floor and thinking, 'What happens if I just keep on wanking?' (I've had a lot of great moments on bathroom floors. The first time I took heroin, I remember being in a similar situation.) Lying in a state of pre-opiated innocence

on my mum's bathroom floor. (Oh that is the telling adjective –
or pronoun, or whatever it is – my mum's bathroom floor. She
wasn't there, of course. It was the floor that she owned, but from
which she was at this point absent. And I was lying upon the bath
rug – which was pink, with a fringe.)

Normally at that stage of sexual immaturity, you'd get an
erection, carry on wanking for a while, and then stop. But I
started wondering what would happen if you persisted beyond
that barrier. The answer was a kind of dry orgasm, which set my
leg twitching against the pink artificial fibres, and left me with an
embarrassed, awkward feeling, reminiscent of how I would later
feel when receiving oral sex from a vacuum cleaner. (Of course,
it's not really oral sex in that instance, it's pipe sex – an oft-
overlooked category of erotic endeavour.)

Growing up in Grays, there were two main landmarks looming
above you. One was the Queen Elizabeth II Bridge across the
Thames (little did I know that lurking on the other side of this, in
Dartford, just south of the river, was the infant Matt Morgan).
The other was Thurrock Lakeside shopping centre – a huge,
great, hovering spaceship of consumerism. I did shoplift quite a
bit from there. But newsagents in Grays were not safe from my
wandering hands either.

For reasons that may have had something to do with my
incipient dishonesty, but could equally have been rooted in the
lunchtime porn video club I had enterprisingly set up with a few
like-minded friends, Mum and Colin did not trust me with a key
to the house. They didn't like me to go home in the middle of the
day, but they'd leave a key out for me to let myself in with after
school.

One time, I'd tried to sneak home at lunchtime, but there was
no key there. So when I got back later on and the stone in the
garden where the key usually was hadn't moved, I just put my

sleeve over my hand and punched through the glass panel in the door to get in.

'Good,' I thought. 'That'll show 'em.' My mum got home a couple of minutes after I did. 'You alright, Russell?' she asked, slightly nervously. I explained that I'd had to let myself in because there was no key. A short while after that, Colin returned. He asked what had gone on, and when I said there was no key left out, I could see him whitening with fury.

The hostility between us was mostly unspoken. It was a silent war, constantly in motion. Colin went into the back garden – wearing the blue overalls that he had for work. He looked under the stone, and came back, full of terrifying adult man-rage. My mum was all panicked – 'Oh Colin, Colin.' As he dragged me out into the back garden, I fell over and pissed myself. I was at an age when it was horrible to have done that – school trousers clad about my thighs. He threw me on the ground, screaming, 'There it is!' with an incandescent rage that had to be about more than broken glass.

It turned out that at some point between my two attempts to gain entry to the house, he had returned home and replaced the key.

There's a theme that runs throughout my childhood of adults taking me to one side to utter these unbelievable things. I'm not sure if it was on this or one of the other five or six occasions when things between Colin and me got really out of hand – but I distinctly remember him taking me into a vestibule and hissing, 'Why don't you fuck off and leave us alone?' And me just thinking, 'Fuck you! Fuck you!' and having to hold myself together. 'Why are these people saying these things?' I would ask myself. 'This can't be right.'

There have been times over the last couple of years – as things have started to work out for me in career terms – when I've stopped to reflect on what the legacy of all this formative unhappiness has been, in terms of the ultimate goals of my ambition. When would I stop? I've realised that my ambition is actually beyond the designs of the Third Reich.

When I used to sit in the front seat on car journeys with my dad, he always listened to motivational tapes: Anthony Robbins, people like that. The one thing I got from them – something my dad endowed me with himself, as well as through these self-help brainwashing cassettes – was that you can do whatever you want. Now if I want something – whether it's a job or a woman – I will determinedly, resolutely, remove anything that's in the way, until I possess the object of my desire.

My dad's philosophy was (and I think still is) that life is a malevolent force, which seeks to destroy you, and you have to struggle with it. Only those who are hard enough will succeed. Most people get crushed, but if you fight, in the end life will go, 'Fucking hell. This one's serious. Let him through.' ☛

10

'Boobaloo'

Until I encountered the Grays School drama teacher, Colin Hill, I had no intention of being a performer. I'd always hoped my dad would be my way out: in Steinbeck's *Of Mice and Men*, Lenny's dopey gaze is forever fixed on an imaginary horizon where he'll finally get his rabbits and alfalfa plants; I dreamed of an unlikely Brand and Son enterprise, like *Open All Hours* but more sexy; perhaps we'd have a casino or a brothel or be guns for hire. I'd not developed a business plan, but the name I liked.

Colin Hill was a big, bovine man with a deeply creviced face and ashen hair. He was also the first teacher I thought of as human, the type of teacher who ushers you across the wobbly, *Indiana Jones* rope bridge into adulthood. I imagine he may have been a teacher that you could address by his Christian name or smoke a fag with. Before that, when you find out a teacher's first name it's like you've seen them on the lavvy wanking, a glimpse of a world so terribly private that while they rattle on about Wilfred Owen or geological stratification you can think nothing but, 'Well, I can't accept all this from a Derek.'

Colin Hill said I was good in drama classes. 'It's just showing off,' I thought, 'sanctioned showing off . . . Oh my God, I've found a loophole.' 'Erm, Colin, you like this showing off, do you? You say I'm doing it well? I can also torment dogs and masturbate, do you have any classes for those?' 'No, I don't usually do them simultaneously, but if there's a GCSE in it . . .'

A former protégé of Colin Hill – though the possibility that he might have exaggerated his role in this man's rise cannot be ruled out – was Karl Howman, then starring in the BBC sitcom, *Brush Strokes*, and also the Flash cleaning product adverts where he plays the same character in a more restricted plot that always has to involve him doing some cleaning under pressure from a Mother-in-Law type woman. Actually *Brush Strokes* wasn't as well constructed as the Flash ads, but it did have a theme tune by Dexy's Midnight Runners which was brilliant and puts *Brush Strokes* alongside *Birds of a Feather* as shows that have unjustifiably tear-inducing music. 'Now on BBC1, some light comedy, but before that why don't you have a quick listen to this and consider that no matter what you achieve you will die alone.'

'Karl Howman's one of mine – him out of *Brush Strokes*,' Colin Hill used to say. And I used to think, 'Hmm, interesting.' And the realisation that people who had later become famous had been taught by the same teacher as me parked itself in my nut and gestated.

'We're doing *Bugsy Malone* as the school play – you should try for the part of Fat Sam,' said Mr Hill. That's as significant a moment in my life as there's yet been – him asking me to audition for that role.

I was fat already, so the adjective had been taken care of before I'd picked up a script. All I had to work on was the Sam bit. How hard could that be? I had met people called Sam. In fact, that was my best friend at school's name.

From the first day I started doing Colin Hill's drama group, I remember thinking, 'This is fucking brilliant – why on earth didn't I do this before?' There were all these girls, for a start. It attracts girls, drama. It's not for boys. Well, there was one lad from the year below me, Jeff Bell. He was really good actually. He played Bugsy Malone, and then there was me playing Fat Sam and loads of girls.

A consequence of involvement in this drama group was you'd get to see girls in bras – I suppose they were changing into costumes. The sight drilled itself so deeply into my mind that vital faculties had to be removed to allow it to flourish. Dancing and the ability to form intimate bonds were quickly sacrificed so that the 'girls in bras' department of my brain could be given extra floors and its own DJ; 'Boobaloo' he'd holler whenever he saw some knockers he liked. He's still in there now, spinning the same discs night after night and keeping me tuned in to the screaming frequency of Libido FM.

I enjoyed the rehearsal process enormously. But on the first night the terror I felt was almost transcendental. Euphoric fear, so vertiginous, awesome and profound that I felt it could only be a prelude to death. I now know that the adrenalised fever is my body's preparatory method and is responsible for the energy and speed I can produce on stage. Once or twice I've sought out a reference or a joke in my mind while on telly and it's seemed like an age or, perhaps realistically, twelve seconds, at the time, but when I watch it back it's an imperceptible beat. Everything about the school seemed different that first night. The hall, which had been empty when we were rehearsing, was now full of lines of plastic chairs and the air was neon and flashed with expectation.

All the parents came. I don't know how many people that would've been – I suppose about a hundred. But it seemed to me like a riot in a straitjacket. I locked myself in a lavvy and evacuated liquid dread. 'God, what are you doing?' I asked myself. 'I don't have to do it,' I reasoned. Locked in the lavvy, locked in negotiation with myself. 'Scared, SCARED. RUN!' sang my unconscious, with backing vocals from my bowels. I had drawn on a moustache with an eyebrow pencil, I had a hat from somewhere, and a big suit of my dad's with a pillow stuffed up it to make me even fatter. I went behind the curtain on the stage, and listened to the audience on the other side of it.

This is a noise that I'm really familiar with now. It endows me with mingled excitement and glee. I want to grasp it and have that moment. The anticipation and anxiety becomes almost unbearable as it builds and builds – 'Oh, Fucking hell! All them people. They're just there living their lives now, talking to each other, but in a minute I'm going to have to go out in front of them and perform.' This was where that first scorched into me. It burnt. It got too much so I went up to the stage and put my head through the curtain and looked at the crowd. Mr Hill saw me, and came round the back. 'What the fuck are you doing? Don't fucking do that.' I'd violated a professional code. Admirable that he cared so deeply, but it compounded the fear.

There was five minutes more, standing there with the tension, stifling the urge to vomit, already drained – nothing left to give but a performance. And then I walked out onto the stage for the first time in my life. The light. The light is so bright that all that remains is you and the darkness. You can feel the audience breathing. It's like holding a gun or standing on a precipice and knowing you must jump. It feels slow and fast. It's like dying and being born and fucking and crying. It's like falling in love and being utterly alone with God; you taste your own mouth and feel your own skin and I knew I was alive and I knew who I was and that that wasn't who I'd been up till then. I'd never been so far away but I knew I was home. 'I know everything,' I thought. I knew I'd never leave and I never have. My first lines were, 'It's okay, everybody. It's okay.' I was doing a Jimmy Cagney impression, but with Tommy Cooper hands. And as soon as I was out there the fear became triumph. I felt enormous and strong.

There was a scene early on with this kid Dennis. He was a funny, scrawny lad who lived just around the corner from me. All pale and wan he was – like a baby that's been born too early – and there was a bit where I had to spray him with a soda-siphon. When I did it, his face looked dead funny as he mewled and gawped, and the audience really laughed and I laughed too and improvised. I felt acceptance. Being on that stage was the headiest intoxicant I'd yet sampled. I loved it so much that from that moment on I thought, 'I'm doing this now, I'll do whatever it takes.' I'd had my head filled with my dad's motivation tapes: 'You can do whatever you want. Focus on what your goal is, refuse to fail.'

I once heard Steve Jones of the Sex Pistols say that he thought David Bowie and Marc Bolan had come from space – because they were so weird. Well, I fucking never. I thought, 'I'm one of them. That's what I am. I'm that.' They didn't seem foreign or alien at all.

What was alien was being ordinary, being humdrum, being trapped into appeasing Colin, having to crush and stifle my opinions, not being allowed to be brilliant, tricking myself into mediocrity. And somehow, in this most ordinary, banal of moments – the school play – I felt immediately unshackled from all that.

Bugsy Malone ran for three nights. And throughout that time I was able to accept myself and other people in a way that I never had before. My dad came to every show. He's been really supportive in some ways – not just the cliché of an absent father.

When the last performance came to an end, though, I felt utterly mortified. I went back with him to stay at my nan's in Dagenham and ended up sitting on her settee, completely desolate. I just didn't have any way of coming down from that high. A couple of years later – once I'd crossed the line from child

GRAYS SCHOOL DRAMA CLUB

presents

Bugsy MALONE

by ALAN PARKER

MUSICAL DIRECTOR - VIC "RAZAMATAZ" WADE

DIRECTED BY COLIN HILL

SEE YOU AT "CINDERELLA" IN JANUARY
AT THE THAMESIDE THEATRE

CHARACTERS

BUGSY MALONE   JEFF BELL
BLOUSEY BROWN   MELANIE GILLINGHAM
DANDY DAN   LEE GARWOOD
FAT SAM   RUSSELL BRAND
TALLULAH   MARIANNE LAYBOURN
FIZZY   CLARE MEAD
LEROY   DAVID SMALLBONE
LOUELLA   MADDIE BLAND

FAT SAM'S GANG

KNUCKLES   RICHARD BALLARD
RITZY   STEVEN PATTISON
ANGELO   PAUL LIFF
LOUIE   ANTHONY WEBB
SNAKE EYES   DARREN MARE
GIGO   JASON TILBURY

DANDY DAN'S GANG

DOODLE   ROSS CHILDS
YONKY CHARLIE   STEVEN LEWIS
LAUGHING BOY   SIMON MUNRO
SHOULDERS   JAY LINDNER
BENNY LEE   CHRIS RIVETT
YONKERS   RICHARD DONALD
SCARFACE   DANIEL POWLEY

ROXY ROBINSON   STEVEN COX
UNDERTAKERS   NEIL INGRAM/GLEN GOOCH
VIOLINISTS   LOUISE BLAND/CHRISTINE HOLLAND/SAMANTHA WOOD
BARBER   SUZANNE GILLINGHAM
FLASH FRANKIE   DAVID DODSON
TAP SINGERS   HILARY MARTIN/MADDIE BLAND/CLARK MERCHANT
BABY FACE   THOMAS LUCAS
POP MAKKER   NEIL PROST
PAPER BOY   SUSI MORRIS
RADIO ANNOUNCER   ALISON HERMITAGE
WAITRESS   EMMA BEARD
ENGLISH REPORTER   CLAIR MERCHANT
CELLIST   ELEANOR EDWARDS
BUTLER   DANNY GILLINGHAM
TILLIE   SARAH CURTIN
LORETTA   DANIELLE MEAD

DOTTY   LAURA BURKE
DANGLER   CLAIRE BEARD
VELMA   LOUISE BLAND
VERA   EMMA BEARD
OSCAR DEVELT   CRAIG MCCORMACK
BIG ASSISTANT   KATIE HARRINGTON
AUDITION SINGERS   EMMA BEARD/JOANNE DELWAY
MARRIONT   DENNIS THOMPSON
VENTRILOQUIST   SUZANNE GILLINGHAM
BUNNY   DANNY GILLINGHAM
AUDITION SINGER   NICOLA WRIGHT
AUDITION DANCERS   CAROLINE BEARD/LANSVIR GILL/SARAH REEVES/CHERYL PICKETT
AUDITION RECITERS   RACHEL STONE/DANIELLE COPELAND
LENA   DAYNA COCKILL
O'DREARY   STUART AVIS
SEYMOUR SCOOP   HILARY MARTIN
CAPTAIN SMOLSKY   BARRY AUSTIN
BRADY   ROBERT BURGESS
LOONEY BERGONZI   RICHARD DONALD
CAGEY JOE   COLIN BIGHAM
PICKETT   ROBERT BURGESS
JOE   DENNIS THOMPSON
PRIEST   ANTHONY WEBB

CHINESE LAUNDRY WORKERS - REPORTERS - BOXERS - GUARDS - COOKS - COWS & GIRLS

LINDSEY WATERMAN   RACHEL STONE
MICHELLE THOMPSON   KATY BECKETT
TARA HIGHAM   DANIELLE KIRKLAND
SARAH COX   RACHAEL GILBEY
LUCY JOHNSON   CARLY HOLMES
AMANDA BEARLEY   LEEANN CRONIN
KELLY PAUL   CARA GOSS
CAROLINE BEAD   MICHELLE HAMILTON
LOUISE BUCKINGHAM   CHARLOTTE COOK
CLAIR OLIVER   EMMA PACEY
ALISON HERMITAGE   DANNY GILLINGHAM
LANSVIR GILL   ROBERT BURGESS
SARAH LONG   JENSEN TAYLOR
NATALIE GANLING   ANDY LEAK
HILARY MARTIN   STEVEN LEWIS
CLAIR MERCHANT   SIMON MUNRO
EMMA HUGHES   SAM WOOD
TINA ALMOND   CHRISTINE HOLLAND
SUZANNE GILLINGHAM   NICOLA WRIGHT
SANRAJ SANDHU

to drug addict – I would have doped myself to sleep. I was inconsolable.

How could I get back the feeling I'd had in front of that audience? That was all I cared about. Accessing previously untapped resources of drive and focus, I found out what I had to do and got on with it. Within just a couple of days, I'd started applying to extras agencies and stage schools. My Fat Sam experience had given birth to this ridiculous dream of salvation through fame and success. And ever since then, that vision has been the one thing – apart from the love of my mother – that has been utterly unwavering for me.

It's difficult to be honest about this sort of thing though, because in cold print it seems serious and egotistical. If you strip away self-effacement, charm and the spirit of mischief – qualities that make determination and ambition tolerable – you're left with a right arsehole. ☞

11

Say Hello to the Bad Guy

My mum refers to the play, *Bugsy Malone*, as 'Fat Sam', because that was the part I played. I suspect that, from her perspective, upon the stage those nights stood but one tubby player, alone, reacting, brilliantly, to invisible entities. My mum thinks I'm an excellent swimmer, simply because I've not yet drowned. I found my religion through that play, Bugsy-ism; the next fifteen years were spent in the service of the God of my ambition. Performing was my way out of Grays, conformity and myself. I ignored the advice of *Heartbeat* and 'Wicksy' actor, Nick Berry, issued in *More* magazine in response to the question: What tip would you offer to any youngster trying to make it as an actor? 'Never pretend to be someone that you're not.' Now hold on, you have to 'pretend you're someone you're not' a bit as an actor. Some would argue, Stanislavski for example, that that is acting's essence. 'I most certainly will not murder King Duncan, I've never met him.' 'But you're playing Macbeth.' 'That's a ridiculous name, I am Nick Berry, Wicksy at a push, I'll even consider MacWicksy but I shall certainly not kill that lovely old monarch; no matter how much Lady MacWicksy may demand it.'

My zeal was potent, as is often the case with the newly converted in any faith: 'I'll be famous soon,' I thought, 'then I can get out of here and on with the job of being the new Jacko' – this was the name of Karl Howman's *Brush Strokes* lothario. The main problem as I saw it was to be owning a fleet of limousines before I was old enough to drive. 'I suppose I'll have a driver,' I thought. No further incentive was required, but a new and powerful one appeared. After one of the performances, girls from another school – probably William Edwards about five miles away – turned up, but to me it was as exotic as a troupe of cabaret dancers from Rio de Janeiro – all high kicks and coked-up flirting – arriving. 'Another school? What's the weather like there? What time is it there now? Marry me . . . I mean, if you think we could ever overcome our cultural differences. Can we make a go of this? If I can change, and you can change, maybe the whole damn world can change.' That's how I felt. Except for the last bit, that was from *Rocky 4*.

My life is a bit like *The Elephant Man*. Probably ol' John Merrick had it a bit tougher than me what with the deformity and torture and bronchitis and whatnot but there are certainly parallels. Like how grateful he is if someone's nice to him. Meeting these rare and glorious specimens from a stone's throw away, the scene I recalled was the one where an actress gives the charming and beautiful hero a photo – 'You're not a monster . . . Mr Merrick. You're *Romeo*,' and he, through delirious gratitude, 'Oh, *how kind!*'

It was unfamiliar to me – girls being flirtatious – and initially I was frightened. But I adjusted with characteristic rapidity. I became a schoolboy Tony Montana – rampaging round the playground, indiscriminately spraying girls with chat-up lines. 'Say hello to my little friend,' I hollered in canteens and corridors. No one was safe from me; charged by a white mound of my own newly discovered potency, every female was a potential target.

This didn't go on for long before the natural hierarchy were restored. I was reminded that status in Grays was determined through football and fighting. Johnny-come-lately Fat Sam actors had a short shelf life. Plus, an identity blended together from traits gleaned from John Merrick and Tony Montana is never likely to succeed; had the Elephant Man in response to a bit of attention from the birds become an arrogant pig, the poignancy of the film would've been lost. If during the film's final act John had been pinching nurse's arses and calling Anthony Hopkins a motherfucker, the audience's sympathy would've waned. Similarly, had Tony Montana's terrifying will to get to the top actually been a flimsy veil across a fragile poet's heart, his drug empire would've been a shambles. So I was whooped out of Grays School the way Coriolanus was driven from Rome. Good. Bloody school, what a load of rhubarb, they never learn ya nothing worth knowing anyway. Assembly? Bah! You can poke it mate. The only times I enjoyed school was when a dog got in the playground. 'There's a dog in the playground! There's a dog in the playground! Wahoo! All bets are off, you can't control me, you can't even keep dogs out of the fuckin' playground! Revolution!' Or those dark, mysterious lads that don't go to school turn up like outlaws, moseying on in on their BMXs, gliding across the tarmac with Eastwood sneers and B&H fingers. 'Miss, who are them boys in the playground?' 'Don't look at them,' she'd shriek, frantically tugging at the blind as if it were her petticoat lifted by a mischievous breeze. 'It's all a con,' I thought. 'There are kids out there who don't go to school. They seem alright, in fact look at 'em, they're cool. They're like highwaymen.' 'Take me with you,' I muttered to the God of rascals. When school became untenable after my Terence Trent D'Arby reaction to a speck of local fame, I sought out these rogues.

You're told school is important, and that whole doctrine seems overwhelming, so then what happens if you just stop going, and you discover another culture of people who regard school as dross? Lads like Nick, Ricky and co, who lived in Wallace Road (the next street to ours), and smoked fags and had rings and wore two-tone Rossini tops that were half grey and half blue. I joined this merry band and we'd bunk off and go on the rob. I admire people that seem to have no fear of consequence: I worried about non-attendance and getting nicked; that clan of fearless vaga-bonds lived in the moment, all perfect and serene like shoplifting swamis. We'd go off to the chalkpit where I'd wandered as a child (this had by now been developed into the Chafford Hundred estate, but they left a scrub of wilderness as a senti-memento), where we'd hang about, unwrapping stolen pens and CDs that we'd nicked from Lakeside.

I popped into school on occasion, on flexi-time, which is a silly phrase, because you can't make time flexi unless you go to space or you're Einstein; it was also Sexi-time – I'd see if I could snatch a moment with any of the dames who hadn't been put off me when I was Georgy Porgied out of town. My virginity had yet to be lost, it followed me everywhere, huffing and sighing, rolling its eyes when I wanked and demanding to be liberated. 'Lose me! Lose me you filthy wanker. I've tolerated you for fifteen years, sixteen if you include the nine months of womb prison.'

It happened a week before my sixteenth birthday, with a girl called Marianne Laybourn, Tallulah to my Fat Sam in *Bugsy Malone*. Oh the glamour of it all, how could she resist? – why, she'd witnessed my ascent. She wouldn't have known I was a virgin until the bungling encounter commenced (when it would've become startlingly obvious, as I adopted the demeanour of a man struggling to build a cuckoo clock in oven gloves) because I was careful to cultivate an image of myself as an aristocratic sex-pert.

Marianne lived in the same road that my school was on – directly opposite the MacLean household. The MacLeans. Ah, the MacLeans, how I loved them. They gave me domestic normality and comfort where previously there'd been none. John, my mate, Jenny his sister, Bill the dad and Trish the mum. They were from Liverpool and lived life like a *Viz* strip. I would find solace and refuge with them after rows with Colin. I'd go round to their house and smoke B&H, and they'd give me a lager. They were always screaming and damning each other in beautifully devised colloquial insults. 'You're a hard-faced git John.' 'You cheeky rat.' I watched TV with them and watched them like telly. They had values that I admired. Me and John were once criticising some girl from *Neighbours* saying she was rough and shouldn't be on the telly. Bill was displeased. 'Leave 'er alone, she might blossom in a few years.' Aah, she might blossom. He stuck up for her even though she was just a girl from Australia on a telly.

When I played up they called me a cunt. Or 'coont', which sounds nicer. I miss them a bit. I was round there, peering through the nets at Marianne's house, before I finally got shot of that twit 'my virginity'. I knew that I was going round to hers to get rid of him and I was scared.

In my mind, all the girls in my year were sophisticated, vampish, Marlene Dietrich-like characters, though in reality I suppose they were just silly little Essex twerps, like I was. I wheeled my bike across the street for my last walk as a virgin.

What ensued was not the sort of proper sex that I have now, where I shamanistically disappear and become like some sort of Aztec nomad watching the situation – 'Oh wow! How could they ever have created those giant eagles that span the land? They must have been looking from the sky!' – I was always present in my own mind. I never left myself.

I didn't have the confidence to remove my clothes. Oddly, given the nature of one of my subsequent catchphrases, I *didn't* pull down my trousers and pants, I merely undid my fly and had some sort of nervous, unprotected jab of a sexual encounter. 'Tell no one,' she said, probably uncertain as to whether or not anything had actually happened. 'Babe,' I assured her, 'I just ain't the kind of guy to kiss and tell.' I kissed her on the forehead then calmly made my way down the stairs and out of the house. Once outside I scrambled towards my bike, and if I could've done wheelies, I would've done one. My heart was pounding, my head was swirling, I tingled and panted, far more excited than during the act itself. My virginity was gone, left in Marianne's room, checkin' his contract to see if the tussle that had granted him liberty could ever properly be called 'sex'.

It could by me. I blabbed to anyone who'd listen: instead of telling no one as requested, I told anyone I encountered; Sam, John, Anyone. 'This is the operator, Ambulance, Police or Fire rescue, which service do you require?' 'Which service do YOU require toots, because I just had me a whole lotta lovin' and I'm aching for round two.'

I told Nicholas Hunter and Stephen Norrington. Lads from my year. But Marianne Laybourn sensibly denied all knowledge of the affair.

This left me with no choice but to entrap her into making a confession like that bastard sheikh in the *News of the World* is always doing to people, ballsing their lives up. For me, it was more important that people knew I had sex than having sex. That's daft, if you live for other people's perception you can never be happy, but this was no time to ponder that existential blather, I had a sting to set up. We went to Stephen Norrington's house, and set up a tape recorder on the downstairs phone while I called poor, beautiful Marianne, who'd been kind enough to let me have pseudo-sex with her, from the phone in his parents' room. I dialled her up and, when she answered, clumsily sought out ways to elicit a confession. 'So, the ol' sex we had was pretty hot huh?'

'Not really.' 'Right . . . So you're admitting we had sex?' 'Well, I suppose . . .' 'That's all we need, miss. Hang up the phone.'

Now that I was irrefutably a world-class sex inspector, I could devote myself full time to becoming a movie star. Having discovered that *The Stage* newspaper was Britain's official gateway to show business, my feverish perusal of the agencies at the back led me into the tragic world of 'extras' management. To a man poor, dreadful, cravat-wearing, hang-mole ridden woofters with offices in their spare rooms.

Always in Leytonstone. There was one bloke called Bernard, and another with an agency called 'Bovver Boots' – as if, really, he was trying to recruit rough trade. Like this little tinker.

A chap I assumed to be his boyfriend took this photo of me standing up against a brick wall. There's an opportunity for a homophobic joke here if you want to do it. I'm too enlightened, but if you're a bit prejudiced you can do a 'backs against the wall' type joke. With this photo in my armoury I was equipped to begin my voyage. 'Stardom' – the yearning for recognition – had encamped in my gutty-wuts. 'Doubtless, I shall be making films by Christmas,' I assumed, with cockeyed optimism. I got a few days' work as an extra and auditioned for the famous school for unbearable brats, Italia Conti. ☞

Part II

'Yes you who must leave everything that you cannot control.
It begins with your family, but soon it comes around to your soul'

Leonard Cohen, 'Sisters of Mercy'

'As I looked out into the night sky, across all those infinite stars
it made me realise how insignificant they are'

Peter Cook

12

The Eternal Dilemma

At the age of sixteen, I was accepted into the Italia Conti stage school. And in my first week there I learnt two important things: i) it was full of beautiful girls; ii) to my astonishment, I found that they liked me.

The transition from Grays in Essex to Italia Conti's in central London was dramatic. I'd shed the awful baggage of my past reputation, plus loads of weight as a result of the bulimia. Suddenly, I was rich. In Grays I didn't possess anything people wanted. I was trying to spend a fantasy currency from an irrelevant island.

'Sir, I am rich with doubloons,' I would announce. 'Yeah, well, we don't take doubloons, now fuck off.' 'Drat! And what of these sovereigns?' But now, at last, I was in a land where doubloons were legal tender. It was an economy built on showing off. Although I couldn't sing or dance, in the acting and improvisation classes I was good.

The excitement engendered by the magical vista of girls in bras during *Bugsy Malone* rehearsals was revealed to be as Bostik is to crack. Italia Conti was as raunchy as an institute for learning can be and still be called a school. There was a dance studio on the way to the canteen. All these gorgeous young women would be doing their jazz dancing in black leotards. It was nauseatingly exciting – an overload of sexual information: thick thighs, round arses, sweaty cleavages.

Everywhere there were beautiful girls bustling around – prancing into the canteen with cascading manes of youthful hair. They were all, it later turned out, miniature celebrities; Martine McCutcheon kissed me once in a corridor. She was very pretty – a lovely girl – and she said, 'I'm glad you like me', and gave me a kiss. I wonder if she remembers? Or if she'll sue me. This trivial exchange lit up the no-man's-land of my life like a flare, and that's before she became 'Tiffany' and I inflated the incident into a festival of bumming for the amusement of the twerps I by then consorted with. 'You see Tiffany?' 'Yes, I see her on *EastEnders*.' 'Well, let me tell you, I had sex with her.' 'Oh, really.' 'And by sex, I mean bumming.' 'Really?' 'Oh, yes. Right up the ol' bum.'

Two members of the girl-group-to-be, Eternal, were at the school, Louise Nurding and Kéllé Bryan. There was a dizzying period of a couple of days where they both fancied me. This was lunacy. Just a few days ago I'd have sliced out a lung for a few moments with one member of the girl-group-to-be, Eternal, and now I had to choose between two. I was not accustomed to making choices of this magnitude; my volition had previously been confined to dilemmas no more complex or consequential than which colour Penguin biscuit to eat, knowing that I'd be eating both eventually, regardless. 'I'll start with you blue, but yellow, you too will know the thrill of being devoured by me.' I thought the application of the 'I'll have 'em all' technique would serve me in this situation. All that remained to decide was which one to have first. I selected Kéllé because being from 'white man's last stand' Grays, the possibility of a black girlfriend was stupidly exciting; girls from another school had seemed exotic, so another race – well, that's almost too much. What a soppy sausage I was not to have yet learned the vital Penguin lesson that beneath the wrapper we're all the same. I was punished for this embarrassing rationale when a friend of mine, Matthew Warner, the adorable embodiment of a stage-school pupil, in the closet, scissor-kicking his way down Goswell Road like a real-life *Fame* title sequence, told her of my twittish reasoning. Leading to this scene, almost too awful to write.

DAY. INT. ITALIA CONTI, GIRLS' TOILET.

We see Kéllé, future star of *Celebrity Love Island*, sixteen, beautiful, wearing a leotard and Russell, a twit. Kéllé is furious.

KÉLLÉ: Russell, what's this I hear that you're only going out with me because I'm black?

RUSSELL: (Incredulous) What! No! That's not true. Who said that?

KÉLLÉ: Matthew.

RUSSELL: Him? You can't trust him; he's not even honest about his own sexuality.

KÉLLÉ: (With incredible sincerity, imagine Oprah Winfrey confronting Eugène Terre'Blanche) Look Russell, I'm damn proud of being black.

RUSSELL: (Out of his depth) Me too, I'm proud of you being black, this relationship is like the song 'Ebony and Ivory'. Shall we get married? That'll show all those bloody racists.

KÉLLÉ: I'm not marrying you, you idiot. You're chucked.

KÉLLÉ STARTS TO LEAVE.

RUSSELL: Kéllé! Please, don't go! I can change. And if I can change and you can change, maybe the whole damn world can change.

KÉLLÉ DISGUSTED, SLAMS THE DOOR.

RUSSELL: Kéllé! No! (Pause) Kéllé, could you find out if Louise is free later? Also find out if she's got any ethnic blood in her. CUT TO . . .

I became obsessed with Louise. I spoke to her recently and she reminded me that I'd send her up to six letters a day. What on earth was I finding to write about? I hope to god these letters were bloody short. Dear Louise, please go out with me. Yes? No? I'll write again after ballet. They weren't short, though, they were long, loooooong and filled with longing, emotional more than sexual, for although as I'm sure you can imagine the sixteen-year-old Louise Nurding was pretty bloody gorgeous, I wanted love and a partner, salvation damn it; this was before I'd become a bounder. I often wonder if Louise, when she reads in a tabloid about some loveless bit of smut I've been involved with, glances over at her handsome, intelligent, kind, lovely ex-footballer husband Jamie Redknapp and thinks, 'I've made a terrible mistake.' Almost certainly.

The novelty of being good at something gave vent to the wild, reckless aspects of my character. Previously, these had come in the form of tantrums, self-harm, and smashing things, but from this point onwards, they began to evolve. I started to become aware of and lovingly nurture the archetype/cliché of the self-destructive artist – the perpetually drunk poet.

The drunk part was easy. And when it came to writing poems, 'Oh, I'm depressed and on my own' was essentially my only topic. But the vocabulary was good, and – people liked them. These were boors, knowing nothing of Shelley and Byron. Poetry should be more than just a list of feelings, shouldn't it? Good poets like my mate Mr Gee, from the R2 show (who just read this chapter to make sure I don't come across as a racist nit) can convey truth, beauty and humour

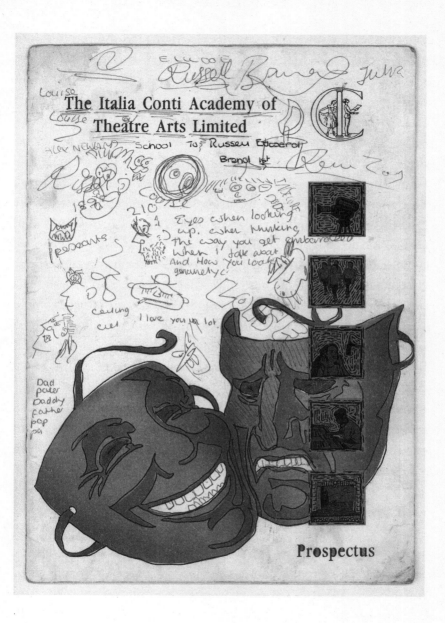

without lapsing into self-indulgence. The poetry I wrote was not about self-expression but about getting people to like me. I'd yet to learn that earnestness was an aspect that was ill-befitting and that I would have no real success, personal or professional, till I focused on making people laugh. But girls liked the poems.

Perhaps overawed by the abundance of varied and spectacular flesh, I opted to go out with this girl called Rachel, who came from Romford. I used to get the train into school with her, 'cos I was staying at my dad's in Essex at the time. She was very beautiful, with long blonde hair, but also a bit insecure and obsessed with getting a nose job.

As will already have become clear, my early sexuality was not characterised by the almost piratical nonchalance that I have developed in later years. I was a nervous and sensitive young man. I suppose partly because of those early filthy encounters – I was really apprehensive about sex, and as a consequence there were a lot of opportunities that I was too nervous to take advantage of.

I'd seen loads of pornography, but I was quite scared of girls, really. What I wanted was to be in love, to have a companion to look after me – someone to replace my mother. But before I could persuade anyone to fulfil that function, I found drugs.

13

Body Mist

I'd never tried social drugs in Grays because I wasn't really a social person, I didn't get invited to parties and the like on account of the ol' oddness. The first notable encounter with marijuana was at Conti's. I was with this lad called Jimmy Black. I really admired Jimmy. He was from Hull and had long hair and was funny and could sing. Me and Jimmy were sat smoking a joint, and he said 'Russell Brand . . . is that your real name?' I said, 'Yeah.' He said, 'That's a good name, that.' I said, 'Oh, do you think so?'

'See all these buildings, Russell? All these buildings were once a drawing on a piece of paper, and before that they were an idea in someone's head. Any idea that you have, you can make manifest.' Wow. Man. That, like, totally blew my mind man. It was my first bit of counter-cultural chitchat. He was one of a spellbinding band of Conti pupils who were out of place in every way but their theatrical abilities.

They were: Justin Edmonds, a mixed-race lad from Moss Side; Jose Vedberg from East London, a handsome lad who was in *The Bill*, and Dean Northard from York, with his ginger hair and muscles and a beautiful falsetto singing voice. Till then I'd only known people from Essex. Talent was anathema. These young men were cool. Although they were only a couple of years older than me, they seemed absurdly worldly. These eighteen-year-old lads, to me, seemed like a crew of rum-drinking smugglers, smoking weed, singing songs and having it off. Charismatic and brilliant, and forever skinning up – and they accepted me into their group and all I had to do was be an unpaid butler carrying out whatever whim my new idols requested. As soon as I saw them I wanted their company as much as I did the stunningly attractive dancing girls. I realised that the easiest way to win their friendship was through grass, so I bought some and nervously approached Jimmy in a toilet which, given the thriving gay culture in that building, the only exemptions being the boys listed on the previous page, was perhaps naive.

He was combing his lustrous hair. I marvelled at him for a while then said, 'Jimmy, I've got some draw – do you want to smoke it?' Jimmy paused and put his comb back in his pocket like Fonzie, surveyed my little face to see if there was any kind of catch – I don't know what that could've been; I was too young to be a government agent. Satisfied that I was legit he grabbed the dope with a curt, 'Yeah, alright,' rolled a couple of joints, and the next thing I knew, he was lecturing me about architecture and opening my mind.

I hadn't really considered when using weed as bait to entice cool friends that it can have powerful psychoactive side effects. We went back to school, my querying in my mind the history of every building we passed. Jimmy bowled off to do some effortless singing, while me and my open mind, listless body and yellow face slumped ourselves into a chair and watched the atoms in the windows vibrating, entranced and queasy, like William Blake watching angels in the trees on Peckham Rye. A teacher saw me sat there, grinning at nothing and reeking of weed, and a brouhaha ensued and a summit was called. 'There's children taking drugs at this school – we'll have to clamp down on it.'

Jimmy Black remarked, 'Fucking hell! We've been here two years, doing this every day. He's had one joint and there's a fucking official enquiry.'

It was obvious that drugs were going to disrupt my life. The first time I went round to Jimmy and Justin's flat, I saw they had a tray full of Rizlas and hash, and the idea of these kind of accoutrements seemed amazing to me. I loved the paraphernalia – the blowbacks and bottles and bongs – and I got so stoned that I went to bed and was there for three days. I didn't eat or anything – just lay there bewildered; people came to look at me, someone took a photograph, I refused all food, I just stared and wondered and became a drug addict. From then on, I smoked draw every day without fail or exception until the narcotic baton was passed on to heroin. Whenever I went to school – or, indeed, anywhere – I would have a joint first.

If I had to go on a train journey, for instance, I used to think, 'This'll be alright. I'll just skin up and smoke in the toilet.' Many years later, when I eventually got clean, I was astonished to learn that I actually don't enjoy my own company. I always thought I loved being on my own, but actually I don't. It was being on drugs that I liked. Here's a tip for you. If you don't have enough money to buy a train ticket but you have to take a train, use this little method I invented. Go into the toilet, hide and smoke weed. Don't lock the door because the ticket inspector can see that the door is locked and will knock or wait for you to emerge. But if you can get your hands on one of these 'out of order' signs, then you're super safe.

There is a risk that smoking soft drugs will lead to harder ones and then any money you saved on the ticket purchase will go on heroin, so economically perhaps my method is flawed. It's unlikely to feature on *This Morning* as a handy financial hint. 'Thank you, Fern. And now we're going live to Fenchurch Street Station where Russell Brand is crying in the toilet.'

BRITISH RAILWAYS
BR 29100/3

DEFECTIVE DOOR

OUT
OF
USE

John Bird said of Peter Cook, 'You met him one day in a quad in Cambridge and immediately decided you wanted to spend the rest of your life with him.' I felt this kind of sentimental awe for this gang of lost boys. I moved in with Jimmy, Justin, and Justin's girlfriend (their Wendy) Julie, in a two-bedroom flat in Bermondsey Street, near London Bridge. I was only sixteen but I didn't really have anywhere else to go. I detested Colin, I stayed with my nan a lot and with my dad, but he'd acquired a barmy wife and a few kids and I didn't feel welcome. Once in the flat my friends treated me like a clothed chimp – sending me on errands – but occasionally they would ruffle my hair and refer to me as 'our kid'. I liked that.

I didn't have keys to the flat. I used to put my arm through the letterbox to open the door: the doors of perception were about to be flung open because Dean had acquired some acid, sheets of it; I'd heard tell of its qualities, of how it made you hallucinate and readdress your life and I thought, 'My God! This sounds extraordinary.' We went over to the YMCA opposite Conti's after school, took some, and went back to his house in New Cross on the tube.

With or without acid, New Cross can be mind-bending, so it's the ideal venue to have something so fundamental as your perception of reality altered, because it just exposes everything – the world as you see it, even your own psyche – as a construction.

All the things you believe to be true are thrown into doubt. And what's so ridiculous is the way that you take this extraordinarily powerful, potent drug: not in a hospital with someone making you sit down and have a glass of water, but on the way home from school with your daft mate, walking though New Cross all fragile and delicate. It's difficult to convey the wonder and horror of LSD: most people who've taken it have at some time tried to document the events that take place while tripping; fancying themselves all Huxley, only to be confronted the next day with a piece of paper covered with the most frightful balderdash. What I recall is becoming aware that my presumed objectivity was subjective and arbitrary and that my hands looked like dead chickens.

There were still raves going on in those days, and the walls of Dean's room were covered with flyers, which I could now see had obviously been expressly designed for people to look at while high. Not as interesting as my hands though. 'They look like dead chickens!'

It's a stereotypical response to taking acid – to become fascinated with your own hands. But it's the transformation of things you are utterly familiar with that makes it such a revelatory experience. The quotidian and unquestioned became the source of rigorous enquiry. Dean had a deodorant called 'Body Mist'. That consumed what seemed like hours, but time no longer conforms to previously agreed parameters but instead leaps and whirls, pauses and rewinds, whizzes by and slithers back so it could've been five seconds. What I am certain of to this day is that 'Body Mist' is a stupid name for a deodorant. What? It's a mist for your body? 'Here, I stink. Has anyone got some mist because I'm pretty sure that this stink is coming out of my body?' Mist. Mist doesn't smell and is by its nature vague and intangible and Body is too general. 'I want to kiss you, I want to kiss you right on the body.' Torso cloud, trunk vapour, corpse fog. It still gets me. Later that night – in the spirit of making the evening as clichéd as possible – I saw the film *The Doors* and decided 'I'm gonna be like that person.' The flimsy identity that I had constructed was instantaneously swept aside: not by Jim Morrison himself, but by Val Kilmer's interpretation of Jim Morrison, as viewed through the cinematic prism of Oliver Stone.

The next morning, I went into Conti's with a dry mouth, some ill-researched but heartfelt views on spirituality, wearing a sheepskin coat, beads and no shirt, with a joint hanging out of my mouth, asking if everybody was in, because the ceremony was probably going to begin. If not now, then very shortly. At any rate, there certainly would be a ceremony.

There was always a sense of being safe inside Conti's, which made it the ideal place for that kind of ridiculous posturing. But when you'd hear of students that had left and weren't famous, it was always a little bit terrifying – 'What? They've left, and now they're just living in a flat? Bloody hell! That's a bit worrying.' It was a reminder of what might become of you. Once you've left stage school, you've got to be famous, or what the fuck are you doing?

When I first went to Conti's there were so many beautiful girls there that I fell in love incessantly. Kéllé, Rachel, Louise and Penny – she was particularly rewarding as she looked like Meg Ryan in *The Doors* and was a bit of a hippy; I saw her a couple of years ago in Camden and I think she may've gone religious, for which I might be to blame. I was so helplessly infatuated with her that I followed her to her home in Wigan at the end of term. She was heading home for the holidays, and I had nowhere to go, nothing to do and no money. She didn't want me to come to Wigan – I was just supposed to walk her to Euston Station as part of my tireless campaign to make her love me. It took longer than anticipated so I got on the train with her – without a ticket, but with my brilliant technique. 'I might as well come with you,' I said, and stayed on the train.

When we got to Liverpool Lime Street, the police arrested me, and I gave them the name and address of an old school enemy. That's another of my techniques, I really should have an item on *This Morning*, I'm gonna phone Fern Britton, plus I fancy her. So, Fare-evasion Tip 2, just get on the train without a ticket, avoid the inspector by remaining mobile; when eventually you are apprehended by an inspector or the police, confidently give the name and address of someone you know but don't like. IMPORTANT, it must be a corresponding name and address, don't make one up, also don't give away that it is an enemy's address by saying, 'That bastard Stephen Reynolds, number two

THE ITALIA CONTI ACADEMY OF THEATRE ARTS LIMITED

Name: RUSSELL BRAND   Subject: ACTING

Term/Year: SUMMER 1992

RUSSELL HAS DONE AN EXCELLENT YEARS WORK IN MY CLASSES. AFTER A TENTATIVE START HE HAS GONE FROM STRENGTH TO STRENGTH HE HAS DEVELOPED INTO A VERSATILE ACTOR — WITH A GOOD UNDERSTANDING OF HIS STRONG POINTS AND THE DEVELOPMENT OF HIS WEAK POINTS.

HIS INTEREST IS OBVIOUS, AND HE PAYS CLOSE ATTENTION IN CLASS. MANY OF HIS PERFORMANCES HAVE BEEN MOST POWERFUL AND HE IS AN ACTOR OF GOOD PROMISE.

Teacher: Adam Armstrong

Actual school report

THE ITALIA CONTI ACADEMY OF THEATRE ARTS LIMITED

Name: RUSSELL BRAND   Subject: ACTING

Term/Year: SUMMER 1992

RUSSELL HAS DONE AN EXCELLENT
YEARS WORK IN MY CLASSES.
AFTER A REMARKABLE START HE HAS
GONE FROM STRENGTH TO STRENGTH
HE HAS DEVELOPED INTO A STRIKING,
VERSATILE ACTOR — WITH A GOOD
UNDERSTANDING OF HIS STRONG POINTS
AND THE OBLITERATION — OF HIS WEAK
POINTS.
HIS INTEREST IS OBVIOUS, AND HE
PAYS CLOSE ATTENTION IN CLASS
ALL OF HIS PERFORMANCES HAVE
BEEN MOST POWERFUL AND HE IS
AN ACTOR OF GOOD PROMISE.

Teacher: Adam Armstrong.

Cleverly doctored report for subsequent drama school auditions

Wallace Road' – you'll arouse suspicion. You may as well have these tips an' all: Tip 3, pretend to be Spanish – 'No tengo un ticket, lo'siento.' Tip 4, pretend to be mentally ill – 'The ticket office was shut and when I tried to use the machine my willy done a burp.' Tip 5, pretend to be dead – just lie there. This time I used good old Tip 2, the police wired the info through and it all checked out, so I was released and that arsehole Stephen Reynolds got another ten-pound fine.

Penny didn't want me to come to her house but I used charm and relentless pig-headed persistence to persuade her. I'd pursued her with poetry and promises, neither of which were original or true, for months. I tackled the nobstacle course with such dogged aplomb that when night fell I was allowed to sleep in her bed top to toe. I spun gags and yarns till she let me turn round, I painted verbal pictures and begged until she kissed me, I lied and danced and evoked the spirit of Pan till reluctantly she removed her bra, I used tears and emotional blackmail to secure the immolation of her knickers. We were naked, and cautiously I went down on her. She whispered, 'Russell, put a condom on,' and – this is how much of an idiot I was – I bellowed, 'YES! Thank God Dean and Jimmy made me take one.' This, I suppose, indicated that 1. My pursuit of her was a topic of conversation, which it was. They thought I was like Adrian Mole in his ineffectual wooing of Pandora, and 2. That I was a bit immature. It was romance though that compelled me, not lust; I wanted to lose myself in a woman, to have an ally, a partner, a girlfriend. This sweet and touching perspective on women was about to be challenged. ☞

14

Ying Yang

Perhaps it was in seeking to cope with this sudden upturn in my sexual economy – this huge shift in the quality and quantity of available women – that I developed my 'cloak of love' identity. 'How did you do that?' I hear you ask, all aquiver. Well, first I got myself this cloak. It stretched from the top of my head to the tips of my tiny toes, like a curtain, and I used it to veil myself and my true intentions, right in it, as I stalked the corridors of Italia Conti.

It were very helpful, that cloak of love. What I liked about it, and what I love in general about inventing catchphrases or jargon or nomenclature is that sometimes other people are forced to say the ludicrous words you've come up with. There was a teacher who used to do an impression of me. Adam his name was. 'Ooh, c'mon girls, get into my cloak of love.' (Instigating a trend that continues – of making me indistinguishable from Janet Street-Porter, which is good, cos I like her.)

Most of the girls at Italia Conti had graduated from the school course (for those aged up to sixteen), which meant they'd been trapped in that place for years with homosexuals. So when I arrived there, still knowing how to communicate with girls because I was all feminised and everything, but being hysterically heterosexual, it was perfect.

'Hello dear,' I would call them over – and I would have spoken in the same slightly camp voice I do now – 'perhaps you might like to join me in my cloak of love?' And they would, the fools. I'd open my cloak of love and . . . It weren't that bad, it was all quite light-hearted. I didn't have a hard-on, I'd only kiss 'em a little bit.

Dear Dean Northard once passed me in a stairwell when I was with Julia – she was so beautiful and little, and I was tall, and she was enshrouded in the cloak of love – and he went, 'Russell, you're like a fucking paedophile with that girl in your fucking cloak of love.' He still called it the cloak of love, like that was its official name, as if there was a protocol that had to be observed. Like when the Australian Prime Minister Paul Keating put his arm round our beloved Queen and we as a nation went 'fucking cheek'. Even staunch antimonarchists put aside their principles and thought, 'That's bang out of order, get your dirty Australian armpit off our Queen.' Even as Dean attacked the cloak of love he adhered to the terminology that the cloak demanded. He didn't just call it what it was when stripped of mystery and tradition: a Burton's mac.

One of my greatest pleasures in life is coining a mischievous phraseology that other people then have to accept as a linguistic fact. It's exciting to be able to interrupt and alter language. It's anarchic and subversive to lay dirty lingo eggs that people are going to have to say, then watch like a voyeuristic cuckoo as they hatch – 'There, speak like that. Now, talk all stupid.'

When everything is homogenised and bland, nothing needs to register; if you put things in an unusual fashion – even if it's just saying someone's name in a silly voice, or changing the way it's pronounced – it always makes people listen more.

When I was doing *Big Brother's Big Mouth*, I always used to begin the show by saying two random words, and then my own name. Everyone knew the programme was about to start, and I was happy for people to be watching it, it's obvious. So I'd amuse myself by saying a couple of words that meant nothing. The Dadaists, an artistic movement who began dicking about around the time of the First World War, reasoned that if rational thought and logic led to war they ought be dispensed with. I think many of the boundaries that convention has placed upon us are arbitrary, so we can fiddle with them if we fancy. Gravity's hard to dispute, and breathing, but a lot of things we instinctively obey are a lot of old tosh.

I felt that even as Dean Northard and, later, the Sheward family who ran the school condemned the cloak of love, they too fell under its spell – in a way, they were as much inveigled by the cloak of love as any of its more formal victims.

Part of the justification the Shewards gave for expelling me at the end of my first year was, 'He's always in the corridors in that stupid cloak of love.' 'And he's on drugs all the time and he hardly ever turns up and he can't sing or dance.' But by then, it was too late, I'd switched off, they'd been forced to say 'cloak of love' and I'd won. It was meant to be an introductory course, and the other two students who were on it were accepted for the full three years, but they didn't want me there for another second. They thought I was a maniac.

After I got chucked out of Conti's, I got an agent and a series of dead-end jobs. It was during this already turbulent period that my mum got cancer again (of the lymph glands, this time). I was convinced she would die; rather than helping her through this terrible ordeal, I buried myself in drinking and smoking dope.

I had this friend called Michael Kirsch, who had been at Italia Conti before me. He was the middle son of a Jewish merchant-banker, a talented and volatile young man capable of incredible compassion and insight. He didn't have a bedroom in their grand

CURRICULUM VITAE

NAME:	Russell Brand
AGE:	16 years
DATE OF BIRTH:	4th June 1975
PLAYING AGE:	15 - 20 years
EDUCATION:	Grays Comprehensive School 1986-1990
	Italia Conti Drama School 1991 to date

CERTIFICATES:

Drama	A
English Literature	B
English Language	B
French	C
History	C
Maths	C

SCHOOL PRODUCTIONS:

Bugsey Malone:	Leading part (Fat Sam)
Pantomime:	Leading part
Pantomime:	Leading part
Drinking Companions:	Leading part

WORK EXPERIENCE:
<u>Television:</u>

Part of young villain with dialogue
Warner Sisters (Rides)   "   "
Streetwise (Child's Play) Featured biker
Eastenders: Assistant Stall Holder

<u>Commercials:</u>

Barclays Bank:	With dialogue
Abbey National:	Crowd scene
Unemployment Video:	Educational, with dialogue

<u>Stage Plays</u>

Wizard of Oz: With dialogue

<u>Pantomime</u>

Jack and the Beanstalk: With dialogue
Pinnochio: With dialogue

<u>Films</u>

Bye Bye Birdie: Teddy Boy with dialogue
Rif Raf

<u>Pop Videos</u>

Numerous

Sports Activities

Varied

Interests

Acting, singing, dancing, socializing with friends, going to the cinema and theatre.

Eaton Square house – he slept on the dining-room floor. Although he'd left the school he had remained friends with people still at it. Mike smoked loads of grass – as all of us did – and was quite an intense character; he looked like De Niro in *Mean Streets* and occasionally behaved like him, once smashing me in the face while we were arguing on an escalator. During that ridiculous period when I lived in Bermondsey Street with Justin, Jimmy and Julie, he took it upon himself to steward me. It was like being counselled by Keith Moon. We decided to write a play based on *The Tibetan Book of the Dead*. The fact that neither of us had ever so much as glanced at *The Tibetan Book of the Dead* made it much more of a challenge. I've still not read it, I don't think many people have, I believe it's quite an esoteric religious text aimed mostly at monks, but I'm confident the play *Ying Yang* will stand the test of time. Even though it ought to have been called Yin Yang. In years to come, scholars will say, 'This play really encapsulates the message of *The Tibetan Book of the Dead*, let's put it on at the National.'

There was this woman at Pimlico School (a huge comprehensive in central London) who lent us a space to perform in. She was a lovely boho character in her forties – with short, cropped hair and ethnic beads – and she let us use the room to rehearse. She even paid for an advert to go in *The Stage* saying, 'New Play: If Interested, Please Call . . .'.

Because the acting community is peopled by millions of desperadoes, we were inundated with responses and had to hold a week of auditions. All day long, me and Mike Kirsch sat in this room, stoned, auditioning people for a play that we hadn't written, based on a book that we hadn't read, absolutely confident that nothing but good could come of it. Not once was the possibility of reading *The Tibetan Book of the Dead* raised. We assumed it'd be boring. Neither did we fret unduly about writing a script for the actors to perform in the castings or rehearsals. We simply looked them in the eyes and told them the script was secret. An extraordinary variety of characters came through that door. The ideology we employed was: 'Let's cast people that we'll be able to manipulate, not people that scare us . . . and – obviously – good-looking women are in too.'

There were two women that were particularly sexy – Claudine and Maria. Maria was an Asian girl with all this tumbling black hair, who turned up in this red dress and looked impressive, and we were just a couple of jerks sat there, high. 'OK, right, this play . . . do you want to improvise a scene?' 'Will you do kissing? There's lots of kissing. And bras, *The Tibetan Book of the Dead* is full of women kissing in their bras. That's what makes it such a fucking good read.' There was also an Australian bloke called Mitch who I think knew we had no script, and this feller Danny, who looked like a live-action version of Inspector Gadget, and whenever you called up his house, his mum would answer. We gave him the part of 'the vicar' and on the cast list for the programme we got printed, in spite of never writing the play, he was credited as 'Danny Vicar as "the vicar".' We'd cast this ensemble of two good-looking women and a couple of nincompoops, and we just kept on rehearsing this play. For months. Me and Mike Kirsch had nothing else to live for. We'd both been thrown out of school, he was signing on, and I wasn't old enough to get benefits. For us, life was a rehearsal.

Matt Morgan said recently, all the best people get thrown out of art or drama school. They should go, 'Right, you're expelled. Now get out and stay out . . . Pssst. Not really, come round the back, this is the *real school* for the creative people who can't be conditioned.'

During the months of pointless rehearsals of nothing, I took a few days off to write the script. It was rubbish. RUBBISH. This is my interpretation of *The Tibetan Book of the Dead*, without

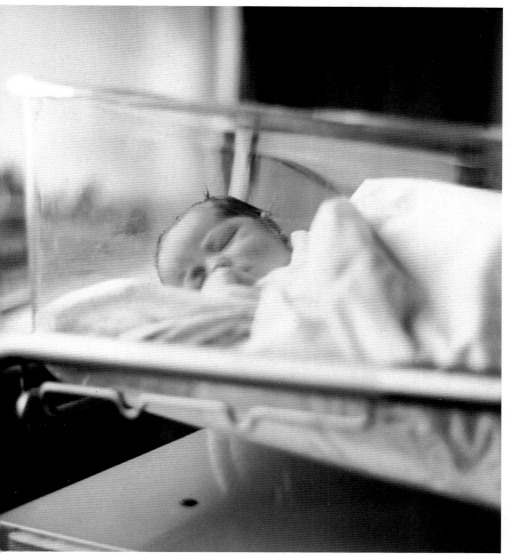

I'd just arrived on the planet when this was taken. Lazy really to sleep when I can't have achieved anything.

Babs and Ron looking to an imagined future. Attractive, aren't they?

An early gig – looks like it's going well.

On holiday in Clacton with Mum, inexplicably blond.

I'm in my aunt and uncle Janet and Jimmy's garden. Ferrets were nearby – that's why I'm confused.

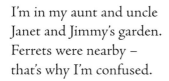

Dr Dolittle.

Disgusted by the shoddy quality of St Nick,
I contemplate atheism.

My beloved Nan.

Topsy. My mad hound imagining scoffing dosh, the twit.

Oddly, the I.C.F. refused me entry.

An imaginative haircut, which I still regret.

I'm suspicious of Baden-Powell – these clothes suck. I never got any badges either.

If you look into that rabbit's eyes you can see it's planning a Woundwart style attack. I cut my own fringe.

This is the exact moment when I decided to act gay to attract girls. It took fifteen years to produce results.

reading it: well, there's these people in a waiting room, but, get this, it's purgatory, oh yeah. But, none of them know they're dead so they just wander into the waiting room, all confused, and a bloke with a clipboard, played by Mitch (we called his character Foster like the beer because he was Australian) evaluates them. Mike played Adam who had raped and murdered Claudine's character (that scene was rehearsed very responsibly, with Mike saying his erection was proof that he was in character), but because he felt guilty about it in the afterlife he was basically let off. Danny the vicar meanwhile (brilliantly played by Danny Vicar) went to hell because he'd nicked money off the collection plate. So there was quite a powerful message – not all vicars are nice and if you say sorry you can rape and murder as many people as you like. I played a bloke who'd killed himself and spent most of the scenes trying to get Maria to resuscitate me.

The play and the lunacy surrounding it demonstrate a couple of things: even though I was only seventeen, I was really dynamic and organised; also I was mad. The day before it was meant to open, me and Mike did acid and thought, 'This play's shit – and so are we', so we sacked everyone and hid. I phoned Danny's mum – 'Is Danny there? Tell him the play's been cancelled.' We didn't even tell the nice woman from Pimlico School (in fact, I'd like to apologise to her now. Sorry).

The loss of this last precarious foothold on the show-business ladder was a terrible blow, but drugs made everything softer. After some time living in Bermondsey Street, I couldn't afford the rent, and went back to my nan's and eking out a precarious living-out-of-a-bag type of existence, hiding from my mum's illness.

Strangely, given that I was so much older and should have been better able to deal with it by then, the third time she got cancer probably had the worst effect on me. I closed myself down and felt dead lost, and no one had any sympathy for me.

Brand & Hersh Productions Presents Ying Yang.

Playing at Pimlico Theatre, Pimlico School

From Mon 26th April to Fri 30th April and
from Mon 3rd May to Fri 7th May

Performance time 7.45pm

Prices £3.50(£2.00 concessions)
Box office Tel:071 828 3817(2-8pm weekdays)

Even when she went into remission, and her hair was coming back after the chemotherapy, it was still a really bleak time. Obviously it was good that she was getting better, but Colin was still there, and things between him and me had become totally unbearable.

I was also a right little petty criminal at this time in my life. Drug-taking, stealing and not paying for bus, train and tube tickets (all of which I considered to be victimless crimes) were fairly integral to my day-to-day life in those days. I used to fare-dodge pretty much everywhere I went. And steal food. I used to go into a supermarket, get a basket, fill it up, eat a sandwich while I was doing it, then put the basket down at the checkout, having eaten the sandwich, and leave the store. I got caught doing this once on the Kings Road, and it was very embarrassing. My life was very disrupted and unsettled. What I really wanted was to escape from the mess I seemed to be making of everything, and to get a girlfriend. But I had no sexual confidence. It was the graphic sexual encounters that took place on the trip I was about to take with my dad to Hong Kong and the Far East which would really begin to instil that. ☞

15

Click, Clack, Click, Clack

Socrates says the male libido is like being chained to a madman, and the links in my chain are these:

1. I love sex, like everyone, because of the ol' biological programme.
2. I enforce my identity and status as a man through sex and the seduction of women.

And:

3. I have a hopelessly addictive nature.

Perhaps you're wondering what formulated my peculiar sexuality? It ain't that peculiar. I'm a bloke from Essex who likes birds with big bottoms and big boobs: Lucy Pinder, Lindsay Dawn McKenzie, Maria Whittaker, lovely dolly-birds. I don't mean to be dismissive, they might be incredibly dark, fretful Sylvia Plath-style heroines for all I know, but if they are I'd rather not find out because life's difficult enough without women who superficially resemble a 'Disneyland for my Dinkle' thrusting me into a tortuous realm of introspection.

Although I sometimes like to portray myself as a rakish fop, meandering up corridors, waltzing around squares, foxtrotting across quads, nimbly tottering through dormitories and boudoirs – I like the same women as readers of *Zoo* and *Nuts*. Strip away the innovative barnet, mascara, inky, bejewelled wet suit and the ol' gift and I'm just a West Ham fan from Grays – a straightforward, red-blooded sort of fella.

The episode that defined my relations with women – and with myself – occurred in Hong Kong with my dad. I was seventeen. His third marriage had just broken up so he needed someone to go on holiday with. I was unemployed, penniless, birdless and desperate for his approval; we were the perfect holiday companions. On the plane home he said, 'I went away with a boy and came back with a man.' Both of those people were me, so what happened to induce such a significant transition?

When I think of my father his face is obscured by a newspaper, which in my mind he was forever behind, turning over the corner to flick me a glance, rebuttal or gag. We get on best when reciting lines from comedies that we both like, *Fawlty Towers*, *Blackadder*, *Fools and Horses*, or chatting about West Ham. Trips to east London kept our relationship alive but when we travelled further east like bizarro pioneers we found a new land of hope and opportunity.

In addition to Hong Kong we visited Bali, Singapore and Thailand, and in all those places we saw incredible things and if you'd like to know more I recommend you go, or get a *Rough Guide*, because as an adolescent there was only one sight I was interested in seeing and it would be disingenuous of me to proselytise about sleeping buddhas or monkey forests or floating markets when you know and I know that that trip was about one thing. One thing, done repeatedly. One thing that chewed its way into my barren little soul and gave me, at long last, a physical pursuit that I was good at. Sex. Disposable sex, sex as leisure, sex for pleasure, sex you sordid little treasure, drag me from monotony and give me kicks too hot to measure.

Day one: we went to some sleazy dive hidden behind a thick black drape where women from the East traipsed louchely along the mirrored promenade in garish beachwear. That promenade was a conveyor belt from which produce could be selected; I didn't know that then but my cock did, twitching, preparing frantically, trying to recall correct procedure. 'This is not a drill, repeat, this is not a drill.' My dad sat there next to me, familiar with this glistening and foreign terrain.

I didn't understand what I was witnessing, but by jingo, I knew I liked it. Dumbstruck, I sat looking at the women, their hair, each single strand identifiable as it responded to a fan that had been placed there to elicit exactly the reaction I felt in my pantaloons, their toenails, painted and perfect, each solitary toe a match for me. They walked with the ease of women that fuck for a living. They didn't seem enslaved or exploited – to me they weren't; they were mistresses, goddesses, salvation. 'I don't care if there is no God because she exists, she's there. She can resolve everything with a redeeming kiss. She can heal me with a smile, a touch, a word.' In the beginning there was the word, and the word was 'fuck'.

'I can't wait to tell my mates that I saw these women in swimsuits.' Before long, I was sat on a barstool with a Filipino girl called Mary-Lou, or something similarly unlikely. I thought, 'I can't wait to tell my mates I was sat talking to Mary-Lou.' That quickly became, 'I can't wait to tell my mates I was kissing her.' The velocity so severe that I could but smile for the g-force. Then we were leaving, a street, a cab, perfume, hairspray, the three Asian prostitutes that my dad was drunkenly herding – Mary-Lou, another girl and the madam of the club, who had come along just for sport (when I learnt that she'd come along without payment, I thought that a testimony to my dad's powers). Arriving back at the opulent Mandarin Palace Hotel we revolved into the lobby, like fairground teens dismounting a waltzer, the knowing staff boredly ignoring the 'Click, clack, click, clack' of hired heels across the marble floor as they beat the well-trodden path from door to lift. And I, with nervous downcast eyes and butterflies, made my way to the elevator and then up into the room. Once there, the room was illuminated by the TV, and the two twin beds waited like sentries, pre-emptively guarding the orgy.

'Get some champagne, Russell,' my dad said, so I called down to room service. 'I'll order not the most expensive champagne, but the second-most,' I hastily calculated.

My dad set about unwrapping his two prostitutes, like pass the parcel where the music never stopped, and I sat nervously on the edge of the bed with Mary-Lou, kissing her and thinking she was beautiful and falling in love. I'd only had anything close to sex once before – jabbing my silly prick at poor Marianne Laybourn.

Naked. I was shy about my body then. I had trouble getting hard, the blow job seemed daft, the way it feels when a customs official pulls your trousers down, or a doctor puts his finger up your arse: not sexual, just giggly and intrusive.

After the un-sex, I carried her in my weedy arms out onto the balcony to look at the view of a great, looming skyscraper, disapprovingly observing.

She was a good prostitute, Mary-Lou, she played her part very well. She didn't make me feel embarrassed, and was incredibly romantic really, given the context. I stroked Mary-Lou's hair and kissed her cheek and traced my finger down her perfect nose, scored by the cacophony from the adjacent bedlam, 'Yeah, come on!' and 'Phwooar, you're juicy!'

As she was about to go, she said expertly, 'Russell, I must leave now before I fall in love with you.' My heart skipped, and I heard,

'Oh, fucking hell, I'm gonna be sick' – a disapproving announce-ment from dear old Ron.

Awake. Yesterday's shadow lay heavy on the dawn – half-full champagne glasses, discarded bottles and underwear, perhaps even a lipstick and a broken heart.

My dad, concealed behind a newspaper, folded down the top right-hand corner. 'Did you wear a condom with that bird last night?' 'Oh, no I didn't, Dad.' He sniffed, 'You should've.' Then the corner of the page flicked up once again, and he was gone. In the course of the rest of that holiday, I fucked loads more prostitutes; always got a hard-on, never wore a condom, and never fell in love. In Bangkok when bar girls in Pat-Pong left their posts to follow me down the street, cooing and touching my hair, I felt that I had my dad's unequivocal approval.

When I came back from Thailand, I was much more comfortable around women – sure in the knowledge that I had 'come back a man'. Some of the attributes of a man included, 'I have now had a prostitute stick her finger up my arse while sucking my cock' – I remember the first time that happened, thinking, 'Bloody hell, this is an interesting way to live your life.' I still didn't become utterly confident, but it had hardened me. And my sexuality had morphed forever from bewildered innocence into something more complex and rapacious.

This change was apparent as soon as I came home from the Far East. One of the first things that happened when I returned from that holiday was I got an acting job on this show called *Eddie and the Bouffants*. It was an Anglia TV programme about the evolution of a hairdresser's – there were scenes set in the '50s, '60s and '70s, with all these different wigs. It's not a show that has gone down in TV history as a landmark of quality and innova-tion, but David Morrissey – a really good actor – was in it as well, fresh out of RADA, he was.

On the shoot I was sharing a room with this gay lad on the make-up team, who told me about going to gay orgies and sticking a puppet of a policeman up some fella's bum. And there was this woman on the crew, she was thirty-two, which to me – being seventeen – seemed preposterously grown-up. And I fucked her, well . . . as best I could. I struggled a bit with getting an erection again – this was my first encounter post-Thailand – but she helped me get into the swing of things by being kind of rude and unabashed. On our first date she stuck her finger in her own pussy and then in my mouth. I thought 'Oh my Gawd! What kind of world are these people living in?' So these were the folk that initiated me into a more sexualised world – prostitutes, that thirty-two-year-old and my dad. After that, I started to get a bit more confident about sex – and popped love in a self-storage facility in Finchley Road. ☞

16

'Wop Out a Bit of Acting'

The first time I was arrested it was for cultivating marijuana. I had about thirty dismal plants – optimistically nurtured from the seeds that you get free in weed, not good weed; 'No stems, no seeds, no sticks' is how Snoop Dogg describes proper grass, and he should know. After my holiday with my dad there was a period of eighteen months where I moved back to Grays with my mum and Colin – it was fraught. I kept myself as anaesthetised as possible and signed on. I grew the plants to save money – pointless business, I'd have got a better buzz from bludgeoning myself over the head with the pots they were planted in. For someone who smoked as much weed as I did, I was pretty enraged, and carved into my arms as a kind of medieval release and as a palpable demonstration of internal trauma. One of my mum's friends advised her, 'Next time Russell cuts himself in front of you, just call the police.' She did. I went berserk in the midst of some tiresome conflict and slashed myself with a knife. My weary arm yawned bored blood, and Mum called for an ambulance; the police came too, perhaps for something to do, they were always on the lookout for an interesting collar in Essex. Before they arrived, I'd gone. I must have been eighteen by now, and I'd been doing a kids' TV show called *Mud*. There was a car that I'd bought myself with my wages parked outside. I couldn't drive it yet, but the only way I ever used to get anything done was by setting myself a deadline: 'If I get a car, then I'll have to learn to drive it.'

As sensible as it was, this plan did not allow for uncontrollable losses of temper. I went outside and gave that car a Basil Fawlty-style thrashing while it just carried on being a car much in the same way as it would have if I'd given it a glass of wine and combed its hair. I broke the windscreen and kicked the door in – then sobbed off round to the MacLean's house, carrying the knife that I'd cut myself with and loads of grass in my sock – and I was smoking a joint and calming down with the sympathetic surrogates when three carloads of riot police in shields and helmets arrived simultaneously through the front and back doors as if they were about to nick 'Leon'. As the police poured in through every orifice of his house, Bill MacLean – a great big hod-carrying Northern man bemused by this overkill – shook his head and said, 'Fooking 'ell, it's only Russell.'

I'd managed to get rid of the knife in the house, which wasn't an incredible operation – it was a domestic kitchen-knife, I just put it down, I didn't have to hide it in the concrete of a flyover or feed it to some pigs, but when I was escorted into the police car, cuffed and crestfallen, I still had the grass in my sock. At the station I encountered all the shoelaces and belt business and the realisation that there are forces in the world that can curtail and contain you. I didn't want to be in that cell. I wanted to leave. But the police left me in there for ages. It was sad and annoying, full of sick and shouting. Plus I was meant to have a bird coming round.

I did have to go to court, and I was convicted of possession of marijuana. They dropped the more serious charge of cultivation.

I was able to employ this experience creatively when I got a part in an episode of The Bill playing a teenage racist. When I sat in the pretend 'Bill' cell I did some spiffing acting on account of my recent troubles.

3. INT. CUSTODY AREA. 6.45 DAY

DEAKIN AND MEADOWS STAND BEHIND BILLY, WHO IS
BEING PROCESSED BY LAMONT.

LAMONT IS ITEMISING THE CONTENTS OF BILLY'S
POCKETS; CHEWING GUM, A CIGARETTE LIGHTER, A
BUS PASS.

BILLY: (TO LAMONT, SARCASTICALLY) What
you going to do me for? Going equipped?

LAMONT DOESN'T RESPOND.

BILLY: (CONT'D, TO DEAKIN) I have got
the right to a solicitor, ain't I?

DEAKIN: (WITH DISINTEREST) Sure. If you
think it'll help.

CUT TO:

A week later, I was arrested again. I was sitting in Carnaby Street, waiting for an audition for a Tango advert – not those daft slapping ones, but that same campaign. I was smoking a joint when a big meat wagon went past, all full of police like they were off on an outing. I thought, 'If you act suspiciously now, you're fucked.' So I made eye contact with one of the coppers, and took a big draw on my joint as they went past. The van stopped and reversed back. 'Alright young man, what's going on?' This policeman conducted my arrest with such urbane and ironic self-awareness that I was still chuckling when he cuffed me and threw me in the van. 'Nothing up my right sleeve, nothing up my left sleeve,' he said like a TV magician as he searched my bag.

They took me to Bow Street nick, where Wilde was held, so I pretended I was in Oscar's cell and ranted at that idiot Bosie who ballsed up Wilde's life. They dropped the charge. The Met are a bit more grown up about that kind of thing, whereas Essex police it's, 'Reefer Madness! Have you any idea what this stuff does to a marriage?'

These comic arrests became more and more frequent as I became more and more drugged and less interested in observing laws that seemed abstract. I swapped my bike for a load of acid and set about re-evaluating my life. 'Russell, you do not re-evaluate your life on a trip,' said Dean, as if I'd breached one of acid's central tenets. It really made him rather cross. He was actually a lovely chap, and when in the course of my re-evaluation I started to cry he gave me my bike back, which I was then able to exchange for some amphetamines the next day. We were conducting this symposium in my mum's shed having returned to Essex from wherever the hell we were staying especially to collect collateral. We were both high having taken a couple of tabs and while I wept and hugged my bike's front wheel, for in that moment my bike became a talisman of childhood, innocence and the soul, Dean chatted with my mum with the grace and ease of Lady Diana visiting a children's ward.

We went into the house, Dean charming my mum's friends and delivering perfectly judged anecdotes while I had a mental breakdown because the plates they were dining from were slightly different to how I remembered them. It wasn't the acid, they were slightly different, it was a very subtle difference, they were still brown and cream floral plates but a bit different, that's what threw me, the subtlety. If you're gonna get new plates, get new plates. They were so similar that I couldn't understand the logic of the replacement. It was like looking at your mum's face and noticing that her eyes were a centimetre closer. Which they were, but that was definitely the acid.

I left Dean doing card tricks to the enchanted gathering who were oblivious to his expertly concealed intoxication and went into the garden to continue my maligned evaluation. With the help of my constant mistress, the moon, I decided I needed to go to drama school. I dashed into the house, told my startled mother of my epiphany, smashed a couple of my crockery-foes and disappeared into the night leaving Dean to apologise and close with a song.

There were two places that I auditioned for in the hope of rebuilding my life. One of them was RADA, and the other was called Drama Centre, which was built around the teachings of Stanislavski – the great Russian dramatic theorist, who popularised method-acting. You had to pay twenty or thirty quid to audition, and that was a pain in the arse to get hold of. I probably tried to swap my bike for auditions.

I can't remember what happened at RADA, but I didn't get in, so I assume it didn't go well. I'd developed the habit at Italia Conti of drinking and taking drugs when I performed. And when

I rehearsed. Or read scripts. Or moved about. Before performing I used to get so nervous that it was impossible to cope without chemicals. The nervousness is not vague, but overwhelming – almost crippling. It loosens my stools. It affects me bio-chemically and anatomically.

This is what the auditions are like: two students from year 2 sit on the panel with Christopher Fettes, the intensely charismatic inspiration for his ex-student Anthony Hopkins' Hannibal Lecter, his partner, Yat Malmgren, a Swedish Yoda who once danced for Hitler – why he did this I've never understood. Why did Hitler even need dancers? No wonder we won the war, Hitler was dicking about watching ballet while the Eastern front was being compromised – and Reuven Adiv, who was a contemporary of Al Pacino at the Lee Strasberg Actors Studio. You go in and do your two pieces, one modern, one classical, while they sit in a line behind a desk in front of you like on a TV talent show.

It was an intimidating atmosphere. Christopher was snooty. And Yat muttered mysterious things; he asked me what my favourite colour was. 'I like purple,' I said. 'Oh. purple.' He responded as if my answer had given him all the information he'd ever need on me as a person. 'People who like purple are vain and are unable to cope with the adult world.' A lucky guess.

I'd got all nice and drunk before the audition. One of the second years who was on the panel – Adam – later reminded me of some of the things I did, so I can now recount them with clarity. I do remember being formally announced – 'This is Russell Brand' – and swaggering drunkenly into the room. 'So,' said Christopher Fettes, in his perfect clarinet voice, 'what are you going to do for us today, young man?' And my reply to Christopher Fettes – this elegant, Oxbridge-educated man (Fettes College in Edinburgh, which is where Tony Blair went to school, is named after the Fettes dynasty) – was, 'I thought I might wop out a bit of acting.' When Adam recounted this to me, he placed particular emphasis on the word 'wop'.

'OK,' he continued crisply, 'so what have you got for us?' Over the thirty years that they've run that school they've trained Simon Callow, Colin Firth, Paul Bettany, Tara Fitzgerald, Pierce Brosnan, and numerous other very good actors. I walked into the performance space, took the chewing gum out of my mouth and stuck it out on the wall, did a piece from Pinter's *The Homecoming* ('One night, one night, down by the docks . . .' that bit), then pulled the gum off the wall, put it back in my mouth, and sat down again.

Next I had to do a piece from *Antigone*. It's a speech where Haemon implores Creon to show clemency to Antigone, who's buried her brother's body after some war – obviously I didn't read the whole play, so I'm not sure what the fuck went on, I was doing it how I would talk to my dad if I wanted something from him: 'Oh come on, show a bit of clemency. You're a powerful man, let's not fuck about, people listen to you . . .'

I didn't know how to take direction at that time, I bristled when they offered guidance. 'He's educated, so it's like a lawyer in court,' Christopher said. I just went 'Yeah, alright,' and did it the same again. I didn't like people telling me how to act, I found it insulting, so I'd pretend to listen then carry on with my instinctive interpretation or, depending on how drunk I was, argue. Or cry. Despite my surly, drunken behaviour those three brilliant men saw fit to accept me into the Drama Centre, snatching me from the dole queue and handing me back my dignity. Actually I continued to sign on throughout my time there and my dignity was diminished. If anything. ☞

17

The Stranger

It was obvious that Drama Centre was a magical place from looking at the building. The school was in an old Methodist church in Kentish Town, where it was rumoured that the brilliant Irish poet W.B. Yeats and devil-worshipper Aleister Crowley had once engaged in a bizarre cult.

Central to the training are the teachings of Stanislavski. The basic principle of method-acting is that you should draw on your own personal experience – 'You know how you felt when you were seven, and your dog died? Well, think about that when you're playing Hamlet.' It sounds simple enough, but it involves learning lots of techniques to heighten your capacity for emotional recall. Those techniques were westernised from the original Russian templates by people like Lee Strasberg, who taught James Dean and Al Pacino, and Stella Adler – another teacher in New York at the time – who taught Brando.

Drama Centre London transplanted those ideals from New York, along with at least one teacher who had trained there (in the form of the aforementioned Reuven Adiv), and set out to teach its young students how to approach acting like a craft. Fettes was an articulate, stylish and brilliant homosexual man who could also be quite clipped and brutal on occasion.

The students deified Christopher, Yat and Reuven. They were great men – excellent teachers and wonderful characters – but obviously that gets exaggerated when you're a young person trying to learn acting and these people hold the key to knowledge and they're in absolute authority and they've created this system where their word is law. As a result, Drama Centre was a very intense place.

It was no coincidence that its nickname was (and still is, even though Christopher has moved on, and Yat and Reuven have both died) 'Trauma Centre'. Going there was like being a member of a cult. The first day I went to Drama Centre, I didn't like it. I scanned the room to get a sense of my contemporaries. There was Romla, the daughter of George Walker, who owned William Hill – his brother was Billy Walker, the boxer – she was quite an imposing character. Then there was Jamie Sives, a really good Scottish actor, who went on to work in some excellent films. And Karl Theobald, the brilliant comedic actor, who would later be in *Green Wing*. Initially these people seemed quite intimidating.

The ideal of the impoverished artist really pervaded that school. They liked people from modest backgrounds, who were good-looking and talented. And drinking neat liquor from the bottle, with all my long hair and my shirt undone and my beads, not so much the lizard king, more a gecko duchess, I fitted in nicely with their idea of what a creative person should be.

The social make-up of Drama Centre was based around a fairly clear divide between the working-class kids, who were there on grants, and those from the middle-class families which could afford to send their kids to a place like that. I'd managed to wangle myself a grant from Essex Council. As if determined to uphold the county's reputation for philistinism, Essex Council only give out three grants a year for the whole of the arts. I was

June 19th 1995

The Stanley Picker Trust
35 Marlborough Gardens
Lovelace Road
Surbiton
Surrey   KT6 6NG

Dear Sirs

        re: Further Education Awards
        Russell Brand, 12 Grays End Close
        <u>Grays, Essex   RM17 5QR</u>

The above named presented himself for audition on the 20th
May 1995 and was immediately accepted by an unanimous vote of
the entrance committee consisting of the heads of all
departments and two second year students.

He appears to use to be a lively imaginative, young man with
a maturity and a background which would guarantee that he
will make full and rapid use of the very strenuous training
that he will receive.

He seems to have made careful enquiry into the various
possibilities and given his own nature and the requirements
of the profession unusually careful thought.

Yours faithfully

Christopher Fettes
Principal

   copy: Russell Brand

proud to receive that grant, especially in the knowledge that I'd fought off competition from all of Essex's poets, painters, dancers and stage hypnotists to get it.

A charity, the Stanley Picker Trust, gave me a thousand pounds a term in response to begging letters that I sent. I don't know who Stanley is, or was, but thanks for that money; it went to a good cause.

There was also a fund, Friends of the Drama Centre, which gave the financially insolvent students – myself included – extra money for maintenance. I did my best to spend every penny of that money on drugs, while living on people's floors, wearing shit clothes, and drinking filthy five-quid-a-litre vodkas named after Russian authors. Tolstoy Vodka, Dostoevsky Vodka. I may not have read their books, but I was devoted to their stinking booze.

I selected friends that were in a similar financial situation from comparable backgrounds who were as mad as I was: Mark Morrissey – who claimed to have been in prison for robbing a post office when he was seventeen, which I thought made him incredible glamorous, but was never sure it was true – and Tim Renton, this Geordie bloke who was a bit nuts. I ended up living with these two above a pub in Kentish Town.

Mark Morrissey was an amazing character. He'd been brought up by his nan. I love people who've been brought up by their nans: nan-kids. They speak funny, because they've missed a generation of talking – 'Alright, nan . . . *Countdown*'s on in a minute. Shall I get some working-out paper, it looks like we're in for a cold snap?' Although Mark wasn't a square like most nan-kids, or a boffin, he did waffle on in an anachronistic vernacular.

Here's an example of something Mark Morrissey said which was funny. In the first year at Drama Centre, they make you build the sets and work as crew, including preposterously dangerous work with electrics for the final year students' productions. When they allocate which department you're in – set, electrics, make-up, wardrobe, front of house – you pray for one of the cushy numbers like make-up or front of house, like in prison, where as far as I can assess from *Porridge*, you want to work in the library or in the kitchen. I got the equivalent of breaking up rocks in the unforgiving midday sun for every one of my three terms – electrics. On wardrobe you just sit drinking tea with actresses. I, however, was drilling holes and running wires through walls and ceilings. It was terrifying, 'I could actually die,' I thought. 'This cable doesn't know I'm a student being taught a valuable life lesson, it's a conduit for electricity, it's going to assume I'm qualified.' It's not like a rollercoaster, where no matter how scared you are you know that it's sanctioned fear, you can't actually die. Life is not a theme park and if it is the theme is death. They make you work eighteen-hour days.

I was especially stunned by it because – as may already have become clear – I prefer not to work on anything where I'm not being looked at and there's no chance of getting clapped at the end. I didn't like doing electrics. I'll do magic tricks. I'll do card tricks. I'll do sex tricks, tricks of the mind, tricks of the heart and soul, but electrics – that's no job for me.

At three o'clock in the morning, all tired and pissed and stoned, doing everything I could to avoid work on trying to get theatrical flats erected – I shouldn't have to write a sentence like that, I'm not saying it's beneath me, it's above me. It makes me confused and emotional. Putting hinges on planks, trying to work out angles, banging my thumb like Tom out of *Tom and Jerry* – why did he have to do so much carpentry?

Mark Morrissey looked like Humphrey Bogart and Rodney Bewes (the dark one from *The Likely Lads*). He stood in overalls smoking roll-up fags like Sid the Sexist, with his eye-rolling, factory-floor sense of humour – and his 'Oh Christ, what's the point?' attitude to life. He looked at my shoddy work, tutted, shook his head and said, 'I dunno. [pause] Men on the moon?' I loved that. That's the sort of thing people said in the '70s when lunar travel was a big deal. It implied my workmanship was so poor that it was detrimental to mankind as a species. He also, on one occasion, when I passed on the accurate accusation that he'd nicked a mate's textbook, charged me with 'listening to the ravings of a madman'.

It was a mark of how successfully Christopher Fettes had created this environment where we were all constantly clamouring to impress him with our vocational devotion that Mark – a natural rebel – piped up in class with the incredibly insincere statement, 'I went down to the National Gallery the other day and just stood in front of Van Gogh's *Sunflowers* . . . And I'm not ashamed to admit this: I wept.'

'Ooh Mark, you're so fucking sensitive,' I sneered afterwards; jealous of the attention Morrissey's outrageous gambit had garnered him. 'This world was never meant for one as beautiful as you.'

For most of that first year at Drama Centre, I lived like the Hulk, or the Littlest Hobo, peripatetically drifting from one girl's flat or halls of residence to another. Simone Nylander – the girl in *Grange Hill* who was always going 'I want to help you Ro-land' – was one of them. She wasn't like she was in the programme, though. She was sexy by then. She was a Ghanaian princess.

A lot of Ghanaian people seem to be royal, in my experience. I think their royal family is badly structured, because about eighty per cent of the Ghanaians I know claim royal lineage. I don't wish to cast aspersions on their socioeconomic system, but it is, I imagine, pretty grim for the other twenty per cent if four-fifths of them are kings, guzzling pearls.

I stayed round at Simone's house for a while. She had very good manners and was really well brought up. I was a little thug. I once spat in her waste-paper bin. She thought that was bad. In fact, she reacted to this lapse in etiquette by throwing all of my stuff out of the window in bin-bags. That was always happening. I've squandered the best years of my life watching bin-bags arcing out of the windows of disillusioned women. I shouldn't bother to unpack, I should just leave my stuff outside by the bins.

Once I moved into the Queens Arms in Queens Crescent with Mark and Tim, life got ridiculous. It was a problem pub that no one could ever run properly. We had to do three shifts a week behind the bar in lieu of rent. I had all the worst possible traits you could have as a barman: I gave drinks away for free, stole from the till and got drunk at work. I couldn't pull pints, I didn't know how to change a barrel and I was an alcoholic. They had moody twenty-pound notes stuck up on the wall, and I'd take them down and spend them. They were free money those notes. Me and Mark Morrissey, every morning on the way to school, would pour a tumbler of vodka or gin, or on Friday, cocktail day, both, then go in to Drama Centre and recklessly do ballet drunk.

One night me, Mark, and the landlord – this Scouse feller called Alan – were downstairs having a drink after hours. Mark wandered over to the piano, announcing that he was better than Liberace – and I didn't see him again till the next day. The piano was only six yards away. God knows what happened to him.

I noticed two women outside – Norwegian – and we invited them in, gave them booze and chatted them up. As is always the case when there's two or more women, it was a question of working out which of them was most likely to have it off. That's always a difficult call to make, which is why one of the fundamental tenets of womanising is 'two birds is worse than none'. You've got to divide in order to seduce. Obviously the rules change when you're famous. In that case two is often better than either none or one.

'Now, you're both very attractive, but would you be so kind as to tell me which one is likely to have sex with the least fuss?' That's what you want to say but many people, squares I call them, consider that to be impolite. 'Do you want to come back with us?' they asked. 'We only live over the road. You'll have to be quiet, though, because of our landlord.' So we went over the road and carefully did the drunken creep up the stairs, where we carried on the evening, with me endlessly skinning up and chopping out lines because booze was no longer accessible.

After hours of fruitless living Alan, the gutless coward – like most men, not as committed to the womanising cause as I – said, 'I think I'll turn in now', and went back to the pub. I thought, 'No, I'm sticking this out to the bitter end.' By that stage I'd selected the more suitable target, Petra, the brunette; the other one had mentioned religion and that's always a bad sign unless it's paganism.

We got into bed. I was a bit delirious by this stage, but we got off with each other for a bit, and then I fell asleep. The kind of sleep you have when you're pissed and on drugs, where sleep mugs you at the end of the night. Not a gentle, consensual dropping-off, where you think, 'Right, I'll just have a read of my book.' Sleep loutishly koshes you off to nod as if its true intention were to put you in the grave.

I lay contented. The day's triumphs and disasters all nonsense now as half-baked dreams cavorted through my bonce, showing off like toddlers. I felt a shove on my shoulder, my dream weaver worked to incorporate it into his script. 'Ooooh, you're in a meadow, but instead of corn, it's a field of eels, growing in slithery acres . . .' SHOVE HAPPENS. 'Erm, don't worry about that shove, it's all part of this brilliant dream I'm weaving . . . one of the eels has shoved you . . .' There was another shove. The dream weaver frantically tried to hold his narrative together. 'Oh what's this? An eagle is swooping down to eat the eels and has accidentally shoved you on the shoulder . . .' At the third shove the dream weaver gave up. 'Alright I admit it, there is no eel field, no eagle. I was making it up. You might wanna look at your relationship with sex though, I was trying to tell you through symbols but it's bloody difficult with all this shoving.' 'Yeah,' I thought. 'What is all this shoving?'

I concluded that I might need to open my eyes if any closure on the shoving were to be reached. When I did, I was greeted with a sight that was as ridiculous as the dream eel field. Directly in front of me, at the opposite end of the bed, was an old woman, beige and alarmed. Toothless with a shawl, it's difficult not to think of her as a crone. If you see the words 'refugee woman', an image will come into your mind. That image is what I was looking at. To her left were two huddled, baffled children. To her right were two more huddled children. 'I don't remember going to bed with all these children,' I thought. 'Perhaps if I continue looking round the room an explanation will appear.'

To my left, children. To my right, more children. 'Well this is a turn-up, there's certainly no shortage of huddled, refugee children in here.' Finally, and with due trepidation, I glanced in the direction of the shove, and there, standing next to the pale and embarrassed Petra, was a man.

Upside-down he was, or I was because I'd not yet moved. Moustachioed and saronged, shouting and angry like a baddie from *Indiana Jones* or that bloke in the Territorial Army advert before the soldier takes off his sunglasses granting eye contact and delivering the advert's core message: 'In the TA you learn stuff.' Obvious stuff, like if you're taking over a village don't strut around in shades like George Michael.

'Well, this is unusual,' I thought. 'Perhaps I'll go somewhere else now where this isn't happening.' I tried to think of a facial expression that would make everything alright but there wasn't one. There is no facial expression that says, 'Sorry, I drunkenly, nakedly got into bed with your children and your mother. No hard feelings. Jesus, no hard anything, there are children present. Oh by the way, I think that there oughtn't be such rigid laws on immigration – as far as I'm concerned the earth is one place and we should all travel with impunity. One love.' So I just done a sort of grin, cupped my nuts and walked out of the room.

I went upstairs, got back into her bed and went back to sleep again, confident that the dream weaver would have nothing to match the lunacy that reality was churning out. What I suppose must've happened was that I'd got up in the night to vomit or wee-wee, and on the way back I'd just wandered into the nearest room – which happened to be harbouring scores of refugees.

What fascinates me about this incident is that there must be a moment in the 'black box' of my brain, when I just walked into that room, found that bed full of people, got into it, naked, and went to sleep. Then all the kids and the old crone would've had to have dealt with the admin, fetching the sarong man and Petra, all confused.

When I left the house, having slept for a few more hours, I walked down the stairs, and all them little children were milling around in the stairwells. Two of them looked at each other, and one pointed and said, 'The stranger! The stranger!' I was the stranger. I liked being the stranger. And I skipped off to drama school, still drunk, secure in the knowledge that this was one role I could cope with.

A few days later, when I was going to sign on for my housing benefit at Kentish Town job centre, I bumped into sarong man. We had a moment. He went 'aah' and pointed, I went 'aah' and pointed back. He smiled. I smiled back. We nodded at each other, and I shrugged apologetically and gestured tipping a drink into my mouth. He in return made the gesture where you put your two hands together as if in prayer, and then make a pillow. After this wordless yet eloquent communion, we forgave each other and all was right with the world. Except not for those two girls who were, quite rightly, evicted.

Over the road from the Queens Arms there was a quite rough estate which a load of Irish travellers had, for some reason, been forced to live on. They were cheesed off about it, and they used to come in the pub to eat, drink and be angry.

The children were really naughty. They'd come in, throw ice around and cause all sorts of bother. I like children, and naturally empathise with that kind of insubordinate behaviour, so I'd just go, 'Oh, come on you lot,' and play with them. Mark and Tim would throw them out, they were good barmen, they looked alright behind the bar. I looked like I was wearing a big wooden tutu and the wind had changed.

Tommy 'The King of the Gypsies' used to pop in, which was nice. He was said to have reduced pubs to matchwood when irked so I tried not to irk him; I could never be entirely sure what would irk him so I just gave him booze without charging him and laid off my brilliant Ian Paisley impression. One afternoon, Tommy's brother, having paid his debt to society, came to the pub. 'I'm Tommy's brother Eddie,' he said, menacingly, and demanded to be able to drink for free all day. I used to give people free drink regardless of whether a threat of violence hung heavy in the air or not, but he wasn't to know that, he was just out of nick, wearing a suit from the '80s all peeved about decimalisation.

He was obviously a gifted fighter; all his stories reached thrillingly gruesome climaxes, at which I'd smile encouragingly and politely applaud. I was getting a bit tipsy myself, what with all the booze we were drinking, so I popped round to the lavvy to dispense with some winky-water. 'You'll have to excuse me old bean,' I said and ambled off.

Eddie came after me – 'That's sweet,' I thought, 'we really are becoming the best of chums' – and I began to imagine a sitcom where Eddie and I lived together and, in spite of our differences, somehow, made things work.

'You're a good-lookin' boy,' said Eddie in his beautiful Irish lilt.

'Well thank you very much, and you too are of peculiarly noble bearing,' I replied.

He craned his head round to peek at my privates.

'I'd like to kiss you,' said the King of the Gypsies' brother; I suppose that makes him the Duke of Edinburgh of the Gypsies.

'Well, that's very flattering, Your Highness, but I much prefer the company of a woman,' I demurred, 'but know this, dear Eddie, if I were gay I'd be lobbying for conjugal visits for your next stretch.' That dealt with I zipped up my adorable penis and went back to the bar. Eddie seemed to be taking this turn of events badly, if the death threats were anything to go by. 'You've got forty-eight hours to get out of Kentish Town,' he screamed. Now I know the Northern Line can be unreliable, but even on foot I could get to Camden in five minutes.

I would like to be able to say it was my sense of professional duty that kept me in that pub till the end of my shift, but that instinct was not in my repertoire. My motivation actually came from a more familiar source: this was one of the first times I'd met this beautiful doctor girl, Kerry, who lived over the road, and I was about to fall in love with her. So throughout the rest of the evening I was busy trying to flirt with her while ignoring the fuming duke drinking free Guinness at the end of the bar. ☛

18

Is This a Cash Card I See before Me?

I went very quickly from living in the Queens Arms and working behind the bar, to moving in with Kerry and doing no job at all. I'd not known her long but I was sure I loved her and I was certainly sure that I didn't love working in the pub and getting death threats. Even though she only lived across the street, her house was in Chalk Farm as the Crescent formed the boundary, so I'd obeyed Eddie's banishment – although it took a week, so wasn't within the recommended forty-eight hours. I kept the keys to the pub though, and we'd go over there at night to get crisps and booze. Kerry was a junior doctor at the Royal Free Hospital, and she was my first love. She'd been to Cambridge University, like Peter Cook. I think I fell in love with her a bit, because she seemed to come from another world.

She went parachute jumping and broke her leg; the plane hadn't taken off but she fell over boarding it and landed badly. I liked that she was a bit clumsy. I had to push her up the hill to the Royal Free Hospital where she worked in a wheelchair every day. I think there's a certain type of pervert who gets off on going out with people in wheelchairs because they want to look after them; I became one of those for a while, it was alright. After I'd got her into work, I'd eat some hospital food (OI, do you like hospital food or something? I do when I'm in love, thanks), walk down the hill and go to Drama Centre. It was romantic. I liked it.

British Red Cross
London Branch

Camden Centre

119 Finchley Road
London NW3 6HY
Telephone 071-586 2199

0171

MR. RUSSELL BRAND.
Flat 4,
63, QUEENS CRESCENT.
N.W.5. 4ES

MEDICAL LOAN DEPARTMENT

INVOICE   4TH SEPT '96.

You have on loan from us the following item(s)

...... a Wheelchair with leg extension ......

....

at £ ..12 = 00.... per week.

The amount due for hire of this item(s) is £.48 = 00..

from ..8/8/96.... to ..4/9/96....(4 weeks)
(INCLUSIVE)

An early settlement of this account would be much appreciated.

PLEASE RETURN THIS INVOICE WITH YOUR REMITTANCE, to the above address. Cheques made payable to the "British Red Cross Society".

6/9/96

569

One day, when I was up at the hospital, Kerry showed me a room with shelves all stacked up with these formaldehyde-filled jars, containing hands, fingers, genitals and malformed foetuses. It was brilliant. I told Mark Morrissey about it; he reflected then said, 'Let's steal a foetus, leave it in the park, then phone the *Sun* and tell them we've found an alien.' 'Good idea Mark,' I said. 'We should definitely do that.'

We took some drugs to relax us and waited for nightfall before embarking on our flawless plan. It's quite easy to get into a hospital – just sidle in through the casualty department and then use elevators and your imagination to get right into its core. Wisely we'd taken a couple of Kerry's white doctor coats and blue scrubs so we looked exactly like normal doctors and not like scarecrows on their way to surgery, on drugs. It was much harder to find those foetuses than we had envisaged because the Royal Free is quite big, foetuses are small and it's hard to concentrate when you're on acid. It was fun walking endlessly round and round that hospital till four o'clock in the morning, past wards full of ill people sometimes stopping to practise our bedside manner or do one of them red zig-zag mountain drawings at the end of someone's bed. We couldn't find those bloody babies though so we contented ourselves with some boxes of rubber gloves, sample jars and syringes. Our shift at an end, we trickled off back into the world like a couple of woozy Doogie Howsers.

To get my hands on some money for drugs I took part in clinical trials once – like the one where people got horribly ill at Northwick Park Hospital; Kerry got me on it.

They said they'd give you a grand, but you couldn't drink or take drugs for the duration of the trial. That was ridiculous. I couldn't not drink or take drugs for the duration of the conversation where they told me that I couldn't drink or take drugs. I had to pop to the toilet for a line while they told me it was imperative the conditions were observed. 'How will they know if I've taken drugs or not?' I thought, 'these rules are unenforceable. It's like taking candy from a baby. Or a baby in a jar from a hospital. By which I mean easy.'

The trial worked thusly: you'd take the drug the whole time, then one night a week you'd go and sleep at the hospital with a tube up your nose taking samples out of your gutty-wuts. I didn't like that at all. I did it once – sleeping over – and then thought, 'I can't do this any more.' They said, 'Hold on, you're one of our guinea pigs, you can't go – it'll ruin the test,' but I didn't care. I just wandered off – away from that situation and into a new one.

I don't know exactly how long I was with Kerry for, but it felt like a long time; I was stood on the balcony of her beautiful flat enjoying the spectacular view south to St Paul's Cathedral and thought, 'Wow. Life's actually okay, I'm with this doctor, who went to Peter Cook college, I'm doing well at Drama Centre, they all think I'm great at acting. Don't fuck it up.'

It was around this time that I was in a play by Pirandello called *Six Characters In Search of an Author*. Even though it's quite old, this play is postmodern as well – they all know they're characters in a play and they're trying to look for someone to write it, but there's some lurking tragedy hanging above their heads. Because I was not deemed to have done very much work, I got given this little part as a stagehand.

I was onstage all the time, but had hardly any lines.

I lay in bed, spurned, and vengefully decided to work hard. I transformed. I stuffed my hair into a hat, I padded out my cheeks with tissue, and wore a fake moustache, a boiler suit and hobnailed boots. I had a utility belt with tools in it. During the performance, which was just for teachers and the students from other years, I bent over to pick something up, my pockets emptied, and twenty or thirty screwdrivers and a hammer fell out, stealing the scene.

When we had to sit around afterwards for 'crits' (an annoying abbreviation but that's what they call it), Christopher and Yat described the performance as 'flawless' and 'genius'. 'I should think so too,' I mused. 'A hat, a moustache, I'm the new Dustin Hoffman.'

Christopher Fettes taught us of the narrative line – from biblical times to the modern era, from Ancient Greek theatre, through the Spanish golden age, to German expressionism, the significance of ritual within religion, and the way theatre grew out of that; while I was learning all that, my life was swinging between comedy and tragedy, triumph and disaster.

I was feted and condemned over the course of a lesson.

I was also in a production of *Macbeth* soon after, and it was a typical fuck-up on my part. I decided that the best way to prepare for playing Macbeth was to snort loads of cheap speed, that I was supposed to be selling for a friend, and drink half a bottle of Scotch.

Alongside my chemical and narcotic groundwork, I had made myself sick, and cut my hands smashing things with a hammer. What better way to establish a connection with an over-reaching Scottish thane? 'I think what Macbeth would've done was be sick and smash things up with a hammer.'

We rehearsed for the play with a guest director; during the first session I did coke off my cash card so I didn't get bored or shy. I hid behind a piece of scenery to keep things secret, just popping my head out, nodding at his directions, then hoovering up more confidence, until he asked, 'What are you actually doing?'

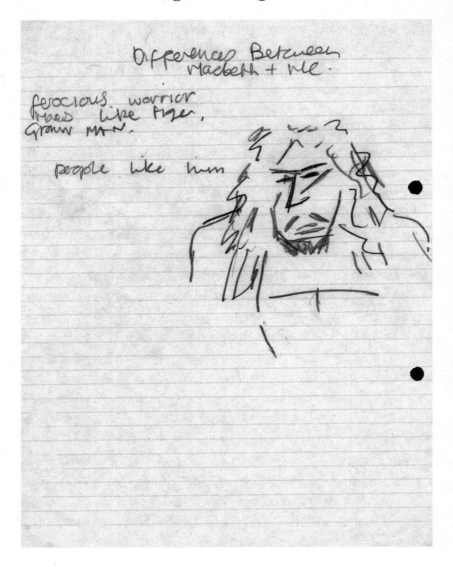

I thought, 'If he finds out I've been taking drugs while he's been talking, he'll be all sad.' He started walking towards me to find out what I was up to; there was still a bit of coke on the card. A wiser man would've thrown it on the floor to prevent an altercation. I just tried to hold the card out of his line of vision. But he moved his neck, and there it was, a card with a tiny amount of drugs, right at the extremity of my fully extended arm as if I was reaching out to pinch a faraway arse. He told people at the school and their response was, 'Oh yes, Russell does do drugs – we've all noticed it.'

I was 'a right skanking little cunt'. I used to get coke, put it on the toilet seat, take away my half and cut the remainder with crunched up Rennie indigestion tablets (I always had indigestion for some reason), then sell it to my close friends. After Kerry threw me out, bin-bags crossing the border back into Kentish Town, I used keys I'd had cut for such an eventuality to return to the flat and steal things. I was a total cad. ☞

19

'Do You Want a Drama?'

Christopher Fettes was into teaching us about tribal societies and the importance of ritual; this filtered through into the culture of the students. Every twelve months, when a new year joined, the third years would hold an initiation party for them.

There was nothing sinister about it: just a little revue-style play where the teachers at the school would be parodied in a jocular fashion and we'd all have a bit of a drink. The whole of the school would come, and maybe even some ex-students (tragic characters, lurking around, still not famous yet).

When we had ours it was a great night, and I ended up getting off with some girl called Chloe who I told a ridiculous pack of lies to. She came up to me, brown-eyed and Joplin-y-fied and said, 'Are you Native American?' The answer she obviously wanted was 'Yes' and the truth was 'No' – I had less than a second to respond. 'Yes. Yes I am a Native American.' 'Wow, what tribe?' Okay, don't panic, come on brain. She was beautiful, bohemian, she was the sort of girlfriend Val Kilmer playing Jim Morrison in Oliver Stone's *The Doors* would have. 'The one from *Dances With Wolves*, I'm out of that tribe. I don't like talking about it because of the hardship my people have suffered under the tyranny of the Americans, the bastards.' Brilliant. That was enough to get me through the night. I could do some research some other time. I kept that charade going for weeks, putting my ear to the ground when I was nervous, crying when I saw litter, smoking um peace-pipe. She didn't suspect a thing.

Two years later, though, this function ended in carnage for 'Lies without Shame'. We held it above a pub called The Enterprise on Chalk Farm Road, from which I've been barred three times; I still drink there. This is how I got barred the first time.

The function of the party was to welcome the first years – 'Yeah, wahoo! We're at drama school. Let's be happy, everybody. Remember my name – Fame!' That kind of caper. People were doing impressions of Christopher Fettes as if he was Hannibal Lecter and Yat Malmgren as if he was Yoda. Everyone was having the time of their lives.

I was to be a lovely teacher called Jenny Litman who sort of . . . spoke . . . very . . . slowly – as if language were made of Hubba Bubba and she had to chew and pop every word. The place you entered from before doing your little turn was the corridor running into the kitchen. They stored the booze up there, cheap filthy Chekov vodka, my brand, before decanting it into the Smirnoff bottle above the bar. There were all these boxes piled up. And as we were all getting ready, me and Mark Morrissey and this other lad Olly nicked a couple for ourselves. I then took a litre bottle of vodka and drank it down all nice in my tum.

When you do that you get a ten-minute grace period before your body realises what an idiot it's housing. One moment you're thinking, 'Wow, I'm Oliver Reed. This hasn't touched me, pass another bottle.' Then it hits you – like a vodka lorry smashing into your cerebellum. Your mind and body split in two, head in opposite directions, and agree to meet up the next day.

Dear Jenny,

Silence is required in my opinion ~~than~~ during the initial stages of the exercises when ~~every~~ the ACTORS ARE consumed by the scene, however ~~my humble~~ when the Ambience is perperated by your instruction I see little harm in my quiet discussion. I accept that to disturb people while they're acting is unforgivable but Stephan's (Erdman) complaint was not derived from his tremendous respect for the craft but rather his desperate adherance to order, born from insipid insecurity.

but I do apologise for distracting you when you were offering post Exercise advice, whether the root of the diversion was my audible or physical presence

love
Russell x

On this occasion, my transitional phase coincided with the time between me standing in the corridor, and me going onstage. The lovely young actors formed a circle. It was all just a bit of a laugh. I began my performance. My hair was in pigtails, I was wearing a skirt, a bra, a blouse, for some reason no shoes or socks and bright red lipstick. The people present still believed themselves to be at a party; I though had decided that I was about to give a groundbreaking performance of 'Jenny Litman', as important to the English theatre as Gielgud's Hamlet. That's why it was vital that no one spoke, drank or did anything other than watch with astonishment my magnificent impersonation. Some people were just getting on with their lives, chatting, being young. It simply wouldn't do.

'What the fuck is going on?' I slurred, enraged. 'Why ain't you listening?' I eyed the crowd with menace. Menace, lipstick and a bra. 'Isn't this dramatic enough for ya?'

The small crowd grew edgy. 'Oh, Russell, he's such a laugh, he's mucking about.' No he wasn't. It turned out that this hastily assembled transsexual was serious and seemed to have abandoned his parody of a tutor in favour of a kind of bent Ray Winstone. 'Want something a little bit more dramatic, do you? You fuckin' mugs.'

Some of the first years began to query whether they'd made the right choice of school; this chap was unbearable and his grasp of the character terrible. 'Well, if you want fucking drama, I'll give you fucking drama!'

I drained the glass of vodka I was holding (it was part of the character), smashed it on my head and plunged it into my chest, raking it up and down my arms. 'Well, the party's been fun but I don't think I want to be an actor any more,' said one plucky newcomer.

'You get back here and watch this masterclass.' 'Russell! Russell!' People are shouting. 'What are you doing?' It seemed I'd misjudged the mood. 'I'm an actor, you must watch me in awed silence . . . I'm . . .' 'Russell, this is your brain, we're going to shut you down now, please don't be alarmed. We apologise for any inconvenience this may have caused.' 'NO . . . I . . . must . . . finish . . . the . . .'

I'm slumped outside the pub with Elia, beautiful Elia. Girl-friend. Spanish. She loves me. She's crying. OUCH. Someone is slapping me round the face. VOMIT. 'Elia, I love you . . .' 'Why you do this Russ?' OUCH. 'Can you stop hitting me . . .' VOMIT. 'Don't worry Elia, he'll be okay.'

This lad in my year, John Turnbull (he's had cancer since then, I hope he's alright) managed to get me into a taxi and back to his flat to sleep on his settee.

'Good morning world! And what's this sensation?' Why, that would be urine, Russell, your urine. 'I didn't do anything to embarrass myself last night did I?' No, of course not, oh maybe a little. After the self-harming ego show you came back to your friend's house, tried to fuck his flatmate then pissed all over his sofa. 'Nothing out of the ordinary then?' No. You carry on son.

John gave me a pair of jeans to wear home, but he didn't have any shoes he could lend me, so I walked barefoot through Ridley Road market in Dalston, across the rotten fruit and the chicken guts from the halal stores. 'What this situation needs is heroin; any fool can see that.' I had taken it once before, when I saw two Turkish lads smoking it on the train to Elia's house, just kids they were. 'You ain't done this before 'ave ya mate?' They saw through me, because my skin was becoming so thin. I smoked it in her bathroom. Yes. Heroin. It was warm on that bathroom floor and my brain was silent; not chattering like now in this dirty market. I couldn't find heroin. I was shoeless. I had no money. Of course I couldn't score.

I got back to Elia's, on Graham Road in Hackney, which she shared with this vegan lad John: a pale sort of fella he was, well-meaning and new age. He wasn't a student and never looked well.

Elia was unhappy about the episode at The Enterprise. We quarrelled. I smashed a glass and stuck it in my arm. It was only a tiny little cut – but it generously laughed out blood. The creases in the duvet filled with beautiful red pools.

I get fixated when I'm bleeding – I can see why they went in for blood-letting in medieval times because it makes you feel a bit better. When I cut myself, the drama of it kind of calms me down.

It doesn't usually have that effect on other people, though. She was a lovely gentle girl, Elia. She went downstairs to call an ambulance, and then John saw all the blood and started going, 'Oh God – suicide! Suicide!' So that was how it was formally reported.

When the ambulance arrived, Elia had fainted, but I – characteristically – was over the worst. Usually by the time the ambulance or the police or whoever it is that's going to take me away turn up I'm generally feeling pretty upbeat. I was in quite a jolly frame of mind as they took me off to Homerton Hospital. 'You should be helping old ladies,' I joshed as I boarded the ambulance.

When we got there, they interviewed me and put me on suicide watch – a list on which I believe I remain to this day. So should I ever find myself in Homerton feeling blue (and it is a part of London quite renowned for its capacity to induce melancholy), I at least know that the emergency services would be in a state of readiness if I opted to do anything rash.

I know it's difficult to imagine how a man like me could be thrown out of drama school, what with all the talent that I've got in such abundance, and all the goodwill I'd earned with my earlier performances as a drunken, amphetamine-ridden Macbeth staggering out of Duncan's chamber, clutching a terrifying selection of butter-knives (it's all they had in the canteen). But thrown out of Drama Centre I was.

In the final term of the final year, I were awarded the title role in *Volpone* by Ben Jonson. As you might imagine, the part of Volpone is pretty much the best one there is in the play *Volpone*. Jonson was a contemporary of Shakespeare's, and *Volpone* is the story of a confidence trickster – the literal translation is 'the fox' – who pretends he's dying, to trick his cohorts (who all have the names of different animals) out of money.

I'm not sure why it was that I never got it together to play that last big role. Perhaps I knew that I was soon going to be leaving Drama Centre, and the idea of actually finishing something that I'd started for the first time in my life became too much to bear. Either way, I remember panicking and thinking, 'God, I've got to do something about this character.' So I went to Boots and nicked some white mascara to bleach out my eyebrows and facial hair, in the hope of changing myself a little bit from the outside in.

After I had been arrested for shoplifting, I was taken straight to Kentish Town police station. When I'm arrested, the police are normally quite nice to me, because I do my best to be charming. I can see the other people in the cells at the same time doing dreary clichéd things like swearing and banging tin cups on bars. What a welcome relief I must be to the police with my bright and breezy manner and 'Gorblimey Guv'nor' forelock-tugging.

I was in there for a few hours. I used my phone-call to ring up the school and tell them I was going to be late for rehearsal because I'd been arrested. They were bored of me by then. When I was in the first production of our third year, *Arden of Faversham*, or 'Black Will' as my mum calls it, since that was the part I played, all agreed that I was on my way to the RSC.

One of my brilliant gimmicks was to have a mouse living in my hair. I kept this going for quite a long time – at least a month or so. I'd gone out and got a mouse from a pet shop, and let it live on my shoulders and in my hair. Mice are incontinent. They poo and wee whenever they feel like it, so my hair was all full of mouse excrement and urine. I'd put it in a little Tupperware box when I went to sleep.

Tim, when my mum called to speak to me on the phone, said in his Geordie accent, 'Barbara, you won't believe this, he's got a mouse living in his fooking hair, like.' It sounded funny. What a character I must be I thought. He was a little white mouse, called Elvis. He escaped and ran off when I was in the middle of smashing a window or opening a vein but he built a new life for himself with the mice and rats that lived in the school. Once in a while someone would say, 'We saw Elvis, we saw Elvis' after a ballet lesson. People told me that he looked all scruffy and weather-beaten. I imagined that he'd got in with the rats and now had a leather jacket and was a real bully-boy.

I was brilliant in that *Arden of Faversham*, and lots of agencies were interested in me. 'This is good. I'll leave this drama school and be all nice and famous.' But I suppose I just couldn't take the pressure. I was always being warned about my behaviour but lionised for it at the same time. They'd always be telling me I had to pack it in, but it was also clear that this was an industry that had revered Peter O'Toole and Richard Burton, and as long as you could come up with the goods, you could get away with just about anything.

What I've learnt – to my cost – on several occasions in my life, is that people will put up with all manner of bad behaviour so long as you're giving them what they want. They'll laugh and get into it and enjoy the anecdotes and the craziness and the mayhem as long as you're doing your job well, but the minute you're not, you're fucked. They'll wipe their hands of you without a second glance.

When I was thrown out of Drama Centre, Christopher called me up to his office – the same office where so many times before I'd been praised and approved of, or told off even, but told off in such a flattering way ('I wouldn't like to work with you, Russell,' Yat told me once, 'I would be afraid to work with you. You are like Peter Ustinov'). On this occasion, Christopher was up there drinking a glass of white wine. Everyone who's ever been to Drama Centre can do an impression of Christopher Fettes – you can do that as sure as you can cry on command. In the read-through for *St Trinian's*, a film I've recently done with Colin Firth, I really wanted to say, 'Hey, show us your Christopher Fettes,' but I was too shy. This was the only expulsion that didn't feel triumphant, the apotheosis of the rebel. It was gloomy, him saying in his beautifully modulated voice, 'Sorry, Russell, we're going to have to let you go.' I pleaded, 'Please give me another chance.' 'Sorry.'

I went downstairs into the canteen and Karl Theobald was there. He was to become the most important person in my life so it was serendipitous that he should be in attendance. 'You alright, Russell?' he said, but he knew. 'I've been thrown out,' I cried. Karl's not comfortable with physical contact with blokes; I don't really cuddle him that much even now, ten years later. We communicate through jokes. He must've known I needed to be held up then though because he put his arms round me.

The drama ended when I left the Drama Centre. From that moment it was comedy. When Karl graduated – literally a week later – we started writing sketches together. ☞

Part III

'But, truly, I have wept too much! The dawns are heartbreaking. Every moon is atrocious and every sun bitter'

Arthur Rimbaud

'I started doing comedy when my girlfriend left me; after all, my life's a fucking joke'

Karl Theobald

20

Dagenham Is Not Damascus

I imagine most people live their whole lives without encountering a comic genius. I'm lucky enough to have two among my close friends. One is Karl Theobald; he's in *Green Wing* as Dr Martin Dear, in which you get to see a slither of his awesome talent. He's sometimes funny by mistake, like Hancock. He emits comedy, while he drinks tea or looks out the window. I watched him do a sketch at school and thought 'I want to work with him.' It's difficult for me to acknowledge others, what with the only childhood and solipsism, but I told him afterwards and the Gods of comedy approved and just a few years later we were performing together. Above pubs. For nothing.

'Theobald and Brand on Ice' we called our double-act. It's a mark of my respect for his talent that I didn't get obsessed about having my name first. We had to do everything ourselves, from stringing up the curtains across the back-room of the Queens Arms where I'd previously lived, to create the illusion of a stage, to making tapes of the music. The pair of us constantly tramping through the Soho rain to give out flyers, and deliver endless cassettes to all the big, indifferent comedy management companies.

We were both signing on and getting housing benefit. I lived in Finsbury Park, and my life at that time centred on, every day:

Theobald & Brand On Ice

For five Wednesdays from April 21st

8.30pm

Armegeddon approaches. The End is nigh. Let's face the Apocalypse laughing.

If you want to see Reggie Kray, the Elephant Man, Hitler and Christ, and what finally made Jack the Ripper crack, as Elvis Presley might have said, "You've come to right place".

A show incorporating comedy, Vaudeville satire and sinister sketches, the highly acclaimed Theobald & Brand turn up at the Hackney Empire Studio Theatre.

Tickets: £4.00 and £3.00 concessions

HACKNEY EMPIRE STUDIO THEATRE

289 Mare Street, London E8
(above the Samuel Pepys pub)

Box Office: 0181 985 2424

turning on the TV to watch *Richard and Judy*, eating Weetabix, reading the odd chapter of Camus, Kierkegaard or Chomsky for beginners, acquiring references, watching films, being ambitious.

A lot of the administrative and financial burden of mine and Karl's low-budget artistic endeavours inevitably fell on our two girlfriends at the time. I was still going out with Elia, who I'd met at Drama School. She was Spanish and took me to meet her family in El Escorial in Madrid. It used to kill me, that sort of stuff – going to stay with people's families, pretending to be nice. She left me in the end, because I was a right little twerp and slept with one of her friends.

Before Finsbury Park we lived at my nan's house in Dagenham. It was an impecunious period and I had to make my own entertainment, mostly through psychological cruelty; I was trying to make Elia smoke a joint or drink some booze or summink, and she was going, 'No Russell, I don't want to, please don't make me, Russ.' It was quite light-hearted, not proper torture.

'Nan,' I said. 'If Elia don't drink this wine, I'm going to turn the telly off so you won't be able to watch Corrie.' My nan, instead of saying, 'What? Don't be ridiculous that's not a proper rule,' looked at Elia and with a sympathetic smile said 'Just drink it darlin.' Like my ridiculous game had been sanctioned by FIFA. I loved her so much for that. She used to give me her pension book so I could sign for her money and spend it on drugs – 'Bring me back a bit though eh, Russ?'

I used to love winding her up more than anything – she was such a laugh. I'd pretend to turn on her telly, pause and sombrely announce, 'Nan, I think the telly's broken.' 'Don't say that Russell, my programme's gonna start.' I'd say, 'It's definitely broken, Nan, you'll have to adapt to life without it, don't make a scene,' then turn it on and she'd be all happy. She accepted me unquestioningly, my nan. I was always skinning up in the front room; eventually she yielded to curiosity, 'Russell – is that drugs?' 'No, it's not drugs, Nan – it's marijuana, and it opens your mind, you square.' 'Well, you wanna be careful with that Russell, 'cos I've seen it on Kilroy: it leads to worse things.'

'Oh Nan,' I muttered, 'you're so parochial.' But it turns out my dear ol' nan was right. My nan's 'Kilroy drugs ladder' led inexorably from marijuana to amphetamines, to LSD to ecstasy to cocaine and then crack to – cue fanfare – heroin: the drug addict's jackpot. I should have listened to her. My drug addiction was a cliché that could've been avoided by listening to Robert Kilroy-Silk.

Stoned, and in the mood to wind her up, I once naughtily crept from the kitchen, the smell of which will remain forever with me – chips, chops, chocolate – to the living room and was about to burst in and tell her there was a fire or a ghost or a murderer, when I spied her through the open door, sat in her chair, the TV off, just staring. I realised that she spent a lot of time alone, that she existed when I wasn't with her, that her body was tired. She looked ready to die.

The last time I saw my nan she said two things to me. One that she'd said every time I'd seen her from the time I'd had the facility for language, the other she said only once. 'You got any money?' as an offer, not a request, and 'Look after your dad Russell.' She'd never said that before. That's all she said from where she lay in Lillechurch Road, her bed having become her deathbed without anyone having been informed. I owe her. Sometimes I wish she'd lived to see me succeed and get famous but it would've made no difference, to her I was famous already.

I phoned my dad the next day and asked him, 'Is Nan alright?' He goes 'No, she died.' 'Oh right, OK then.' The phone went dead – he later said that he was in the car, and drove into a tunnel. I was in a call box in Elephant and Castle. I went to a pub and cried and drank loads, I wrote a poem for my nan that I read at her funeral. I scribbled it out longhand in biro on a series of little scraps of paper, while tears fell on it. It's the only poem I've ever written that is about someone else. Not meant to prove how deep and clever I am, it's just a simple thing that I meant.

I didn't cry when I read it at the funeral – I just recounted it blankly, almost phonetically. And after the funeral, my cousin Gaynor copied it out, and made it into a card, which she sent to everyone. I remember glancing at the photograph – a black-and-white picture of my nan looking joyful and beautiful with my cousin's little boy, Sam, who's all gorgeous with his curly hair. 'Ah, that's so beautiful,' I exclaimed to myself, 'she's done it so tastefully, on that parchment paper.'

At that moment, my eye caught a crucial couplet early on in the poem, where 'Damascus' should rhyme with 'ask us', but Gaynor had inadvertently left off the 'us'. It wasn't just the rhyme scheme this messed up, but all the stresses as well. Of course I had no option but to fly into a blind fury of artistic perfectionism – 'Fuck! That's wrong, that's not my poem. How many copies of this have you sent out?'

Silly really.

On the day of the funeral, though, there were no such lapses in decorum on my part. In fact, it felt at the time like my transition to adulthood. In the poem I mention every member of Nan's bloodline, which was a plea for them all to stick together, 'cos the family was falling apart.

We had to carry that fucking coffin through this huge graveyard by a flyover off the A13. I've never been back there since, but I'd like to. All that throwing dirt and stuff, so full of bleak pageantry. I gave my cousin James my jacket because he was cold, but I didn't really feel the chill of the midwinter air, because my senses were overwhelmed by things that were much more

Dear Bobs and Colin

Thank you for the ... lovely
flowers, they helped make
Mums ... day 'special'.

... you being ... and ... a
great ... support as usual.
Mum loved ... Jim Bobs, and
you will always be a
very special person to us
all

Love to Rex Jan Jim and
Ron.

Mum – by Russell Brand

Dagenham is not Damascus
It's a long way from being divine
But most people here, want you to walk, wi
would say Littlechurch Road to a shrine.
(still) 593 6579, just a number again
Not sympathy and anxieties, sanctuary no more.
'Thank you' is all that is left.

Which becomes a slight reward at that
when we consider all you've given
Your children, grandchildren, friends, strangers, dogs,
A heartbeat and next door's tempestuous cat.
forever to 'Sunset Lane.'
'got my money and' 'can its a shame',
... morality stories of ... and parents.
Valhalla is no longer my name.
when I think of you ... life and the very times long about
There's a hole in the Nobel, now the ...
God sooner always entertain in life
So I don't accept ... your kindless and magic
has just slipped away from us now. You're still here
In Sean's strength, Tom's warmth, Ron's determination,
Karen's charisma, Jaywer's smile, Guy's honesty- he's a
lovely boy- Diana's integrity, and in Sam, beautiful Sam.
Amidst all these ... gifts you've bequeathed,
There's a day we owe you, no, just tears and wreaths
So if you could ... one last thing it would have to be
Hold me close, hold me like Christmas, let us agree
To ... this holiday's continued, it's finally ...
And with our custodians let us agree
To leave you in heaven, later finding Jesus with tea.

powerful – like duty and family, and other pressing issues that I wouldn't normally think about.

At one point, when I simultaneously ran out of money and girlfriends who were willing to be financially exploited, I even had to go and live back with my mum in Grays again for a while. I signed on with a temping agency, and they told me that there was work over Christmas assisting the postal service. I didn't realise that the reason they needed assistance was because the postmen were on strike (not that I would probably have cared that much anyway, as my political sensibilities were still very much in their infancy at this stage).

I don't think there was even an interview – you just went down and said you could do it, and started there and then. You didn't even have to wear a uniform – which disappointed me a bit to be honest. A uniform might have made it easier for me to cope with the indignities of this form of labour. The first of these was that each morning my mum would drop me off with some sandwiches and a few pre-made joints in my lunchbox. This made me feel slightly bad, 'cos I don't think many other postmen in their early twenties were still getting dropped off at work by their mums.

No one ever wanted to have it off with me while I was being a Postie: this infuriated me. Unless the films of Robin Askwith are a complete fabrication (a possibility which I find too horrible to contemplate), then postmen should fall comfortably within the remit of casual early morning how's yer father. And yet the entire time I was working for the postal service, not a single wanton housewife propositioned me.

As I tottered round the great big estates of Ockenden, trying not to come a cropper in the frosty ground in my dead slippery shoes, I would make the time pass more quickly by stealing some of the letters and packages. I thought that would lighten the mood. When I made that confession previously in a brochure for forthcoming Channel 4 shows that was distributed free with the *Evening Standard*, someone in the Ockenden area tried to press charges saying that I could easily have been their postman. But unless they're missing a *Best of Frank Sinatra* CD then it's unlikely.

Down the end of one of the streets was a recreation ground or a rec as they're commonly known in the Essex area, and perhaps the world over, for all I know. There was a group of men playing football and so I thought it would be nice to watch them for a moment or two, instead of just trudging onward with my breath freezing in front of my face. I paused, heart as heavy as my sack, laden with resentment and parcels of unfulfilled ambition, to watch their game.

They seemed to be quite good players these men – charging around on that chilly early morning pitch. At one point the ball came bouncing towards me, filling me with that immediate sense of dread which always accompanies this eventuality. If a ball comes in my dad's direction in a park, he nimbly dances up to it and elegantly, with the side of his foot, sends the ball swooping back to its place of origin, like a footballing Enoch Powell callously repatriating immigrants.

When a football comes towards me, however, I know this precedes a moment of terrible embarrassment. I'll either hoof it skywards, or step on it, or it'll go between my legs. When it came towards me in this instance – although on the outside I was simply placing my sack on the ground, trying to act as nonchalant as possible – inside my head I was screaming, 'Oh no, that ball is coming towards me, I'm about to be humiliated, here it comes, this is the moment of humiliation . . .'

Sure enough, I swept my foot into the ball with all my might and it skidded about eight inches in front of me. At the same instant as the man who was sprinting to receive a pass saw that he was going to have to come all the way towards me to retrieve the ball, he also noticed that I had a postbag. 'Here, what are you doing watching football?' he demanded. 'Why don't you get on with your job? You fucking scab.' The other players, seeing the confrontation, soon began to join in the chorus of condemnation – 'Yeah, you scab, get on with your fucking job.'

These men were striking postal workers, playing football to distract themselves from the harsh realities of industrial action, and while they were forgoing payment in a bid to improve their working conditions, I had stepped in to take their wages. I was embarrassed and frightened by my own naivety. This further reinforced my sense of not belonging to my own culture.

I was never very good at sustaining jobs – it always seemed a bit pointless, 'cos you never seemed to get the money for ages. My mum was always on at me to get a paper round when I was younger, and I tried it for a bit, but I quickly realised that it was much easier just to throw the papers away. I had a job collecting for this hospital lottery once as well, but I just used to give them the bare minimum I could get away with and keep the rest of the money. I realise now how disgraceful that is, but I just didn't have a work ethic, and if anyone ever challenged me on it I'd just quote George Bernard Shaw to the effect that 'a true artist would see his family starve, rather than work at anything other than his art'.

My dad was (and is) a confident, masculine, working-class man, and Colin, while somewhat less ebullient, was still very much the embodiment of the big, heavy manual labourer – always working, always drinking. I presume that feeling ostracised and alienated from them, even within my own home growing up, encoded within me a deep sense of alienation. That's why in any group dynamic my identity will always be defined as an outsider rather than from within.

This is also the reason why stand-up comedy is the perfect career for me. Not just because I'm constantly scribbling notes inside my own mind to deal with the embarrassment I perpetually feel, but also because I'm always observing, always outside. It's a perfectly natural dynamic for me to stand alone in front of thousands of people and tell 'em how I feel. The fact that I've managed to make it funny is bloody convenient, because I can't think how else I would make them listen. ☞

21

Don't Die of Ignorance

I got very close to Karl Theobald in that confused and anxious time after leaving Drama Centre. He comes from a working-class background in Lowestoft. He's a real autodidact, who always knows loads about books, culture and art, and is very clever, quick and funny. He was my first comedic soul-mate. There was a period when our impecunious circumstances even led us to share the same bed – like Morecambe and Wise, dreaming of better things.

It's a shame that it has to be me that tells the following story, 'cos Karl always said he would tell it in his autobiography (though obviously the fact that I've got there first doesn't mean he won't get the chance, and the more different angles people get to hear this from the better as far as I'm concerned). We were in bed reading Shakespeare together (oh yes, ours was a very cultural household).

At one point I broke away from the text and was just making stuff up as I went along, but Karl hadn't realised and kept looking at the book, struggling to find out where those lines were coming from. Now obviously I'm not saying that I'm as good at improvising dialogue as Shakespeare was at writing it – that would be ridiculously conceited – but this story does seem to suggest as much. Just look at the evidence.

It wasn't all late-night Shakespeare readings and off-the-cuff brilliance, hanging out with me at that time, though. My egotism and the single-mindedness with which I pursued potential sexual conquests could often make me uneasy company.

Karl and I would often muse that in this secular age where man no longer believed in or devoted himself to God, salvation could only be sought through love, that love was a new religion – romantic love, devotion to the female, a return to pagan roots – and women were goddesses who could be saved through worshipping. Thus I was forever on my knees before women, hungrily devouring truth, seeking out redemption wherever it may lie – usually squandered between someone's thighs.

After about six months to a year of working together, my alcohol and drug use and erratic behaviour with women eventually drove Karl away. We didn't have a formal falling out, we just sort of stopped phoning each other. I think it was partly the pressure of both being poor and me drinking too much and taking too many drugs. But either way, I adored him, and missed him terribly once we stopped working together.

That summer, I went up to Edinburgh with a group of students to do a series of short plays by the bloke who wrote *Moonstruck*, in a fifty-seater room. That was the first time I'd been to the festival, and I loved it. Me and this other guy who was in the play had a league to see who could pull the most women (I believe I won). I remember there being lots of big parties we couldn't get into, so we just kind of blagged our way around.

It was in the midst of these misadventures that I did my first solo open-mike spot, above an Edinburgh pub called The Blind Poet. It only lasted seven minutes, and it was terrifying and difficult – even though there were only about fifteen people in the audience, most of whom were in the play that I was doing – but I loved it.

I sat in a laundrette writing jokes about swans, which are quite a staple of the surrealist lexicon. When I finally performed the piece, I was every bit as scared as the first time I stepped on the stage as Fat Sam, but this time there was no character, no hat, and no accent to hide behind – only me and material about swans (remember this is ten years ago: at that point no one had found out just how funny swans were; you could say I was a real pioneer).

My first gig was yet another profound epiphany – I've been lucky enough to have had several in my life. I hope I reach the point where epiphanies become so commonplace that I scarcely bother to register them: 'Oh look, another epiphany – as we acquire knowledge we become mired in the ignorance of the educated, delivered from the wisdom of innocence by a cor-rupted midwife. Now what's on telly?' (That's probably why I put the stuff about Saul on the road to Damascus in my nan's poem, because I recognised how it feels to suddenly be rendered holy and complete by a realisation of the exact nature of your destiny.)

Obviously doing *Bugsy Malone* as a kid was my main incidence of what Jack Kerouac called satori, but since I've been thinking about it, I've realised that there was probably one even earlier than that – when I had to read at a school poetry competition in the third year. The fact that this happened at all was probably down to Mr Hannebury – this English teacher who would sometimes show me a bit of encouragement (when he wasn't slamming his hand down on his desk and saying, 'Russell, have you done your homework? No? Case proved!'). In my mind, he seems like a very worldly-wise, almost avuncular figure, but in reality he was probably younger than I am now.

The piece I read was called 'The Nightmare before Christmas' (I presume it was written by Richard Curtis, because it was in a

Comic Relief annual). I remember it had the word 'bastards' in it, which they wanted me to change, and right up to the moment I read it, I thought I probably ought to say it anyway. In the end, I toned it down to 'rotters', or something similarly ridiculous. In a sense, I've never really forgiven myself for that – probably because somewhere within me I knew that when it came to tell the story in an autobiography, it would sound much better if I could write '. . . and then I said bastards.'

But I suppose now I've managed to make a virtue of not saying it, so all's well that ends well. Still, if you were looking for early motivation for my subsequent reluctance to censor myself in any way whatsoever, this would probably fit the bill. I came second in that contest (Ranjev Mitra won it, as he did every year – he was a thoroughbred when it came to that competition), but this was probably the first time I experienced that euphoric feeling – 'Thank God, there's something I can do.'

I felt something like it again in 1994, when Channel 4 broadcast a tribute screening of Bill Hicks's show 'Revelations' at the Dominion Theatre, and an accompanying documentary. Seeing Hicks for the first time (ironically, just after his death) affected me incredibly strongly. I thought he was extraordinary – a funny, powerful, poignant, passionate, clever, erudite, brilliant and moving man. And I watched that video so many times that I learnt it off by heart.

I'd grown up on *Blackadder*, *Fawlty Towers* and *Only Fools and Horses* – rewinding my dad's tapes and playing them again so many times that the rhythm of those programmes is forever ingrained in my mind. I wasn't madly into music growing up. Comedy was my music, and the same way other people can always call upon the songs they loved as teenagers, the contours of my emotional landscape were shaped by lines of dialogue from minor characters in BBC sitcoms of the 1970s and '80s.

As I started to get more interested in comedy, I began to feel the same way about Hancock, Peter Cook and Richard Pryor. I loved the fact that Pryor made big Hollywood films and did brilliant stand-up shows at the same time, because that's what I wanted to do. I loved the iconography of Cook – the rakish bohemian sophisticate, who had seemingly achieved everything he wanted by his early twenties and then became bored of life, but still remained a beautiful, debonair genius. And I loved the way Tony Hancock perfectly articulated how miserable and out of place and bored and snooty I felt. But when I was taking my first tentative steps as a stand-up – a few years after I'd first seen him on TV – it was Bill Hicks's confrontational – almost hectoring – style and radically politicised subject matter that were the clearest influences on what I was trying to do.

After that first experience at Edinburgh, I came back to London and started doing other open-mike spots at places like The Purple Turtle, on Essex Road in Islington. I was cripplingly nervous, even when doing tiny five-minute spots. What the fuck can you do in five minutes in those bawdy loud rooms where people are hardly listening? It's so fucking difficult. But even when I was waiting nervously in North London pub toilets, having diarrhoea and smoking grass to calm down, I could still cling onto a new sense of purpose.

I felt that I was finally in alignment: that at last I was doing what I was supposed to be doing. From this point onwards, the seeds that had been planted in me with my endless hours of watching comedy videos could finally begin to germinate.

I've seen Matt Lucas talk about how angry *Vic Reeves Big Night Out* made him initially (I think he even made a complaint to Channel 4), but then he really grew to love it, and I was exactly the same. I was about fourteen when the first series came on, and I thought, 'What does he mean, "What's on the end of your stick?" What is this rubbish?' But then I watched a couple more and realised it was the most amazing thing in the world.

It's funny and charming and specific in its language and its references. It taught me that you should never pick the first word people would think of, you have to train your mind to sift through the obvious stuff until you come to something that's really funny. I remember when Bob Mortimer came on *Big Brother's Big Mouth* last year he referred to Mikey as 'the perfumed labourer': that's just beautiful.

Around the time of those first stand-up gigs, I was going out with this girl called Josephine, whose dad was a high-court judge (I remember seeing him on the front of the *Evening Standard* once). I think she's married to a rabbi now – I don't like it when ex-girlfriends get married. I always think, 'Come on, you never really ever got over me did you? That wedding – be honest with yourself, it was a sham.'

I was quite diligent at first, as a stand-up comic. I took it very seriously and worked very, very hard on it. Sitting on fucking night buses with a cassette Walkman, playing my own set over and over – learning it by rote – as well as spending hours educating myself further about Woody Allen and Lenny Bruce. Even though I'm almost congenitally self-obsessed and solipsistic – in the same way that Allen is – I always wanted my stuff to have a spiritual and political agenda.

When I was working with Karl, I'd met these people doing this kind of political sketch-show troupe thing called Article 19. One of them was called John Rogers, a writer of satirical songs, who now researches material for me, in the hope of making my forthcoming stand-up shows a bit more politically valid than their immediate predecessors. A wonderful, erudite man, he sits there, patiently tolerating my rants about socialism and revolution – topics that he himself is very well informed upon, never embarrassing me, just diligently pointing out the numerous errors, inconsistencies and lies like a tutor for arrogant spastics.

As soon as I met John, I imagined that I'd know him for the rest of my life, and probably go on yachting holidays with him in my fifties. He'd still be married to Haidi – the lovely Australian wife, with whom he has two obscenely beautiful sons – and I'd be there with some seventeen-year-old dolly-bird. Of course I'd be all bloated by then, like Michael Winner, but perhaps with braids in my hair and gold teeth, wearing a moo-moo (I think that's what they're called – either way, one of them things you wear when you're fat).

In London – as I suppose in all major cities – there are all these people slogging away at the arts: writing things, performing for nothing, taking B.Tech courses, just trying their best to get somewhere in show business. And the further down the line you get, the more you realise there's often very little logic separating people who are actually making money, from those slogging themselves to death in some destitute pit of bedsit boredom. I consolidated my position in the latter group by moving in with Mark and Andy, a couple of chancers from South London.

The flat was above a branch of Barclay's Bank, just south of Tower Bridge. Mark Pinheiro was a beautiful black lad, who'd been orphaned young; all daft and full of dreams he was, his ambitions and astonishing awareness of pop culture perpetually at war with his love of sleep. Andy Dobson was a brilliantly gifted electronic musician – a great big ginger cupboard of a man, always sat poised above his various Moog keyboards, battering out tunes. The two of them had one of those relationships which is like a traumatic heterosexual marriage. They were constantly bawling and screeching at each other, and would sometimes have ridiculous fights that never amounted to anything: once Andy came running up to Mark with this kitchen-knife that was still in the container with egg whisks, ladles and spoons, like a murderous pastry chef. Along with John Rogers, Andy and Mark became like a second surrogate family to me, the same as when I'd moved in with those Italia Conti lost boys Jimmy and Justin when I was sixteen. Oddly, that flat was just around the corner – which showed how much progress I'd made up the property ladder. This time, though, I was at least going in with a bit more status. John Rogers had a day job in a language school – one of those ones in the West End, in Oxford Street, where the students indiscriminately distribute leaflets saying 'learn English'. I asked him if he could sort me out an interview and it turned out – luckily for me – that they take pretty much anyone.

It's a job that could be done by a tape recorder. They give you this book to read out – 'Janet opened her umbrella', that sort of stuff – and it's like a script: you're not supposed to deviate from it by one word. The students have got the same book, and they have to repeat it back after you.

I approach jobs where there's no chance of getting either sex or applause at the end of it with a mixture of reluctance and resentment. This language-school job fulfilled at least the first of my conditions for productive employment.

The first time they actually left me in a room with the students and this book, I thought, 'There are no adults here – how are they gonna make sure I do what I'm supposed to?' That feeling of 'I can't believe people are actually going to let me do this' has preceded many of my most gleefully decadent interludes. The whole affair was utterly ridiculous. I starting reading the book, but as I did so, I was just scanning the room bedazzled by the selection of glorious females over whom I'd been granted authority.

It took maybe two weeks before I realised my classroom was a sexy library from which I could borrow lovely women from all around the world: Italian, Brazilian, Japanese; I remember I brought back these two Polish women once and Mark Pinheiro said, 'They look like them girls in *Schindler's List* that put blood on their cheeks to avoid being executed.' I liked them.

There were male students in the class as well; they didn't get as much attention from me, but they joined me and the girls when we went to Soho Square to smoke draw instead of learning a language that I already knew. It was alright that job, really. I think it was about eight pounds an hour. And the shifts would vary, but it was roughly eight hours a day, five days a week.

I was working hard at practising my stand-up in the evenings. And after a handful of five-minute sets I got to the final of the Hackney Empire's New Act Of The Year competition.

This was really important to my career. The first round of the competition you just do in a pub in front of about thirty people, but the final is in front of an audience of two thousand. I was really committed to making the best of this opportunity; I went to the Hackney Empire in advance, to walk around on the stage and get used to it.

By the time the night of the actual final arrived though – with my mum, my dad and loads of my mates there (Karl Theobald, who I hadn't seen for months, left me a good-luck card with a picture of Tony Hancock at the stage door) – a few complications had arisen. Two Danish girls had moved in with me, Mark and Andy in Bermondsey. Mark liked one of them – Zenia. When my friends like a girl, sometimes it makes me fancy them a bit; their interest seems like an endorsement. 'She is beautiful,' I find myself thinking. Now that I'm not so insanely selfish, I force that feeling into my stomach and leave it there to fester into a tumour. But when I was younger I flew into action like a sexy, disloyal cobra. Zenia and I had a relationship, which must've been annoying for Mark, although he did end up seeing the other girl so, in a way, I'm a bit like Cilla Black, a manipulative saucy Cilla Black. Once I weed in her bath so that it seemed like a fountain; she swore she'd get revenge, but I hubristically claimed that I was too brilliant to be tricked; whom the Gods wish to destroy they first make mad. Or they just get them to drink a big hearty glug of girl wee instead of the water to which they're acclimatised of a morning. It was like drinking a cloud, I didn't mind it.

It was while I was with Zenia that I met Amanda Alguero Alejos, and began what was to be one of the most significant, romantic and destructive relationships of my soppy life. The teachers at Callan language school used to go out for drinks on Friday night, in order to exploitatively work their way through the students (at least, that was why I went). Amanda – this beautiful Spanish girl – was there one night, and the first thing she ever said to me was 'Hmmm, you a good-looking boy – come to the toilet for kisses.' I got a bit obsessed by her, not least because she was a very intense person, and we argued a lot.

She came to that Hackney Empire final, looking really gorgeous. At that point I – ever the gentleman – said, 'I think you should probably know I've got a girlfriend', and she just smacked me right in the face. We spent the whole night in Arthur Smith's dressing room, drinking and getting off with each other, while he was onstage compering the show. By the time it got to my turn, I was properly slaughtered.

I didn't come anywhere in the competition (well, I was fourth, but that's not even in the medals, is it?). However the *Time Out* comedy critic Malcolm Hay wrote this really lovely review of the whole night, mostly about me, saying, 'He's from Essex, and he could be the real deal.' There were a lot of industry people and managers there as well, one of whom – Nigel Klarfeld from Bound and Gagged – signed me up, and became my first agent.

He's a funny feller, Nigel. Very short-sighted – he can't see anyone who's more than a yard away from him. He had a dog called Harvey – one of them whose skin is all wrinkled up, so they look like their face has been pulled forward. I would eventually part company with Nigel in a characteristically dignified fashion – hurling a glass of water at him, shouting 'Fuck you, Nigel' and walking off out of his life forever. But for the moment, signing this deal was a huge step forward, and I felt like I was finally starting to get somewhere.

Shortly after the Hackney Empire final, I wanted to go to Spain with Amanda, so I asked the people at the language school if I could have a fortnight off. When they said, 'No, you're supposed to be working,' I just went anyway. On my return my employers were curious as to where I'd been and the truthful answer – 'the holiday upon which you expressly forbade me to go' – was likely to cause me all manner of bother which I couldn't be expected to tolerate. If you have to do some lying, you may as well commit to it. Hitler said, 'The bigger the lie the more people will believe it.' I'm not holding Hitler up as a role model, the man was a filthy swine, but as I stood in the suspicious glare of my boss I thought, 'What would Hitler do?' He'd probably have had her killed; she was a lesbian. Plus she was shouting and pointing and I don't think he'd have stood for that. Then I remembered Hitler's lie theory. 'Sorry I've been away, I know it looks bad, and probably you think I went on that holiday that I requested and was denied. But the truth is, and you better hold onto your hat 'cos this is a belter, I've got AIDS.' Silence. 'Yep. You heard me correctly, I'm standing here, looking you right in the eye and telling you that I've got AIDS. Now it's over to you in the studio, to see how you're going to cope with this big, stupid, atrocious lie.'

My boss was speechless. The good thing about my evil lie was that it was so terrible that no one would ever tell such a lie. That's why the lie worked.

Luckily, I was starting to get more and more stand-up work at this point, so I was able to leave that job before they either got up the courage to sack me, or I had to start faking symptoms. ☞

22

Firing Minors

I went up to Edinburgh in 2000. Me, Mark Felgate and Shappi Khorsandi – both of whom had finished above me at the Hackney Empire final – put on a three-hander doing twenty minutes each.

I was still being quite disciplined at that time. I actually had some material – about twenty minutes of quite good, pseudo-Bill Hicks-type stuff about care in the community. But I suppose the most notable thing about that show was the children I put in it.

They were rough little kids, aged between five and ten, from the surrounding estates. They were always playing with matches and spitting at people, and they stole stuff from the production office. I still have this letter from the Gilded Balloon (which was the venue that had put me on). Sadly I couldn't find it in time to include it in this book, but this is the rough gist of what it said: 'Dear Mr Brand, I am writing to complain about the children you've got working for you. Firstly, to have children working for you in any capacity is against employment law. Secondly, these particular ones are very badly behaved.'

I liked the fact that they were naughty, though. I used to have them onstage and say, 'I've just got a natural rapport with children,' and then they'd put a sign on my back saying 'Wanker'. Sadly, after receiving that letter I had to tell 'em that they were sacked – it's not easy to sack a child. When I broke the sad news they just said, 'If we can't work for you no more, we'll just go back to stealing.' They're probably old enough to earn their money killing people now.

That Edinburgh I also had a part in a play by Trevor Lock, who would later work with me on my 6 Music and Radio 2 shows. A good play that was, by old Trev. It was called *There's Something You Should Know*; he played a character who died but didn't know and turned into this kind of earth-bound angel, and I was his best friend watching him go all religious and spiritual.

I was womanising a lot already at that time – Amanda having fucked off back to live in Spain, leaving me to wallow in a pit of my own debauchery – and then Trevor Lock and his wife Sem, who was from Peru, bought me a copy of that book *Women On Top*, by Nancy Friday. It's a collection of women talking about their sexual fantasies – proper rude they are. It turns out some of them want to fuck dogs, which made me think 'Crikey, the sauce of it all.' So I rampaged through Edinburgh having a fantastic time, and getting some great, sexualised reviews in the process. People compared me to Heathcliff from *Wuthering Heights* and said things like, 'Brand, who has star of the future tattooed beneath his Calvin Kleins.'

Some people from MTV came to see me perform up in Edinburgh, and asked me to audition for them when I got back to London. Getting that job would provoke possibly the clearest ever demonstration of my astonishing capacity (and it's even astonishing to me) to descend in the blink of a proverbial eye from enormous, obsequious gratitude, into indifference, cruelty and pompous affectation.

I was incredibly thankful that I wasn't going to have to sign on any more, and could shrug off the indignity of standing in dole queues, knowing that in every encounter with a clerk they're trying to withdraw your benefits. Particularly if they know you're in the entertainment industry – you can see their sneering cynicism with regard to your career: 'Oh, like you're ever going to make money from show business.' I remember experiencing that in Grays job centre when I was sixteen, then subsequently in Bermondsey, Kentish Town and Finsbury Park: an odyssey of social insecurity.

Apart from the odd bit of acting, this was my first regular work on telly. And when MTV gave me a contract to make ninety shows I thought, 'That's it – what a relief, I've made it', and went from 'Oh, that's ever so kind of you' to 'Where's my fucking taxi?' in about ten seconds.

It was the delightful Andy Milligan who gave me my first break – he was a skinheaded lad from Newcastle who looked a bit like Tom Thug, a character from a short-lived Southern *Viz* rip-off, *Oink!* When I cast my mind back across the porridge-coloured mindscape, one of the best moments of my life was arriving at MTV after I'd done the pilot for our new show, and seeing loads of people gathered round a TV set, really laughing. I thought 'what's going on there?' and peered through the crowd to see they were watching the tape of me.

The idea for the show which ended up being called *Dancefloor Chart* was a very simple one. Me going up to people in nightclubs and talking rubbish to them when they were off their heads on pills. Sample dialogue:

RUSSELL: You know Postman Pat and his black-and-white cat?
LAD: Yeah.
RUSSELL: How do we know it's his cat?
LAD: Well . . . we just do.
RUSSELL: Can he prove it though?
LAD: It is his cat. It says at the beginning. In the song.

RUSSELL: Can we trust them though?

LAD: Look, it is his cat . . . Why would they . . . ? (The lad tapers off into a drugged confusion.)

RUSSELL: They can't prove it. There are no papers.

LAD: (As if realising the CIA killed JFK) Yeah, you're right. It's probably not his cat.

That was the format of the show. The lad was high on ecstasy, but I was by now quite the connoisseur of opiates and crack. 'Don't you think it's out of order taking the piss out of them pilled-up people in clubs?' people would sometimes enquire. 'I was on crack and heroin,' I'd reply. 'I didn't even know I was in a club.'

Then, late as usual, I met the second comic genius that was to blight my life. Matt Morgan. He was just an intern there when I met him. He came from Dartford, which is just the other side of the river from Grays. He had a similar background to mine, as well as sharing my taste in comedy. The first conversation we had was on a plane flying to Ireland. I had these giant African snails with me (even though it was the time of foot and mouth, so you weren't even supposed to have apples on planes, let alone snails).

I said, 'Look at my new pets, they're great – what shall we call them?' He said 'Wiggins', which is a name in a Peter Cook and Dudley Moore sketch about a headmaster who sexually abuses boys. Then we talked a bit about Cook, and Chris Morris's *Brass Eye*, which we both really loved, because it's so clever and dangerous and acute, and I immediately recognised him as a kindred spirit.

Matt, like me, was from a small estuary town (he actually went to the same school as Mick Jagger). He also felt sort of ostracised and alienated growing up, and shared that same kind of darkness to his sensibility that I have.

He would tell me stories – which we later turned into a very scary sketch called 'Mr Natterjack' – about there being a bird trapped in a vent in his bedroom wall when he was a child, and none of his family believing him. He was afraid to go to bed because of the noise it was making: 'Mummy, there's a monster in the bedroom,' 'There's not a monster – go to bed.' And he had to listen to this crow dying in his air-vent.

We went over to Dublin (MTV's on their regular telly, so I was a bit famous there), got with some girls, got in a little bit of trouble, and he quickly became the only person at MTV I'd hang out with – or indeed talk to. We've got in all sorts of sex adventures together over the years, but there's never been any actual rhubarb between us. Not that there's anything wrong with that, it's just not our way.

Part of the special affection I felt for Matt is because he's a couple of years younger than me. When I first met him, Matt was like Rodney in *Only Fools and Horses*, and prior to that I'd always been the Rodney. Not just in my own family – where my dad was a bit like Del Boy, a sort of upbeat Thatcherite go-getter, and my nan was like grandad, sentimental, lachrymose and lovely, and I was kind of gawky and aspirational, trailing along behind – but in other relationships too.

Karl Theobald was older than me and senior. Whereas while Matt is very clever and funny, he was the first person I'd really been friends with in adult life who was demonstrably my junior. Because I was a TV presenter and he was an intern, that meant I had status in the relationship. This just made him more sulky and adolescent, which I found very entertaining.

Matt would never go and get drinks for me, 'cos he was too lazy, but I did make him score heroin for me a couple of times later on (he refused initially, but I bullied him into it, saying, 'I'll still get it, Matthew, you'll just inconvenience me. I'm not going to give up heroin because you don't go and get me some now'). When he wrote an article called '10 things Russell should be ashamed of' in my tour programme, this incident was one of the ten.

Meeting Matt was the beginning of a period which in retrospect feels like quite good fun. There's an episode of the MTV show *Jackass* where Johnny Knoxville and the lads recreate a stunt from the film *Cool Hand Luke*, to see if they could eat a load of hard-boiled eggs without vomiting, like Luke does. To promote *Jackass* in the UK, MTV re-staged this all around the country, which meant I had to go to every major British city – Glasgow, Edinburgh, Leeds – hyping up *Jackass* through a microphone in shopping centres, doing this competition, and posing for pictures in local papers, while trying to avoid streams of egg-strewn vomit. Even quite recently, when I was back at MTV doing *One Leicester Square*, I would bump into the people that were my PR handlers on that trip. One lass reminded me that I put lap dances and prostitutes on her gold card, and got the hotel to give me cash on her account without her prior knowledge. Looming larger than any of these misdemeanours, though, was the saga of the aforementioned giant African snails.

I bought them at Brixton market, took them on tour with me for a bit, and then grew a little tired of them. They were good for a while, but once you've grown used to the fact that they're bigger than normal snails, they get a bit boring. After a couple of weeks the novelty has all but worn away: it's just like they're normal snails and you're closer to 'em. I had to order them room service; spinach they liked, though 'not with Hollandaise sauce – any kind of salt will kill them.'

In the end, I left them behind at the Leeds Hilton. I was at some shopping centre – normally they're called the Corn Exchange, so let us assume that was the name – with all these Leeds yobbo lads scoffing eggs and puking them up all over a tarpaulin on the floor, when the MTV PR girl comes up to me with a phone and goes, 'Erm Russell, it's the North Yorkshire police on the phone – they've had a call from the RSPCA about you leaving giant African snails in your room at the Hilton, do you want to speak to them?' North Yorkshire police? RSPCA? Hilton? 'Sounds like a lot of aggro,' I thought.

'You take it, you're in PR.' But later on, the story got out, and I had to talk to some syndicated press people about it – it was only ever picked up by local papers and the Irish press, for some reason. They asked, 'What do you say to these charges from the RSPCA that it was gross neglect of a rare and endangered animal?'

This was ridiculous, because they're normally food – you buy them at the market either alive or frozen, and you're meant to put them in a stew, so effectively I had saved them from certain death and taken them on a once-in-a-lifetime adventure. So I said, 'I miss them pets – Sebastian and Jake, they were called [I gave them different names every time someone asked me], they meant the world to me, and I'll do whatever it takes to get 'em back. They lived like proper little toffs with me – Burlington Berties they were, accustomed to the finer things of life.'

I remember reading this Irish newspaper and seeing they'd put this load of rubbish in it verbatim. I suppose that was my first taste of a form of public notoriety with which I have subsequently become all too familiar. I remember seeing that clipping stuck to Andy Milligan's desk at MTV, and thinking, 'This is good.'

Me and Matt just used to fuel each other's madness when we were doing that *Dancefloor Chart*. We'd both be off our heads in some club somewhere, I'd ask him to think of an image and he'd pause then say, 'Worzel Gummidge at the Berlin Olympics lying to Jesse Owens about Teen Wolf's dreams,' then I'd go off and present this alternate reality to some hapless sod, and they'd have to come to terms with it. There were a lot of '80s films involved – it was just my childhood being reconfigured as jokes – and it was sort of a cult hit.

I thought, 'This will be the thing that makes me famous: in a tiny, insular, cable TV way, but still famous.' I was meeting loads of women when we were out in those clubs, and getting a lot of blow jobs in toilets. Amanda had come back into my life, so I was seeing her as well, and it was the first time I'd ever had a bit of cash to spare. I spent it mostly on too tight t-shirts, which I wore with most of my abdomen visible and highlights in my hair. Matt said I dressed like some kind of swarthy Latino lover. That place above the bank where I lived with Mark and Andy was like the house in *Fight Club* – dirty plates piled up everywhere, people riding round on BMXs. And after I'd been at MTV a little while, I moved out and got a room with their old next-door neighbour Daniele. He was a juggler, but he had a good job selling commodities or something like that, and he'd got this amazing flat in a converted church in Hackney Road.

This was the first time in my life that I'd lived somewhere nice. There were three or four different flats, attached to a cool bar that held interesting events, leading off a beautiful courtyard, and Daniele's was on the top floor. It was a really interesting L-shaped space, with a lovely living room, a skylight and wooden floors. I had a great little room, and good money coming in from MTV, so I was always able to pay the rent.

When Matt stayed there I used to make him sleep in the corridor, on an old brown duvet that I'd had since I was about nine. He used to plead with me – 'Can't I sleep in your room?' And I'd say, 'No Matthew, you will be sleeping on "the brown."' I'd only been there about a month when Daniele said, 'Russell, you've made my house feel like a brothel – the whole place smells of drugs, and every time I come in here there are different women.' (It wasn't Matt he was complaining about: I did have other guests.)

He was right. If anything good came my way, I had to fuck it up. Daniele couldn't understand why, because he was a gentle person who really knew how to live. He loved cooking, and once he brought all these slippers back from Morocco in all different sizes, and left them by the door for visitors. That would never occur to me, he was from another world. France.

Daniele perhaps found me a difficult flatmate on account of the antics. I was always up to antics. He never learned of the time I was locked out. This anecdote is an almost perfect representation of instant karma: I did something bad, the universe caught me and promptly punished me. When John Lennon sang, 'Instant Karma's gonna get you', I thought how? It'll never get me, I'm too smart, too swift, too tricky and quick, but he was right. I met this German lap dancer called Michaela – she was one of a long line of lap dancery-type girls who distracted me from the sadness at this time. 'Sisters of Mercy', Leonard Cohen would've called them, offering salvation and redemption. I called them tarts. Karma must've been listening. And waiting. I was going to lap-dancing clubs quite a lot at the time, in particular Spearmint Rhino. Cunningly, I used to phone them up and go, 'Hey, my name's Zack Showbiz. I'm the manager of Russell Brand – the hot MTV presenter – and he's on his way down to your club. Don't make him wear shoes and trousers like you do the normal guys. Welcome him with open arms, show him a good time.'

A few minutes later I'd arrive – 'Hi, I'm Russell, I think my manager, Zack Showbiz phoned?' – and they'd say reverentially, 'Oh, come in, Mr Brand, nice trainers.' Some of the dancers recognised me from MTV, and I'd be able to chat 'em up, and kidnap them. You're not supposed to do that, it's against policy, like touching and feeling and wistfully reflecting that everything could've been so different if only you'd learned how to love. Michaela. She was sexy, in a lap-dancer sort of way, which many might think, incidentally, is the best way to be sexy: other ways include; sexy like a teacher, sexy like a policewoman, a mate's sister, a biblical character, Cher, Eva Braun, a Brontë sister, a babysitter, Madonna, or The Madonna. I like lap-dancer sexy.

I got her delivered to the house in a cab using the MTV Addison Lee cab account, of which I am still the world-record exploiter. I used to hang out in crack dens with a car outside; get my mum brought round, takeaways delivered and my mum's takeaways delivered; on one crazy occasion I had my mum delivered to a takeaway just to mix things up. I had dealers picked up in Camden, so they could drop me off drugs in Hackney and then get taken home. I just exploited that account from the moment I started working at MTV, till the moment they sacked me. I simply didn't use public transport from the second an MTV researcher spoke these cherished words: 'Russell, as a presenter you get an account number to use at Addison Lee, whenever you need to get to work.' I ignored the 'get to work' bit: every single journey I took from then was in an account cab, and not just my own journeys – sometimes I'd have two or three cars out at a time, ferrying my mum around, or picking people up from airports.

Michaela arrived in her car just as someone else departed in theirs – Daniele was away in Paris. We were watching pornography together and having sex in the living room – 'This is the life,' I thought, like a Beano character eating sausage and mash on a deckchair, as I ejaculated. Michaela hadn't cum. My policy was – first sexual encounter orgasm comes free, after that be on your toes 'cos I won't be hanging about. Her orgasm quota had been met earlier in the evening, it was now three in the morning so I strolled off into the flat all nude, to quiet my belligerent mind with a fizzing brown snake of heroin. Michaela began loudly putting her stuff away – in the way the women do when they want you to say, 'Oh, don't put your stuff away.'

I wasn't going to fall for that one; they teach you that on your first day of womanising school. Michaela was angered by my well-tutored ignorance: she came out into the corridor – fully clothed and carrying her bag – walked up to me with rage twinkling in her perfect green eyes, and smacked me really hard in the face. I'm very much of the view that it's wrong to hit a woman, or anyone really, so I had to be innovative when meting out retribution; thankfully the smack had awoken my creativity, I grabbed her shoulders and bum's rushed her towards the front door. I never know whether to say bum's rushed or frog marched – let's call it a frog's rush or a bum march to keep the mood light; it was the manner in which a bouncer would evict a drunk. As I escorted Michaela through the front door, I felt very strongly that I needed to avenge the slap – 'she can't slap me just because I didn't make her cum then swanned off leaving porn on the telly while I smoked gear.' Yes, what kind of man would let such a slur pass unaddressed? Not me, so naked and riled and one hundred per cent sure that what I was about to do was objectively right and what God would've wanted, I spat in her face. Yes that's right, I spat in the face of a beautiful woman that had made me cum. She had slapped me and I was convinced that it was the only course of action and that there'd be no consequences. Then the front door clicked shut behind me. 'Uh oh.'

I discreetly pushed the door to check it was shut. It was. Michaela hadn't noticed yet because she was too stunned by the spitting atrocity. 'Hmm,' I thought. 'This doesn't look good. It's three o'clock in the morning, I'm completely naked, I've got no money, and the only person who could possibly help me has got my spit running down her face.' She still hadn't noticed the door. 'Fuck you, I'm going,' she shouted and started to walk off into the cold, Hackney night. 'Before you go, Michaela, I'd like to take this opportunity to apologise.' She stops and looks back, wiping her face. This will take some charm. 'It was a beastly thing to do, even if you did slap me really hard in my face which is my livelihood, I'm sorry. I'm really very sorry.' She hasn't walked away. Do it, ask, you've got no choice. 'Erm, Michaela darling, can I borrow your phone please? I seem to have locked myself out.'

Selfishly and with no thought for my feelings she starts laughing, but I manage to win her round to the extent that she'll let me use her phone to call Talking Pages and get a locksmith. Unfortunately the first two or three aren't open twenty-four hours, and when I do finally get through to one, I've just started to give them the address when the credit runs out on her phone. At this point, Michaela decides she's not going to hang around for my benefit any more and clears off – never to be seen again.

Time moves very slowly when you're standing naked on Hackney Road at three o'clock in the morning. I can hear music from the bar below, and I realise there must be a party with a late licence, but I can't go down there completely naked. Luckily, there's an umbrella standing up against the door, so I open it up between my legs, like in a Marx Brothers movie, and use it to shield my genitals. Did I mention that the umbrella is pink? That's one detail of this story I often try to forget.

Just then, a girl emerges from the bar to change a barrel. She looks me up and down, with the pink umbrella shielding my dignity (or what's left of it), and says, 'Can I help you?' What a question. It's three forty-five, I'm naked but for the stupidly comic pink umbrella, it's cold and I'm in Hackney. 'Pretty much anything you do would be a help.' Ten pee, a sweet, a match. I've got nothing. Eventually, she offers to call me a locksmith. After I've waited for what seems like an age, but is probably only thirty minutes, she emerges again. I ask her how long he's going to be, and she says, 'Oh sorry, I forgot.'

Finally moved to action by my increasingly despairing pleas, she roots round in the cellar and comes up with a pair of those chef's trousers – giant, musty, stinking things – and lets me come down to use the phone because it's 'quietening down a bit now'. I pull the trousers on – they're much too big – and I have to hold them up by hand with the pink umbrella over my shoulder. I walk into the bar behind this girl and, obviously, it's gay night. Gay night. Really gay it was, the whole night dedicated to gayness. The whole place was full of gay lads, sniffing poppers and GHB. As I'm trying to use the phone – with change that she's grudgingly lent me – my trousers are falling down, and all these gay lads touch me up while I'm struggling to make the call. But I finally manage to get through to the locksmith I spoke to before. He agrees to come, and I go back outside and wait for ages. And ages.

Eventually he turns up, takes out a bit of plastic that looks like a bit of cut-off Coke bottle, and runs it down the narrow gap between the door and the frame, roughly the way you'd swipe a credit card through a machine. The door just opens straight away – the whole process probably takes about ten seconds – and he charges me £250. Instant karma. I spit, almost before the spit lands, the door slams shut behind me, the crime and punishment administered in the same moment. Daniele never found out about this terrible indiscretion.

Once I finally got a bit of success, it became clear that my internal deficit of sadness and longing would not really be sated by the things I'd always thought would save me. This realisation made me turn to hard drugs – specifically heroin – in an even more concerted way than I ever had before.

Ever since the first couple of times I'd taken it, in my early twenties, I'd always maintained a great interest in heroin. I'd sort of fallen in love with the warmth of it – the way it felt like crawling back into the womb. I always knew it'd be the one, because it was the only drug that did what was promised.

I won't lapse into saying that it did exactly what it said on the tin, because I despise advert-authorised idioms, but heroin delivered. LSD kind of does a bit, especially when all the things that are familiar to you peel away and you suddenly realise the fragility of how you normally see the world. Marijuana kind of doesn't really, although it's a laugh for a while (I say that having smoked it constantly for a decade). Alcohol makes you sick and gives you a headache. Crack is like inhaling plastic, but so brief and flimsy and brittle as a high. Normal cocaine just makes you nervous, amphetamines are even worse, and ecstasy never really agreed with me. But heroin gets the job done.

What it mainly does is take you right out of reality, and plant you somewhere more manageable. In short, it contextualises everything else as meaningless.

All of us, I think, have a vague idea that we're missing something. Some say that thing is God; that all the longing we feel – be it for a lover, or a football team, or a drug – is merely an inappropriate substitute for the longing we're supposed to feel for God, for oneness, for truth. And what heroin does really successfully is objectify that need.

My mate Karl once told me he'd been looking after this five-year-old boy who – not knowing enough to have an ironic inflection to his words – said, 'I want something.' He didn't know what it was. Not 'I want sweets', or 'a can of Coke', or 'to watch

The Tweenies', or whatever it is they're into now (I liked *Bagpuss*), but 'I want something.' All of us, I think, have that feeling. And what heroin does when you first start taking it is tell you what that something is.

It makes you feel lovely and warm and cosy. It gives you a great, big, smacky cuddle, and from then on the idea of need is no longer an abstract thing, but a longing in your belly and a kicking in your legs and a shivering in your arms and sweat on your forehead and a dull pallor on your face. At this point, you're no longer under any misapprehension about what it is that you need: you don't think, 'nice to have a girlfriend, read a poem, or ride a bike', you think, 'fuck, I need heroin'. ☞

23

Down Among the Have-Nots

MTV's studios are in Camden – a vibrant, thriving, diverse sort of place, very sexy and self-consciously cool. Drug-dealers lurk down by the canal and up on the bridge, amid the punks. How do punks know to sit there? I wonder who was the first punk who sent out leaflets saying, 'Hello, I'm a punk and I'd like to meet similar – why not come to the bridge over Camden Lock, and we'll sit around punking it up and drinking a bit of cider?'

Drugs, specifically heroin, were everywhere in Camden: little blue bags the size of, I suppose usually, two peas. That's how big a £10 bag of heroin is – half the size of a Malteser, twice the size of a pea; just in case you ever become a junkie and you need to score in Camden, you can take this book with you as a guide to weights and measures. 'That's not ten pounds'-worth, you scumbag, look at this Malteser.' Possibly that'll be the last sentence you utter before being flung into a canal, to drown to the sound of giggling punks.

The dealers keep the bags in their mouths. Then when you buy one they spit it into their hand and you have to put it directly into your mouth. Even though you obviously want the heroin, a little bit of you is thinking, 'Eeugh! He's had it in his mouth.' After a while, though, you stop thinking that. It's a bleak day when that happens. You know that's another little boundary that you've crossed, another principle chalked off to experience, another thing you've put behind you, because there's so little in front of you.

'All my days are empty and the pages of my diary are all silver foil, with nought but an inky black snake carving its way through the days,' I once wrote. Probably to impress a girl.

I became preoccupied with London's Hogarthian underbelly when I was still at Drama Centre – befriending poor, doomed Homeless Jim, who died on the steps of the school and spoke using only three phrases. 'You know me, Right or wrong and not being rude.' He could communicate everything he needed to say with that palette. And scoring off Lucky Ricky. Lucky Ricky were an amazing character – sat behind his great giant glasses, with his wiry, Iggy Pop-fit body and his endless kids. For someone who had failed so spectacularly in socioeconomic terms, this man's genes were powerful: his kids' faces – even the girls' – were identikit versions of his.

These are the main things that I remember about Lucky Ricky. He lived on a North London council-estate, and his wife was called Pearl. You know the one of the Muppets who's got hair that's made out of spaghetti? The woman Muppet, that was in the band? Well, Pearl looked a bit like her. It felt like gravity was pulling her downwards. You could see this struggle reflected in every movement she made – as if she couldn't blink or turn her head without doing battle with Newton's implacable adversary.

There was a picture of Pearl which they had on their wall. A charcoal drawing, I suspect from Leicester Square – not a caricature, a realistic one. The street artist had really captured the tragedy of Pearl as a character, so this thing that was meant to be a memento of a happy trip to the Trocadero was actually a haunting reminder of the family's terminal dilemma.

One time Ricky compromised both me and dear Pearl by showing me a photograph of Pearl's vagina – taken up her skirt. I was sitting politely taking drugs in their house demonstrating that I enjoyed their company as well as their wares when Ricky, beaming, thrust a photo into my eyeline and asked, 'What do you think of that?' I thought, 'How do you answer this question without offending anyone? What is the correct answer? What would it say in *Debrett's Guide to Etiquette*?' 'It's nice' – is that the right answer? 'It isn't nice'? It's just an impossible social quandary. I think in the end I went 'mmm', thinking, 'If I just make a noise, that could be judged either way.'

I've never encountered poverty like it – and haven't since, as a matter of fact, other than among those who are actually homeless. But there were still structures and hierarchy and charm and dignity and codes and protocols. Ricky was a proud man, and I really liked him.

He sold mostly speed and weed and hash. I wasn't really taking too many hard drugs yet. This was the time when me, Mark Morrissey and that Geordie Tim were a little pack of ne'er do wells, living above that pub the Queens Arms. I stole a guitar from one of the students at Drama Centre to swap for drugs once, giving it to Lucky Ricky, then feeling awful about it and trying to get it back, but not being able to.

They had a pet snake – some kind of python it was, not a massive one – and they lost it. It got loose, and then six months later, it came back. What had it been eating? I guess there was an ecosystem in that house which could sustain it. I went round there once and the house was all full of wreaths, because one of their kids – a fifteen-year-old girl – had had a baby, and it had died. I remember them all going, 'Yeah, it's terrible really, but you know . . .' like they came from a time when infant mortality was normal.

Lucy – one of Ricky's surviving granddaughters – had some terrible respiratory illness which meant she had to spend a lot of time at the Royal Free. Even when she came home, she still had a drip up her nose, going into her stomach, and she was only meant to be fed through that until she got better. Their one concession to the medical needs of this child – who they did really love – was that they'd leave the door open while they were smoking. I saw her eating a pack of Frazzles once – this little tottering thing with a drip up her nose, poisoning herself with illicit corn snacks. 'Oh Ricky,' I called out anxiously, 'Lucy is eating some crisps, look.' 'Oh yeah,' he replied, 'she likes them.'

Amazing characters would accumulate in that flat, and I'd sit round there smoking draw for ages when I was supposed to be doing ballet. There was this one woman called Sue – again one of these washed out, almost transparent people. I was just round there for a sixteenth of dope – about £7.50 worth – and she goes, 'Oh Ricky, I'm really depressed, I was thinking about killing myself last night.' He just said, 'Okay, I'll come round and do it for you.' There was no sense of this as a cry for help: he just briskly outlined different ways of doing the job quickly and painlessly (through the eye socket was one that stuck in my mind, for some reason).

There was this other bloke Brian, who spoke like Henry's Cat and was intermittently addicted to heroin but was actually really wise. I used to get all stoned and talk about my problems and feelings with him, and one day he goes, 'Well, you know Russell, it's a hard life, down here among the have-nots.'

That really resonated with me, 'the have-nots'. Later on, when I started hanging out with homeless people in the West End, scoring heroin with them, I realised that there's this secret culture of people going up and down Oxford Street, whistling and yelping to each other in a kind of tropical slang – men on BMX bikes delivering £10 bags of heroin to be purchased with grubby fists full of 50p and 10p and 2p coins; West Indian housewife-type women perambulating past Topshop, cheeks wedged with packets of smack.

You don't see this bustling underworld until you need to. There have been occasions, thrilling to me, when I went off to score, cutting a purposeful stride down past Tottenham Court Road tube station in the company of three or four homeless people, their sleeping bags worn about their shoulders, like the cloaks of Roman legionaries. I must have cut a ridiculous figure, dressed in my MTV presenter attire – skin-tight white jeans, graffitied tops, Ray-Ban sunglasses – jostling along with them, as they set off in search of a bag in Covent Garden. In the midst of Oxford Street, with its perpetual, glum buzz, the constant dull throb of the buses, the normal people busily skittering to work, this homeless sub-set exists – in the margins, along the kerbs – scarcely noticed by anyone. Who else do you think it is that uses phone boxes? They're only there for prostitutes' cards and homeless people to call heroin dealers – no one else bothers with 'em, we've all got mobiles.

Until quite recently – when I gratefully gave up public transport – I would still see people I'd scored drugs with begging in tube stations. There was one bloke – I don't know if he's still around – whose eyes were missing. First he lost his wife then his house then his shoes, then his eyes; heroin is a greedy drug, robbing you by increment first of your clothing, then of your skin; finally when it comes for your life it must be a relief. They're not present those people: if you talk to them, they just look beyond you, they're not really there. That's why the invisibility of the homeless scoring drugs on Oxford Street is almost by mutual consent: they don't want to be seen, and no one else wants to see them.

I was a tourist in that world. I've never been homeless – I've got too many safety nets, too many people that have seen my frailty and vulnerability and are determined not to let me slip through. People like my mum and my nan, that have just gone, 'Oh bloody hell, he's always gonna be a child to some extent – we'll just have to keep an eye on him.'

One crack-house in East London, I used to pop into from time to time, you know, for the atmosphere, where an enormous black woman used to deal drugs from her bed. Like Lady Madonna. People were just nodding out all around the flat – in the bathroom, in the bath. And yet it was just off Bethnal Green Road. Outside, everything was normal and functioning, then you'd walk through a doorway, and be amid all this madness.

Once at Lady Madonna's crack emporium this pimp was arguing with one of his girls, syringes strewn like confetti at a junkie wedding, and I was using with them and I thought, 'I shouldn't really be here.' I had work and a bit of money and people that loved me. That place exists still waiting for me should I err.

I craved the illicit even as a boy in my mum's house. I called a prostitute knowing that I had no means of paying her except for my NatWest cheque book that had woodland creatures on it – 'Would you like a cheque for twenty-five quid with an illustration of a squirrel? I don't know if it's going to clear.' 'What about the badger?'

I'd frequently visit prostitutes in Soho; they have cards displayed in the doorway saying 'model'. I sometimes considered going up with some Italian sun hats and floral dresses and saying, 'Put these on love, it's for Kays Catalogue', but I usually plumped for joyless sex. I'd cross paths with a guilty stranger on the stairs, worse on the way in than the way out. Often they were poor old sods in suits.

I especially liked really big women. One lady had boobs like bin-bags filled with lard. She wheezed her way to the door, and then when she got onto her back, I thought she'd never get up again. I visited her on my lunch break while working at Vera Productions, a liberal TV production company that makes Rory Bremner's and Mark Thomas's shows. Once someone stuck a packet of Kit Kats to the kitchen wall because they were appalled that someone had brought them into the office because of Nestlé's irresponsible marketing of baby milk formulas in the Third World. I thought 'Bloody hell they'll be furious if they find out where I go for my lunch.' And I ate those Kit Kats.

I went to Reading once to meet two gorgeous and enormous women; it was like an away fixture. Huge women, they were. What I don't like – and often this'll happen if you sleep with pairs of prostitutes – is they'll do this really unerotic kind of pseudo-sex talk that makes you feel like you're in an Alan Ayckbourn play. 'Ooh, hello there, big boy, I am feeling sooo hot . . . you're a naughty boy in't'cha?' – that sort of rhubarb.

Luckily, those two giant Reading women eschewed that grisly euphemistic seaside-postcard routine.

After all the sexy fun, it is nice sometimes all warm and simple; we sat and swapped stories, they told me about encounters they'd had with their clients. Cosy it was, like nattering housewives, I felt young and drowsy. The stuff they said was mucky but to them it was ordinary: 'We've got this one client right. One time he came in and put on your underwear, didn't he, Sue?' 'Oh yeah, yeah, he put on my knickers and bra.'

Must've been a hefty gent I thought, but I kept quiet as I didn't want to cause offence or ruin the yarn. 'Then he got into the bath,' Sue continued, 'shat himself, and said "Ooh nanny, I've been a naughty girl, I don't think I can go to nursery."'

I enjoyed the tale wholeheartedly and assumed others would too. The first time I ever spoke to Ricky Gervais, he called me out of nowhere because he wanted to tell a story on his XFM show about something that had happened to me and Karl Pilkington and he wanted to check I didn't mind. He was funny as you'd expect and I was excited because we were getting on really well and I liked his TV shows. I thought, 'This is great – I'm gonna be lifelong chums with Ricky Gervais.' I remembered that Ricky is from Reading and thought, he'll love my prostitute story. 'Hey, Ricky, you're from Reading, let me tell you this story about prostitutes in your home town.' I told him that story, got to the punchline – 'Nanny, I've been a naughty girl. I've just shat myself and now I can't go to playschool.' And Ricky went, 'I'm gonna have to go now.' I just said, 'Oh, Okay,' put the phone down feeling really deflated, and thought, 'Oh no. What did I say?' ☞

24

First-Class Twit

Amanda Alguero Alejos, I still get satisfaction from writing her name, the three As, triple A. A schoolroom endorsement of the woman I came closest to loving. It was a very volatile relationship, but it was fun. I couldn't speak Spanish properly and she couldn't really speak English. But instead of that creating a situation where we couldn't communicate, it meant everything became very simple – we didn't waste time discussing nonsense, we just talked about very simple things. To describe pirates to me without using the word 'pirate', which she did not know (her English teacher, me, was on drugs), she said 'very bad boys only love for gold'.

I was with Amanda for six years in the end – on and off – and lived with her again quite recently, but there was never really any prolonged period when we were what you'd call comfortable together.

I'd go over to see her in Ibiza, and we'd just ricochet from argument, to sex, to argument (I remember chasing her down the street in nothing but a towel once, shouting 'please come back'). Then I'd return home to London, to a life of whores and heroin.

A further complicating factor in what was an already troubling dichotomy was Amanda's job. In the early part of my time at

MTV, she was managing a motel in Ibiza which was affiliated with a famously seedy nightclub. It was the most decadent, vile place. I'd go and visit her there and there'd be loads of drugs and fucking going on everywhere you looked.

This was extraordinary to me, because obviously this was the kind of thing that I was generally into, but at that time I was in love with someone. And it seemed oddly in keeping that when I finally found a woman who I felt quite romantic towards, she was ensconced in the kind of decadent environment that would cause me to constantly baulk at the context of this unaccustomed tenderness.

From the day I met her at the language school, I wanted Amanda with me always, but because we spent most of our time apart, I went through a lot of psychological tumult, and I increasingly used heroin to take the edges off those emotional extremes. When things went well, I'd smoke heroin to celebrate, and when they went badly, I'd smoke some more to comfort myself.

The first time I realised I'd become addicted to it, I was staying with Amanda in a risible '70s-style hotel in Ibiza. It was a horrible beige nightmare of a place, which claimed to provide four-star accommodation. I don't know where they'd got those stars from – they must have tumbled from the heavens, 'cos the AA certainly couldn't have seen fit to award them.

Amanda didn't like me using heroin. She knew I'd been doing it in London, but I'd told her I'd given up, so I had to hide my drug-taking from her. On this occasion, though, there'd been no opportunity for me to smoke it in secret. When I said I thought I might go for a walk, Amanda was (understandably) suspicious and insisted on coming with me. At that point I began to get anxious. I could feel myself heating up and breaking out in a sweat, and then my legs started kicking and jumping. That's the worst symptom of heroin withdrawal – I can tolerate the nausea and the sweating, but I hate it when your legs go all kicky. That's where the phrase 'kicking the habit' comes from.

When I was travelling, I used to smoke heroin in airport toilets. I'd burn it and then inhale the vapour and hold my breath until there wasn't a single bit left. When you do eventually breathe, the smell is so beautiful. It tastes like warm, chocolatey tar, sweet ink, saccharin venom. Obviously I knew it was addictive, but prior to this occasion in that appropriately brown Ibiza hotel room, I hadn't yet realised that this small drawback was relevant to me.

Amanda eventually fell asleep, and I had to go into the bathroom and quietly unfold all the things I needed, which I'd managed to secrete about the place. I got the foil out, sat on the toilet, lit the lighter under the foil, and the tiny lump of heroin started to liquefy and bubble. Then it begins to run along the foil, and as it does so a vapour escapes, and you have to hover above it, sucking it up with a tube.

I remember being very conscious of the sound of the lighter, then almost as soon as the smoke had hit the back of my throat, that feeling – the kicky leg, the sweating – it just went. It was like turning off a light. Then I could lean back and everything was suddenly all relaxing and beautiful. It was at this point that I knew that I was an addict, though the pain of that realisation was greatly mitigated by the impact of the heroin: that's how it gets you.

We filmed a lot of *Dancefloor Charts* in Ibiza, and I got another job there presenting a programme for Sky One with dear, lovely Tess Daly. She was very kind to me. I remember her having to knock on my hotel room door and drag me out of bed to go to work when I was all smacked up.

Haircuts must be high. I persevered with that haircut for longer than my dad persevered with his marriage.

Dagenham Park, elfin, porcine, oddly Puerto Rican; this look has it all. I loved that shirt.

This is the first time I performed. I found the best light on that stage and I lost my virginity to one of those girls.

After *Mud*, a show I did. I look and felt like I'd been superimposed.

The drugs are beginning to work.

Actor cake.

Callan Language School, with my beloved students. I slept with none of these ones.

Me, doing acting in *The Bill*.

Me and Karl in Ilford Park, scrabbling around for fame.

Amanda and me, second day of abortive 'cluck'.

Coming off smack in the Cotswolds, eyeing a reptile.

Cotswolds, trying
to get clean.

Thin from drugs
and angry.

Me and Martino
acting like Wham.

I will pose nude for work.

I was, by now, mad. Look at my eyes. I want to go home. These lads had eaten dozens of eggs.

Flatteringly large censorial letterbox.

I used to get in a lot of trouble going back and forth between London and Ibiza. One time, my pursuit of drugs led me to be shot at with what Matt Morgan describes as 'a tiny gun'. I was on my way to the airport, and I had to go to this estate in Swiss Cottage, taking the dealer with me in the MTV account car (I had dealings with this individual over a long period of time without ever being sure if he/she was a man or a woman).

Anyway, me and the androgynous creature went to the tower-block where Goldie used to live (the drum and bass pioneer turned *EastEnders* star plays no further part in this anecdote, it was just that whenever you had to go anywhere near that place, people always used to point it out and say 'Goldie lived there'). The driver took the dealer's bike out of the back of the car, while he/she went inside to get the drugs, and as he/she did that a pellet pinged off the top of the car – someone was firing at us from inside the block.

It might seem a bit reckless to be picking up drugs on the way to Heathrow, but my need for a regular supply of narcotics would not be constrained by the exigencies of international air travel. I generally travelled with drugs up my arse in the belief that should customs officers decide to pursue this unsavoury line of enquiry my day would be ruined and the discovery of crack or heroin couldn't make it much worse.

You'd think the presence of packages of illegal narcotics within the confines of my own body would have restricted my normal inclination to seek out centre-stage. And no doubt this might have been the case, had it not been for the unlimited quantities of alcohol available in business-class lounges. They've now attached metal teats to the tops of the bottles in those lounges, ostensibly to aid in the pouring of the liquor, but actually to indicate ownership. But at that stage the general understanding was that you could have as many drinks as you liked, so I used to just take the bottle.

I was thrown off an Iberia Airlines jet at Barcelona airport, after I refused to remove my feet from the top of the seat in front of me. Scruffy people are not welcome in any class other than economy. If you find a way of affording overpriced travel without dressing like a boffin it irritates conformists. They've been assured that by relinquishing freedom and dressing all square they will be rewarded and if someone turns up claiming privileges for which they've eschewed good haircuts they get browned off and look for ways to penalise you.

I offered the haughty air hostess the perfect chance to tell me off by being a bit drunk and bawdy and lounging about. She told me off but I ignored her. I thought, 'I wonder what'll happen if no matter what happens I refuse to cooperate with this woman?' I know she was just doing her job but I sensed she was enjoying being authoritative and we all know 'just doing my job' is the excuse offered up for enacting genocide. She became increasingly agitated and elicited the support of the pilot who, honestly, flung open the cockpit door and had a go at me over his shoulder like a dad chastising naughty daughters on a motoring holiday. I ignored that too; I was in a silly mood. The pilot made an announcement over the Tannoy that because of 'passenger disruption', the flight would not be taking off, thereby falling back on a form of psychological warfare constantly deployed against me in childhood, where the teacher says, 'Because Russell's been naughty, the whole class has to stay behind,' in the hope of turning everyone else against you.

I'd put up with that kind of thing as a kid, but now that I'd read a bit of Noam Chomsky and a Che Guevara biography I understood the way that society is formulated; I was damned if I was going to put up with any more of that nonsense. I got defiantly to my feet and (realising I would get no support from the bourgeoisie and the landed classes) swept grandly through the curtain separating business class from economy and stood there, holding my flip-flops in my hand.

'Ladies and gentlemen,' I announced to the packed aircraft, 'you are being told that this plane is being taken back to the airport because of the behaviour of a passenger. Well, I am that passenger, and let me tell you that I have committed no crime. I was simply resting my feet on the chair in front, in the same way that I can see many of you are. Can we be dealt with in this fashion by authority? If we don't take this opportunity to bind together and stand up against the people that have power over us, then surely we will forever be oppressed. They are planning to throw me from this plane. If you refuse to let that happen, then it cannot happen.' Take that society. 'Who's with me?' So came the cry from the obviously drunk TV presenter, newly arrived from business class. I would like to say that at this point all the passengers rose up and marched to the front of the plane, like in the film *United 93*, and overthrew, not terrorists from an Islamic fundamentalist sect, but the terrorists of the corporate sector, who seek to govern us in every aspect of our lives (be it walking through Bluewater, be it working for IBM, or be it – as in this case – on an Iberia Airlines flight). What actually happened was that one drunk man, seeing the chance for a fight, nodded enthusiastically – even though I think he was Spanish and didn't understand, and everyone else just looked at their newspapers.

The plane pulled over and security got on. There was one man and one woman. 'Russell,' said my brain, finally turning up, 'this is one of those decisions that you have to make quite quickly. Are you going to dart under the seats and make yourself really difficult to catch, or will you just go quietly?' 'Well brain, as you're so late, I think I might go for the former stupider option to

punish you.' I began to dart down an aisle. 'I should probably mention that your anus is full of heroin,' countered my brain, the little know-all. The security people took me off into this little room to have a bit of a go at me, and I apologised with such heartfelt sincerity that not only did they neglect to give me a full body search, but the security woman booked a hotel for me, because there weren't any more flights that night. And she gave me a hug when I left.

I had this job in Cuba once, which I got through Nigel Klarfeld (my agent at the time). It was a chewing gum advert, filmed in Havana. I was reading Naomi Klein's *No Logo* at the time, so my head was awash with all these deliciously palatable ideas about capitalism and consumerism – ideas which seemed to be borne out by the endeavour in which I was engaged. Of all the consumer products, chewing gum is perhaps the most ridiculous: it literally has no nourishment – you just chew it to give yourself something to do with your stupid idiot Western mouth.

Half the world is starving, and the other's going, 'I don't actually need any nutrition, but it would be good to masticate, just to keep my mind off things.' Fired up by this self-evident absurdity, I threw myself into learning about Che and Castro and the way a handful of men were able to seize power in Havana because of the corruption of the Mafia and American politicians (I also met Castro's brother in a nightclub, but that is another story).

A short while before this, I had a part in a musical history of Cuba. Martino Sclavi was producing it for a friend of his who was at film-school. Martino is an exceptional man, cosmopolitan, principled and bright, and he facilitated a vital transition in my life. His parents are Italian, but he grew up in America and Germany. He is brilliantly educated and humours me, like John Rogers when I tell him things that he already knows.

The problem with the role I'd been given was that it involved singing and dancing, both of which – but especially the latter – I was very nervous about. My talents in these two areas were simply not up to the standard you'd expect of a man who had once auditioned for the boy-band 5ive; I sang George Michael's 'Faith' into an empty bottle.

I was still working at the language school at this point, and the night before filming, I had a really bad spasm in my back while I was teaching, and fell to the floor in front of the class, completely unable to move. Unfortunately, my students knew me as a bit of a joker so my plaintive cries of 'Help! I'm in agony' were met with a cheery chorus of, 'Oh Mr Russell, you are a very funny man.'

Eventually, I managed to persuade someone that it was serious, but not before several of my charges had tantalised me as I lay on the ground by waving crisps in front of my face. The other staff were a bit off with me because of the whole AIDS thing. I told them back spasms were mentioned in the leaflet and that they ought to be more sympathetic. When the ambulance arrived, they had to wheel me out of there upright, propped up on the same kind of stretcher thing that Hannibal Lecter gets put on, with that grille over his face. Although I didn't have one of those.

Amanda came with me to the hospital, and I went through some work with her in this curtained-off bit of the ward, while they gave me some pain-killing injections. Her pronunciation was terrible, so I kept telling her, 'Come on Amanda, you've got to learn this.' My back hurt and I was being a bit aggressive. This Scottish drunk hollered from the next bed – 'Ah shut up, ye bastard!'

I recovered quickly enough, but I was so fucking glad I didn't have to do that dancing. The guy who was doing the choreography – this quite handsome black lad – stepped up in my place, and ended up lip-synching to my voice. It was ridiculous to see him in the finished film, miming with my voice coming out, like I was some kind of Bollywood soundtrack artist.

Martino (who you'd think might have heeded this warning about my general reliability as a colleague) ended up becoming my business partner when I set up my production company, Vanity Projects, a couple of years later. It was around the same time we started that company that I finally convinced Amanda to leave Spain and come and live with me in London.

Her two conditions for doing this were that 1. I should quit heroin, and 2. I should get us somewhere to live. In pursuit of the first of these goals, Martino booked the three of us a cottage in the Cotswolds. The last night (as I grandly, though ultimately inaccurately, styled it at the time) of my using, I was presenting the annual awards for this dance music magazine, with June Sarpong.

I had a coterie of friends around me, including Amanda. I smoked abundant marijuana, smack and crack, and drank a skinful, as well as taking four tabs of Viagra, so I could still fuck. At one point, I mispronounced the name of a famous DJ (I think it was Danny Tenaglia, but I'm still not sure even now, to be honest) and fell off the stage. Boy George later wrote in his *Daily Express* column that I'd been brilliant and had done these things deliberately. The canyon between the perception of me and my actual reality seemed to be widening on a daily basis.

The next day, me, Amanda and Martino took an MTV cab to the Cotswolds, costing them £400. I took a bottle of Jack Daniel's, an ounce of weed, and loads of videos to get me through my rattle (as we denizens of the drugs underworld term it). It was awful – hot and cold, nausea, and, worst of all, I remained horrifically awake all weekend. The best thing about heroin is it turns your life into a waking dream, but then, when I needed it most, my mistress sleep had deserted me.

I still made it through though, with Amanda and Martino's help, and also managed to fulfil the other pre-condition for Amanda moving to London, by renting this ridiculously gorgeous flat, just off Brick Lane. This glamorously empty, warehouse-style apartment soon echoed with misery, as our relationship almost instantly became a psychological war.

Amanda was a strong, beautiful woman. After a string of infidelities on my part, she finally had the good sense to leave me. I just came home one night, and all her clothes were gone. I thought this a flabbergasting affront, and threw myself with ever more self-destructive intensity into my work, womanising and, above all, a renewed and increasingly all-encompassing relationship with heroin.

I thought, 'Well, at least now she's left me, I can just take loads of drugs again.' The moment when you decide not to try any more is always such a relief with an addiction. Even now, four and a half years since I got clean, there's still a lot of effort involved for me in not taking drugs. But that 'Ah, fuck it' moment, there's some sort of beauty in that – maybe even more so than in the drugs themselves. There's something about the collapse, the yielding; it's giving into death I suppose, but it kind of makes you feel at ease. I've got this sense in me sometimes that perhaps death will simply be blissful – an endless expanse of nothingness, which might be a great relief from the tyranny of life's minutiae.

Throughout this period, my instinctive drive towards the abyss was coming through more and more strongly in the stand-up shows I was doing. I had long since abandoned the idea of actually rehearsing material that was meant to be funny. Instead I'd generally end up out of my mind on a cocktail of heroin and Smirnoff Ice, releasing locusts, cutting up pigs' heads, smashing up dead mice and birds with a hammer and then throwing them into the audience. On other occasions, I'd slash myself with glass and take drugs on stage. I once did an 'industry showcase' at a venue called 93 Feet East – just round the corner from the flat in Brick Lane. Loads of people turned up, including The Mighty Boosh, Julia Davis from *Nighty Night*, and this agent from ICM called Conor McCaughan (who actually ended up signing me, miraculously enough). Both my parents were there too, and Matt's mate Rick nearly got in a fight with my dad when he tried to stop the pair of them screaming at each other. It was one of those nights when everything feels like it's broken.

I decided that a confrontational agitprop approach was the right one to take to this audience full of people I knew and/or hoped to work with. I came on two hours late, having got homeless people to sit outside the venue collecting money from the crowd as they arrived at the venue, so when the gig finally began I could bring them onstage, tip the money out, divide it by the amount of people in the venue, and go, 'So that's all you can manage is it?'

Even – perhaps even especially – when I was at my most self-indulgent, I remained very politically engaged. I was always eager to blame the audience for society's ills, demanding insurrection and revolution, and damning them as 'passive Nazis' and (somewhat more poetically) 'a lazy cluster of atoms'. This almost suicidally militant tendency within my work would eventually reach its peak in a horrendous incident at the 2002 Edinburgh Festival.

On the day Ian Huntley was charged in the Soham murders case, my interpretation of the concept of collective responsibility caused me to berate the audience with cries of 'You killed them little girls.' I then got in a fight, put my leg through a plate-glass door and had to be hospitalised as well as arrested (for criminal damage to the door). The doctors told me if the laceration I'd incurred had been an inch to the left, my leg would've had to be amputated.

Not content with damaging myself physically, I had already set about dismantling my career with a series of strategic acts of recklessness. The most celebrated of these – and one of the most notorious stories of my addiction (if only because I've repeated it so many times) – was the encounter between Gritty and Kylie Minogue.

Gritty was the main drug-dealer I used to get heroin off at the time I worked at MTV. I'd met him through that strange androgynous character I mentioned earlier. He/she . . . actually, I think I'll go with 'they' for ease of reference – they weren't actually a dealer, they'd just ride round Camden on their BMX scoring drugs for me (and probably ripping me off a little bit) with their mad eyes and mad teeth. Once they'd introduced me to Gritty, I moved up the ladder a bit, and dealt with him directly.

I liked the fact that destiny had allotted him the name 'Gritty'. Just as Ned Ludd, leader of the Luddites who opposed the Industrial Revolution, would have struggled to make such an eloquent case against the Spinning Jenny had his name been Fabrizio Zodiac, so that name seemed well adapted to the needs of his profession.

He seemed a nice sort of man, though. He had quite a caring side to him, for a drug-dealer. I remember one occasion when I was buying drugs off him near Camden Bridge. Having just sold me my two £10 bags of smack and two £10 rocks of crack – dropping them into my palm down by the water – he gave me a sincere look and said, 'Be careful with that, won't you Russell.' I was thinking, 'What do you mean "be careful with that"? They're drugs. What does he think I'm gonna do with them?' 'Oh no, I seem to have taken them. Why didn't I heed Gritty's prophesy?'

By this time I'd graduated from wanting to be Jim Morrison to wanting to be Andy Warhol – my life will be art, the streets shall be my canvas. So when Gritty asked me once if he could bring Edwin, his eight-year-old son, into MTV to have a bit of a look round, I said, 'Sure, why not? What could possibly go wrong? "Bring Your Drug-Dealer to Work Day".' The date that the inaugural BYDDTWD happened to fall upon was September 12, 2001, the day after (as is typical with the Gregorian calendar) September 11, the day after the destruction of the World Trade Center – an incident which I was referring to at the time by a series of sarcastic observations about international violence being a two-way street and it being impossible to oppress people endlessly without consequence.

This stuff goes down a bit better now than it did at MTV on September 12: 'Come on guys, get over it. It was yesterday. We've got to move on. We cannot grieve forever.' I should add that on that day when I'd gone into work with Gritty and Edwin, I was dressed in a white Muslim tunic with matching white bottoms, a camouflage flak jacket, a false beard and a tea towel on my head, held in place by a shoe-lace.

I'd been aware of Osama Bin Laden for about a year. He wasn't someone who people of my age group generally knew about, but he'd been involved with some other bombings and he was top of the FBI's most wanted list, and I was fascinated by that sort of stuff. That day, I was going to present this programme called *Select*, where kids phoned in and chose videos for us to play, and pop stars would come on to flog their records. That afternoon our guest was to be Kylie Minogue. Me, Gritty and Edwin went into the toilet and the two older members of our party smoked some crack – Edwin didn't have any. He was just a little boy, and seemed quite upbeat about life anyway. Children don't need drugs, because they have sweets.

We blearily swaggered out of the disabled toilet door. On the other side of the foyer – with its round console, its vast banks of TVs, its trendy turnstile, its endless parade of beautiful young people of both genders and every sexual persuasion trundling in and out – I saw Kylie Minogue, all famous and everything.

Somewhere in my mind, the artist within me – the situationist within me – thought 'I can create a moment here. When am I ever going to get an opportunity like this again?' Before I knew it, I'd walked across that foyer, made a kind of 'woo-ooh' noise – in a mum across a neighbour's fence sort of way – and said, 'Kylie, meet Gritty.' Then I just stood back to watch it unfold.

What were these two gonna talk about? It's September 12, Kylie and Gritty are having a sort of awkward chat, with Gritty trying to be polite and Kylie asking 'what do you do?' Sort of like the Queen would. And there's me standing beside them, still dressed as Osama Bin Laden.

I thought, 'It don't get any better than this.'

And it didn't, 'cos they sacked me about two days later. 🖝

25

Let's Not Tell Our Mums

My stage performances had become mental breakdowns for the handful of shocked spectators. I was steadily getting sacked from all my jobs. My girlfriend had left me. My heroin use was incessant. And the only reason I hadn't made a serious attempt to kill myself was because I just thought, 'I've not done anything yet.'

Luckily, UK Play – a now defunct satellite channel – had decided that this was an appropriate moment (a decision which perhaps throws some light on their subsequent financial collapse) to give me a quarter of a million pounds to make a TV series about whatever I wanted. On American MTV, Tom Green was a really big deal at that time. He did lo-fi, spazzing out in public type of comedy; he's very funny. I originally intended to do something like that.

I'd already got together with Martino, and I told Matt I wanted to carry on working with him, and made him leave MTV at the same time I did. UK Play weren't just going to give us all that money to spend on our own. So we made the programme with Vera, who I mentioned earlier in relation to my cheeky lunch breaks. Vera stands for Vivien Clore, who's Rory Bremner's agent; Elaine Morris, who was one of the executives – a stern, tough sort of woman; Rory Bremner was the 'r'; and Geoff Atkinson, a lovely man who Matt said was like a big talcy baby –

he'd worked on *Spitting Image* and written for *The Two Ronnies* – was the 'a'. Their offices – in Margaret Street, just off Oxford Street in London – was a cosy, woolly liberal, *Guardian*-reading kind of place, but quite sort of stuffy as well.

I was really fixating on street people and those who lived on the fringes of criminality. It wasn't long before me and Matt were cluttering up Vera with lap dancers, rap crews and the homeless. One abortive show starred this berserk lap dancer I was larking about with. I was sucking one of her boobs while holding up this little puppet wearing a Bill Clinton mask to the other one, then we all jumped on Rory Bremner's desk going 'Ooh 'ello I'm Rory Bremner' – the hunter had become the hunted.

When we came to work the next day, Elaine was watching the tape. Elaine was the most austere of the Vera bunch and we thought, 'Oh fuck, this is not gonna look good for our TV programme', but by that time they'd committed to the project, so there wasn't very much they could do about it.

Six months roared by without us getting anything done. The main problem was I had too much status and not enough discipline.

Geoff Atkinson was forever drumming his sausage fingers on his barrel chest with his jolly, Father Christmas-like chuckle and saying, 'Come on Russell, what are you going to do today?' Just sort of humouring me really, and I'd be all full of acrimony and revolutionary bile – furious at society, but ultimately furious at myself.

In the end, after months of dicking around with all sorts of ridiculous behaviour, we just thought, 'We'll hire a camper van, live in it, and tour Britain, getting in adventures.' Vera had set things up for us all over the country, and our first appointment was to go down to Cornwall and interview these Cornish separatists. I didn't really care about Cornwall's historic struggle for independence, I just wanted to capture insanity on screen, that's what it was about for me. I was up for having a mental breakdown on television.

I wasn't at all famous. I had a very limited appeal based on the stuff I'd been doing on MTV. And my stand-up was getting increasingly bizarre. Although I was very nervous and delicate and fragile, I wasn't so self-effacing or self-aware as now, so the way I came across to audiences was very angry and conceited. I would overcompensate for my lack of preparation by being really aggressive, clambering through audiences, getting into fights, and inadvertently insulting people who turned out to be mentally ill. I once stuck a sheathed Barbie doll up my arse onstage at the London Astoria to make some point about consumerism that I can no longer remember.

There'd been another ridiculous incident at the Edinburgh Festival in 2001, the year before I got that leg injury, where I provoked a near riot by stabbing myself with a broken vodka glass and covering myself in fake blood, until Sean Hughes, a comedian I really respect, had to usher me out of the back of the building to escape from the baying mob. Embarrassingly, when I met Sean again a couple of weeks later, I failed to remember the entire incident.

My main problem was that I'd started to allow my capacity for self-flagellation and destructiveness to dictate what happened to me onstage. When it comes to your career, you must always try and allow the positive aspects of your character to dictate what happens to you. Be led by your talent, not by your self-loathing; those other things you just have to manage.

At MTV's suggestion, I had got rid of Nigel Klarfeld when I first signed up to do *Dancefloor Chart*, in the belief that I needed management that was more attuned to TV presentation than live comedy. The agency I joined, KBJ, was run by all these lovely sweet middle-class women, who just didn't understand the full extent of the nightmare they were dealing with. Our director, Will Knott – a handsome, capable, straggly-haired dog-basket of a man – wasn't the sort to get involved in trying to set me on the straight and narrow.

Matt has some capacity for self-preservation, but is also a naughty sort of person, an outsider like me. (Once the police got involved when he was childishly throwing peanuts out of the window of a hotel in Leeds, and Matt said, 'Why do these things keep happening to us?' He seemed genuinely aggrieved, as if this turn of events was proof of the innate malevolence of the universe, rather than the direct consequence of our own action.) Martino – the producer – was probably the only grown-up among us, but he loved me, and didn't have the capacity to curtail my lunacy.

This was probably why Elaine and Geoff insisted we take someone else with us on our proposed round-Britain trip, in case we went too mad. They appointed this guy Duncan, effectively to be our babysitter. He was a lovely bloke, but I remember Matt going, 'Oh, Duncan ain't coming is he?' Like his school trip had been tarnished.

We were supposed to meet up early the next day. By seven o'clock that morning, I had drunk the best part of a bottle of gin. By the time the MTV cab had delivered me to Notting Hill where the camper van was waiting, I was laughing and crying at the same time.

Matt, Duncan and Will had got there before me, and were busy packing up the kit and equipment, ready for our travels. I, on the other hand, became instantly fascinated by the vehicle we were supposed to be travelling in. 'Wow, look at the van, man, it's crazy,' I enthused, on finding out that this touring holiday home had both a shower and a TV in it, 'let's get on top of it.'

'Come on, Russell,' they chivvied benevolently, 'we've got to get ready and go to Cornwall and meet these separatists by half past one.' At this point, I climbed up on top of the van and started shouting, 'Come on, film me now. Film this! Film this!' Duncan shouted, 'Just get down – we've got to drive to Cornwall.' 'You can still do that, just with me riding on top! This is the show – I am the show!'

'Look,' I continued, the gin aiding me in concocting a remarkably plausible theory, 'we're supposed to be making a programme about challenging people's preconceptions and the conformity and conditioning that we find everywhere in society. If you're not the sort of people who are prepared to film me doing this, then there isn't a show: we've got the wrong mentality. I'm not getting off the roof of this van.'

Will ambled up the ladder. 'Come on Russell, get down mate, stop being silly.' I think I was sort of in a panic, really. I could see Duncan thinking, 'This isn't looking good. We're meant to be embarking on a month-long voyage, and ten minutes in, he's already up on top of the van refusing to come down.' When he climbed up the little ladder to try and talk to me, things got worse. I started shouting, 'You make me sick! You make me sick!' Then I stuck my fingers down my throat, and dry-retched gin fumes into his face in a sort of bilious grey cloud.

Duncan started to cry. One by one, a series of other people came to visit me on the roof, like I was some kind of bonkers sage, a lunatic guru or berserk swami – on top of a mountain, rather than a van. But in this case people would come not to seek advice, but to try and talk me down.

Sometimes I flick into this mentality where I think, 'I'm just gonna carry on saying or doing this thing now, to find out what happens as a result.' Like on that plane, or wanking before I could cum, or drinking booze as a lad. At these moments, it's almost like I'm observing my own life happening – not in a conscious way, but with the sense of detachment that I imagine I learnt at an early age, as a way of coping with stress and trauma.

I remember thinking, 'I wonder what'll happen if I just refuse to get down, and stay up here for as long as possible.' First Martino came and pleaded with me. Duncan didn't make another attempt because he was frightened by the gin fumes. But Matt came up, sort of chuckling but trying to take it seriously, 'Stop it, you're being a dickhead.' Then Elaine from Vera called up. They gave me the phone and she said, 'Russell, what the hell is going on? We've got a schedule. We've paid for everything and you're not going to be able to do it.'

I was calm and reasonable. 'Look, there's nothing to worry about, there really isn't a problem. I'm completely able to fulfil my obligations to Vera, and to you.' But even as I was saying this, I sort of giggled to myself at the realisation that I was delivering this soothing message from the top of a van.

At that point, they cancelled the shoot and took the camper back to the depot, and we all went back to Vera's offices. Me and Matt sat in the pub while other people just sorted through the debris and I said, 'This is bad, isn't it? What have we done?' Matt resented the 'we'. 'Let's just not tell our mums,' I said, like when you're in trouble at school.

The upshot was that Matt was suspended, and poor, dear Martino was sacked. Geoff said, 'We expect Russell to do things like that, but we also expect you to be able to control him.' Martino, who'd always encouraged and protected me, just drifted around after that – he'd rented a new house on the basis of the money he was earning from the show, and he had to leave it and go back to Italy. Everyone was really traumatised by this barmy incident – Matt had to move back to his parents' and sign on the dole – and for a while it looked like the whole thing was falling apart.

Eventually, I was able to get Matt back on the payroll because at this stage I was incapable of doing anything on TV without him, and they kept Will on as well. They wouldn't have Martino back though, as they were determined to give us a 'proper' producer. We ended up with this character called Sean Grundy. He was actually from Bolton or somewhere, but he looked like a portrait of an Irish leprechaun hung in a theme-park haunted-house, with little brass buckles on his dolly shoes.

Sean was a little, pale, ginger-haired man, always whispering and pessimistic. The people at Vera teamed him up with one of Elaine's friends – this woman called Trish – so the pair of them could be like our pretend parents. Stung by the indignity, it was at this point that me and Matt finally made a sensible decision. 'Right,' we said, 'let's just do things that are mental.'

From this moment, the idea behind *RE:Brand* ended up being basically, 'Let's challenge different social taboos. Let's look at things that confuse and confound people, and I'll embrace them.'

It was an extraordinary experience making that series. Each episode was such a psychological strain that, had I not already been a heroin addict, I would very likely have become one to cope with this silly show. I still stand by the actual programmes, though. They're painful and poignant and laden with pathos – not only because of the emotionally extreme subject matter, but also because I was in such a damaged place, psychologically. At this point I had absolutely no concern for my own physical or emotional wellbeing and was basically out of control. But while this made day-to-day life virtually unbearable for me, it also made for pretty good TV.

It was Matt's idea that I should have a bath with a homeless person. Together we contrived to take on these taboos: have a fight with your dad to examine the idea of the Oedipus complex, have a bath with a homeless person, get to know a member of the

BNP to see what they're like, seduce an old woman – all these berserk notions which we ended up turning into twisted realities, and ultimately broadcasting to minuscule viewing figures, via the schedules of a little-watched satellite TV channel.

I'd first met Homeless James when I saw him being harassed by the police off Oxford Street, while begging by a cash-point. I'd gone over and got involved – on my Che Guevara tip – 'Why are you hassling him. Aren't we all equal? That could be you begging one day. Hey, I pay your wages.' That sort of stuff. Then I started taking James up to the Vera offices, much to the chagrin of the directors and staff.

They were quite happy to demonstrate social solidarity through Kit Kats but if you actually bring homeless people into their lives, it makes them uncomfortable. So James was forever in our office with his mate Alan – they were the Batman and Robin of the homeless community. One day, we brought him in for a cup of tea and stuff and asked him, 'James, would you like to make a TV programme? We'll give you some money.' Obviously, he said yes. That's how it is with heroin addicts – they're very open to suggestion. If you give them money, they'll agree to do just about anything.

At the time I was still living in that nice flat off Brick Lane. The driving ideology behind the Homeless James encounter was that no one should really be homeless. With all the unoccupied buildings that there are in the UK, it's irrational that home-lessness should still exist. Presumably the reason it continues is that we somehow think of the homeless as dirty and unpleasant, so how would it be if I took a homeless person, brought him right into the core of my life – shared my bed and my bath with him – how would that make us both feel?

The intention was to film with James for a one-week period, but the reality was that after two days he decided that he preferred being homeless to living with me. Also, as a junkie, he needed to get out to score drugs. I stayed in touch with James after the show and used with him quite a lot. We only fell out after I gave him £100 to get me some heroin and he fucked off and didn't come back. It's obviously difficult to have a genuine friendship when one of you is on MTV and the other is a tramp: 'He's a homeless person and I'm a glamorous TV presenter – We're the original odd couple!'

I do have very clear memories of being kept awake by James's snoring on the night we shared a bed together, but the most significant moment in that particular episode was probably the bit where we had a bath together. We were both naked, and James's weeping ulcerated leg was sending clouds of pus into the bath-water. But I just got on with washing James's back and shaving him while he coped with this enormous discomfort by keeping his eye on the ultimate prize of £500, or whatever it was we were paying him.

There were some quite sad and touching moments. I took him out on a double date to a posh restaurant with a couple of birds I was seeing. He'd been scrubbed up and given some clothes that I didn't want, so that he resembled a small-time drug-dealer. We went to a place called Freddie's in Islington. As I recall – from watching the tapes as much as anything else – it was quite sort of stifled, until the champagne started flowing, but even then he was uncomfortable.

One of our least successful notions was to take James into the radio station XFM, where me and Matt had a Sunday lunchtime show. The item that I'd brilliantly created in honour of this occasion was 'Homeless James, your homeless agony uncle – for all your homeless needs.' There was a dearth of callers, on account of the fact that homeless people don't have radios. To make up for this deficit, I had to look elsewhere for problems to solve, and ended up looking through tabloid newspapers – specifically, the *Sport*.

In my opinion, the letters in the *Sunday Sport's* problem page are not real; they are in fact – as most of the paper is – just an excuse to print pornography. The problem I chose to read out in the hope of getting Homeless James to solve it was one where a woman had been having an affair with her husband's father and had been sodomised by him. She was keen for her husband to start sodomising her, but didn't know how to approach the subject. Obviously it didn't say 'sodomise' in the paper, it said 'fucked up the arse'.

I was professional enough to realise that you can't say that at one o'clock on a Sunday afternoon, so I changed it, very cleverly, I thought at the time, to 'f'd up the a-level'. After I finished the item, we put a track on, and the controller – Andy something, his name was – rang up and started using worse language than anything I'd said. The next day, I was fired. Driving home from that show in a cab with James and Matt, I had a terrible nauseous feeling, just thinking 'everything is going wrong'.

The next day we took him to the Ideal Home Exhibition, thinking, 'Oh that'll be amusing, as he's homeless' – some of our ideas were a little stunted – and there was a moment which was actually screened where I said, 'Look James, do you feel exploited by this?' And he goes, 'Yeah, I do a little bit.' When I asked him why, he said, 'You don't really know me. I could be anyone. I could be a murderer or something – I'm not – but having me living in your house is still a bit weird, isn't it?' And I said, 'Yes, I suppose it is.'

So that was kind of how it ended. It's strange booking a cab for a homeless person. Where do you say they're going? We gave him £20 for his fare and they dropped him off in one of his old doorways at C&A (it's Niketown now).

One discarded *RE:Brand* idea which it's probably best we didn't follow up was: 'Let's get a load of prostitutes, make them live with my mum, and she'll be their pimp. We'll change her car into a pimp-mobile and make her put adverts in the paper and deal with all the customers!' I remember that phone-call very clearly: 'Mum, can I have loads of prostitutes come and live round your house for a TV programme?' 'Oh, alright darling. Yeah, OK,' she replied, in that same soft and gentle voice she always used as she continued resolutely in her mission to love me.

That misguided programme idea mutated into me just going to live with an individual prostitute. We picked this woman called Ali, who I'd met on this holiday with Matt on the Norfolk Broads, where we'd had to get this woman we didn't know to pretend to be my wife because the boatyard owner didn't want to rent out a boat to two men he'd assumed were gay (but that's another story).

She was living in terrible poverty. Well, not terrible in a dramatic sense, but just in that way which is tragically quite mundane and common. Her living room door had a hole in it, so that her boyfriend Pete could observe what was going on when she took her clients upstairs.

The premise of the programme was outlined in my opening monologue. 'Hello there, I'm Russell Brand. Now, we all sleep with prostitutes don't we, but would we still do it if we knew a little bit more about their environments?' 'Cut! Russell, we don't all sleep with prostitutes – that's just something you do.'

The idea was nonetheless a good one – would anyone sleep with prostitutes if they weren't able to dehumanise them? If they understood that prostitutes were women with lives and families and problems and hopes and dreams, would they still be able to empty themselves soullessly and leave fifty quid on the table?

I know some people would, but it's partly the surrounding culture of anonymity and exploitation that allows these things to flourish. That's what I wanted to demonstrate by living with Ali and Pete and their daughter for a few days, and then finding out how it would feel at the end of that period to go, 'Right, well, it was nice getting to know you, but here's a hundred quid, let's fuck!'

The operation they were running up there was crackers. Ali was working to support not only Pete, but also his brother. The two of them pimped her out by putting cards around the Norwich area, and then stayed at home to make sure she was OK while she brought clients in. There was one time when the other two were out delivering cards or scoring gear or something and it was only me and Matt in the house downstairs with the baby. We could hear her upstairs working.

She told us heartbreaking stories about the stuff that she'd do. She could make more money offering 'oral without' – blow jobs with no condom – and she told me about one bloke with a syphilitic, tumour-ridden cock, and her saying, 'Oh, you're gonna have to put a condom on that love', and then still giving him a blow job.

They were always going to 'Cash Converters' to convert their TV into heroin. The sign outside the shop read – 'Convert your unwanted goods into cash.' In the window there were things that obviously had a sentimental value, all steeped in emotions (a sitar seemed especially poignant). The wording is lovely – 'Convert your unwanted goods': 'I don't want these goods – what I want is heroin.'

Of course I was a junkie then as well, so I was using with them the whole time we were making the programme. The hypocrisy of it was ridiculous, really. There were bits where on camera I'd be going, 'Stopping using heroin is the hardest thing in the world, but you've gotta do it mate – you guys have got to look after yourselves.' Then the camera would be turned off, and I'd say, 'Right, OK, let's go,' and we'd all have a big use-up.

Ali seemed – quite understandably – somewhat scatter-brained and absent, just as a way of coping with the situation. Her hands were like chorizo bound with twine. The brother was quite an interesting character, always looking off into the distance – where things were more bearable. And I became quite close with Pete, the dad – this pinched man, this mobile corpse.

I had this one chat with him in the garden – which was all on tape – where he was talking about his addiction. He started to break down and he was just sobbing, 'I hate myself, I hate myself', when his daughter came running out and zipped his fleece up around her, as if this coat was the toxic swaddling of their common problem, from which they both peered out desperately.

At the end, we took them out on a boat to film the final scenes on the Norfolk Broads – which was obviously where Matt and I had been when we first came across Ali. Everything was cool, and we got some beautiful footage of them having quite a nice day out. Then I took Ali and Pete into my room, and explained the idea of the show, and the fact that I was now going to offer him extra money for me to have sex with Ali.

Pete just started crying. It was agonising, and made me feel terrible, but I still thought, 'This is what you're doing every day, it's just that you've got to know me.' Of course, if he'd have gone, 'Oh fine, yeah, thanks for the money', it would have put me in an incredibly difficult situation; it was bloody lucky that they didn't want to go through with it, really.

When Elaine and Geoff at Vera saw the footage, they thought it was amazing. I suppose it's not normal to see this sort of thing happening on camera, because 'the talent' doesn't generally behave like that.

In the next programme, 'Wanky-Wanky', we addressed the subject of sexuality. As the title suggests, this episode was a little more juvenile than its immediate predecessors, but still interesting nonetheless. The question was, 'Is your sexuality constructed by environment and experience, or is it innate?' I examined this issue by wanking off a man in a toilet. In conclusion, your sexuality is innate.

I had this friend called Cyprian. He was a gay Jamaican who spoke a bit like Eartha Kitt – 'Oh Russell,' he'd purr, 'you are a very attractive boy.' I'd met him in a club in South London where he'd given me some Ketamine. (Ketamine is an unusual drug – this was the only time I took it, actually. It situates you in a kind of pulse, creating an effect in your head like the high-pitched noise televisions used to make after closedown: 'Shash', I think it's called. Mind-shash, brain-shash: that's what Ketamine gives you; it's like going into a tunnel of shrill sound.)

I thought Cyprian seemed like a good person to give us access to the gay community. We explained the idea of the programme to him, and he agreed to help us out with it. There are some daft bits at the beginning where we wander about and he teaches me blow-job techniques on a sausage, even though I was a vegetarian at the time (that was my main concern, rather than the fact that I was practising fellatio on a West End street). Then we started hanging around outside this gay gym in Covent Garden, trying to pick up men without very much success. But as soon as we went into a gay pub – the King William on Poland Street, it was – our luck changed.

This pub was for bears – gay lads that are big and burly – and the first bloke we spoke to was Gary. I strolled up to him with the cameras and said, 'We're making a TV programme where we examine and explore homosexuality – can I wank you off in the toilet?' And he went 'Yeah, okay.'

Me, Will and Gary went to the men's toilets and arranged ourselves in the cubicle and got on with making the show. The first thing that struck me was the unfamiliarity of male genitals – they looked somehow ridiculous to me.

Of course, there is an element of aesthetics involved. Had Gary been an Adonis or had he been like David Beckham or Leonardo DiCaprio, things might have been different, but as it was, he was too strewn with quirks. My own genitalia were well-groomed, neat and delectable. Gary's genitals, on the other hand . . .

Worzel Gummidge never bared his genitals, but had he one day got drunk on moonshine and savaged the world with his nudity the sight that would have greeted the astonished Crowman and a frightened Aunt Sally would have been very much like what I had to contend with – an angry thicket of pubic hair, clutching skyward like furious Shredded Wheat, as if to escape Gary, sentiments I was beginning to understand.

With trepidation I reached down towards the nub, which was draped in a film of scum – before you baulk, remember these are just anecdotes to you, not mucky little memories.

Midway through, the still flaccid Gary requested, 'Can I touch yours, Russell, it'll be easier for me to get turned on.' No reflection required, no erection desired. 'Fucking hell, mate, do me a favour.' Then Will, from behind the camera: 'Go on Russell, it'll be funny.' Many times in my life I have allowed that sentence – 'Go on Russell, it'll be funny' – to direct me into the jaws of trouble, danger, harm and sackings, and once more I was helpless to resist its siren lure.

At that time, it was my custom to wear colourful Y-fronts emblazoned with icons. I believe on the day in question the honour had fallen to Che Guevara (Elvis and David Bowie were safe at home in my underwear drawer). Gary reached over and peeled my pants down. As he began to stroke my genitalia, I realised they looked like something found in a butcher's shop.

It was a sparse ration that Gary contented himself with that day, plucking at my indifferent cock. But then one of my great gifts and worst curses kicked in: ego. For, in spite of the fact that I happen not to be gay, and found the whole experience quite unpleasant, I'm so vain and egotistical that, somewhere inside of me, I really wanted to be good at giving Gary a wank. So I pretended it was my own beloved winky. Triumph! Grey sperm ribbons decorated the lavvy, a ticker-tape parade for the unknown soldier. I fled immediately from the cubicle and washed my alien hand with hot water and soap.

Watching the tapes, you can see that I was in a proper state after that. Ironically of course, due to broadcasting law, the bit where I wanked him off couldn't be shown. We could only use audio. The whole thing was a really disturbing and unsettling thing to do – and I immediately got in touch with some lap dancers to do some heterosexuality. Me and two lap dancers, one American, one Australian, went out in a limousine and filmed that as some sort of denouement to the episode.

There were a lot of loopy ideas flying around at that time. 'Cut off your thumb, have it frozen for a week, and then we'll sew it on again,' that was one of them. Then, 'Why don't we chop off your foreskin, cook it, and eat it?' This latter stroke of programming genius came from that Trish woman – she'd started to go a bit mad. In truth, everyone was feeling the pressure.

Especially Sean Grundy: he was a hilarious character. Morrissey is a living sign, he was a living sigh. Once, driving into Soho to buy sex toys for the 'Wanky-Wanky' episode, me, Matt, Sean and Cyprian were in the back of a cab, and Sean was on the phone complaining about some dud microphones. He was just being so undynamic that I got irritated. 'Tell them to replace the mics. PRODUCE the show.' 'Fuck you,' he blurted. We then embarked on a physical conflict that was so ineffective and wet that the cab driver had to stifle laughter as he ejected us from his car. I clutched Sean's hand, he clutched mine, and we tussled for a bit; nothing really happened, because we were in a peeved clinch. In a bid to break the stalemate, I used some of my sexy fighting talk, which would lift the whole tone of the most basic brawl. 'Oh yeah baby boy? You wanna sniff Pappa's poo pipe' – if not exactly that, it was certainly from that stable. Then, I hissed at him like a goose. The goose hiss is only called upon when a fight really hots up; it's more of a deterrent, but I was cross so I did a hiss Hiroshima. 'HiiSSsssS,' I went.

Cyprian had bought me a lovely bunch of tulips, and he was a little disturbed because his flowers were all buckled up by this ludicrously effete altercation.

We spent so long making *RE:Brand* that we seemed to pass every major landmark in the calendar while we were doing it – Halley's Comet went by a few times, there were three or four World Cups. So when May Day came round, I dragged Matt and Will down to the West End for the anti-globalisation protests.

Neither of those two are particularly politically minded people, but I was determined to rope them into my plan to 'start a revolution, and then film that.' I'd been to quite a few May Day protests by then, and had a Zelig-like ability to be present at flashpoints. I was there when Winston Churchill had a turf mohican placed on his head by anarchists, and that time when they smashed up that McDonald's on Whitehall.

On May Day 2002, however, I was to be the main event. Aside from the ideological principles and the anti-corporate sensibilities, the thing you really had to experience that year was me wandering around dangling sex toys through the windows of police vans, trying to arrange a football match like the one with the Germans in the First World War, and stripping naked at Piccadilly Circus.

The footage we filmed is ridiculous: I'm jumping over barriers, throwing myself on the floor – mental, I was. The statue of Eros was completely ringed by coppers, and you can feel that atmosphere where at any time it can spill into violence. I find the potential for mayhem exhilarating – society's only held together by a few ideas. I know those ideas are quite entrenched, and the reason we have a police force and an army is to maintain that status quo, but at moments like this, that whole apparatus can suddenly look quite vulnerable, and I find that thrilling.

On this occasion, my tendency to get overexcited manifested itself in a plan to take all my clothes off by the statue of Eros. The police were saying, 'Look, don't strip naked, or else you'll get done,' but I was showing off. 'I pull down my pants, will you lot overthrow the government?'

The mob recognised that they were witnessing the dawn of an age of freedom and cheered. Down came the ol' Che Guevara panty poo-pots, which I'd worn knowing that this was to be as significant a moment in revolutionary history as the taking of Havana or the Paris uprisings of '68 and I wanted to dress appropriately. The police folded in around me like dough and I disappeared into an angry loaf of casual brutality.

I'd picked up from somewhere that if you're being bothered by the police pretend to have an epileptic fit, so – naked and lying on the floor, in the middle of Piccadilly Circus – I started to shout 'I'm epileptic! I'm epileptic! I've lost my bracelet'; a brilliant detail – epileptics wear them, don't you know. I rolled my eyes back into my head and started throwing myself round on the floor, and the police parted from around me, all freaking out.

A senior policeman, who was a bit older and wiser said, 'Look, come on son, what's going on?' So I dramatically leapt to me feet and pulled up my freedom knickers. I was escorted into a theatre doorway where the Reduced Shakespeare Company play. The step elevated me, and the police looked all small. This black bloke with dreadlocks and motorbike leathers stood beside me throughout – the police asked him to move on but he never did, he was my guardian angel.

Loads of photographers and press started asking me about the protest, like I was a visiting dignitary; Matt always satirises the moment I started spouting off quite well – 'Oh bloody hell, the government . . . Jesus . . . Nelson Mandela.' I on the other hand prefer to think I devised some quite brilliant policies there, amid the madness.

Perhaps moved by my eloquence, the police said, 'We are unarresting you' (an excellent innovation in law enforcement, which I had hitherto been unaware of). But they should ne'er have unarrested me, for I was an immediate recidivist.

I galloped off to liberty, which was as usual on top of a van – those ones you see at news events, with satellite dishes on top. It was down the bottom of Wardour Street. The sex-workers' parade had begun – flags were waving, bongo drums were beating, and I was again caught up in the exhilaration of the protest atmosphere. The street was flooded with people, and they all cheered when I climbed up on that van.

I thought, 'I'd really better do something.' So I began to strip. 'People like stripping, and this march is for sex-workers, it is a befitting tribute.' A tribute that would not have altered had it been a march for orphans. I received a standing ovation: yes, they were standing before I began, but I detected that they were standing with renewed intent. They were a very generous audience; they were sex-workers – to them it just looked like work.

A security guard clambered on top of the van after me, so I legged it. Me and Matt ran into Old Compton Street, which by

Continuation of Charge(s)/Circumstances

Police station:	Charge No:	Custody No:
WEMBLEY QD	01DP6551202	0211666
Person:	Other references:	
RE BRAND		

CHARGE(S)/CIRCUMSTANCES

COML049   INDECENCY IN PUBLIC PLACES (ORIGINAL)

ON 1ST MAY 2002 AT WARDOUR STREET, LONDON, WC1 COMMITTED AN
ACT OUTRAGING PUBLIC DECENCY BY BEHAVING IN AN INDECENT
MANNER.

CONTRARY TO COMMON LAW
========================

COML049   INDECENCY IN PUBLIC PLACES (ORIGINAL)

ON 1ST MAY 2002 AT PICCADILLY CIRCUS, LONDON COMMITTED AN
ACT OUTRAGING PUBLIC DECENCY BY BEHAVING IN AN INDECENT
MANNER.

CONTRARY TO COMMON LAW
========================

Officer taking charge(s):   K.BUTCHER (PERM/CUS)   PS 0093(
              Signature   Name   Rank   Nu

              Time   Date

then was cordoned off by the police, because the protests had started to turn violent. We saw some people escaping up a fire-escape, near the Offspring shoe shop, so we climbed up there, into an unseen Soho world of fire doors and air-conditioning vents, and ended up in that cemetery on the corner of Shaftesbury Avenue.

As we squeezed out through the railings, we were stopped by the police, who asked us a few questions and then let us go. It wasn't till a couple of weeks later that the police found me and charged me and I had to go to court for indecent exposure – which sounds terrible – and criminal damage, because while on top of that van I'd smashed up that satellite thing a bit for my encore. One consolation was that the hearing took place at my favourite Bow Street Magistrates Court, where I'd now been held so many times (I think there'd been a bit of shoplifting and drunk and disorderly as well, in the years since that initial Tango ad audition drug fiasco) that I could almost see it as my spiritual home, as well as dear Oscar's.

26

You're a Diamond

Lost, as I was, in a sort of psychotropic fog, it was hard to discern that amid the madness of *RE:Brand*, a kind of ideology was beginning to emerge. The project was so swamped with wilful self-destructiveness that I couldn't formulate anything coherent. But I think that humanity, love, self-expression and truth all played a part in it.

The show where this came through most clearly was the 'Nazi Boy' episode. The idea was to spend some time with this nit called Mark Collett, who was the leader of the BNP's 'youth movement'. We wanted to find out why an idealistic young man who was supposedly bright and intelligent and had a promising future ahead of him would end up allying himself with such an old-fashioned ideology as ultra-nationalism.

Less than a year had passed since September 11, and there was still a peculiar tension around regarding questions of racial and cultural difference, that the BNP was trying to capitalise on. It was also around the time that Jonathan Woodgate and Lee Bowyer were awaiting trail for an attack on an Asian student (which took place at a nightclub called The Majestic, which you could see from our hotel window when Matt wasn't throwing peanuts still in the jar out of the window), so the combination of Leeds and racism seemed pertinent.

I'd spoken to Mark on the phone a few times beforehand, and he seemed quite personable for a fascist. Going to his house was eerie, though. It was on an old-fashioned redbrick street, but there was a security gate across his door and barred windows, and you thought, 'God, this is a person who really does think Britain is on the verge of a race war.'

We went in there and he showed us around. There were all these little bits of pseudo Nazi memorabilia scattered about the house – strange Nordic signs, and other things that had an air of white supremacism about them. There was a picture of the skinhead band Skrewdriver – the lead singer had died in a car crash, and Mark was convinced it was some kind of conspiracy.

When we went in his kitchen, no one had done the washing up, and I thought, 'how is this man going to help lead a racialist revolution if he can't even keep his own kitchen clean?' Less of the ethnic cleansing, Sonny Jim, and more of the kitchen cleaning.

It was at the time of the 2002 World Cup in Japan and Korea, when all the games were on early in the morning, and we met up with Mark for the England versus Argentina match in a packed pub. It was mostly just students in there, but there was also this coterie of racists wearing England shirts, which was odd, as in the World Cup the St George's cross is around everywhere anyway, but in this context it seemed not so much an acceptable show of patriotic pride, but the manifestation of something a bit more sinister and toxic.

I was drunk and smoking weed. I got Mark a drink, he took a sip and asked, 'Is this Carling?' I said, 'No they didn't have that mate, so I got you a pint of black person's urine,' and laughed at my own joke. It was strange how Mark's lack of compassion came out in his sense of humour. He was really homophobic, and rude about women, casually damning the marriage of Lenny Henry and Dawn French, which sometimes I do because I fancy her a bit.

England won of course, by the only goal of the game, and the two men – Mark Collett and his handsome but quite threatening sidekick who'd just flown over from Germany (apparently a coincidence, he was an Aryan skinhead who looked quite fierce and hard) – embraced. For all their homophobia, there was a homoerotic subtext to their relationship. Mark was definitely very keen to cuddle after Beckham's penalty.

I went into the garden, and chatted to other lads from some little town outside Leeds. I asked one of them what he thought about the BNP, and he said, 'I think they're a fucking nuisance – they come round here stirring up trouble between Asians, blacks and us.' I called Mark over, going 'come and hear this': he insisted, 'These people are plants.'

They weren't plants, they were just lads who weren't racist, so I got on my high horse. 'Listen,' I told him, 'you're going to have to confront stuff like this, because your ideas are old-fashioned . . . I'm glad you've had a moment of local celebrity, because you're going to face a lot of conflict and confrontation in your life, the things you believe in are wrong.'

Mark got all arsey and refused to film with me any more. This was a bit of a drag because the other episodes had left a certain amount of collateral damage for the grown-ups we worked with. Homeless James kept hanging around at the Vera offices, asking for money for shoes (drugs), and these rappers that I got a bit obsessed with, called The Joint Squad, they really are jolly good, kept turning up there and stinking the place out smoking skunk. I'd left a lot of chaos in my wake, and we couldn't really afford for anything else to go wrong.

When Matt and Will went back to film without me the next day – which was the condition of his compliance; I suppose I was lucky not to be sent back where I came from – they asked Mark questions about his frankly gorgeous sister. 'Would you rather she had it off with Russell or a black person?' His reply was, 'I think I'd rather she died.' A ridiculous answer in which no one wins. I would've said both. At once. In a saucy new show called 'Russell's Interracial Sex Bonanza'.

In a way the burblings of one racist are irrelevant, but Mark Collett was emblematic of a moment, and it's disturbing to learn that five years later he's become a councillor. I was pleased with that show though – I think because it's not as complicated as some of the others – and it got a lot of positive feedback when it was eventually screened.

The one really significant *RE:Brand* episode that I've not discussed yet – and it's notable that I've avoided it so far, even though I wasn't doing so intentionally – was the most complex of the lot. 'Dad Fight'. Yes, before Bob Mortimer fought Les Dennis, before Ricky Gervais fought Grant Bovey, I took on my own dad in a televised boxing match.

Because we didn't have much time or money to spare, we just trained for a couple of days at a kick-boxing gym called Paragon, in Shoreditch, East London, near that Brick Lane flat I lived in at the time. They were lovely lads those boxing trainers, with the sort of boisterous optimism that I now know to be typical of people in that trade.

'Yeah we can do a lot for you in a couple of days,' they said, and I'd turn up there stinking of vodka and go on a treadmill and do shadow boxing and a few drunken press-ups – all red-faced and bleary and puffed up like a toad. I can also remember a certain amount of jogging and skipping in too-tight shorts. And my dad – bless him – agreed to do the same.

I'd phoned him up and asked, 'Dad, will you have a fight with us for a TV programme I'm doing?' I explained to him a bit about the Oedipus complex, and the idea that to become a man you must kill the father; I used the example of *Star Wars*. He said 'Yeah, alright.'

It was unfair to have involved him because, while a big, healthy man in his youth, he was now getting on a bit. We both had head-guards on, and we did three three-minute rounds. Boxing's fucking knackering. You've got to admire boxers for being incredibly fit. Just doing it against your own aged dad is exhausting enough. Mind you, if you're drunk it don't help.

The first couple of rounds were a bit tentative, then I started to really go for it and hit my dad quite hard, and he fell to his knees; the programme just ends with us talking, afterwards. I just said, 'Shall we go down the pub and chat up some birds? Do something we're both good at.' And that's exactly what we did. It's available on YouTube.

There were a couple more shows. One was called 'My Old Tart?', where me and this lovely elderly actress called Wendy Danvers (I think she was eighty-one) went on a trip to East-bourne to explore the idea of sexuality in old age. I tried to seduce her. That was quite light-hearted. We sort of hung out and might have gone to some strip club or other, and then we were on the beach and I kissed her and told her I wanted to have it off with her, and she just said, 'Oh, don't be silly, Russell.' Finally we troubled the paralysed motorcycle stuntman and heart-throb Eddie Kidd for a few days, with me adding his willy to those I touched over the course of the series when helping him to wee.

Enough was enough. RE:Brand was finished. Vera were over-joyed that it was over and done with at last, and they didn't have to have us and our demented entourage hanging around in their offices any more. Matt had to go and get some other job, which he hated, and I went back to doing catastrophic stand-up gigs.

It's strange that series, though, because for all the chaos that surrounded its making, in some ways it's the most sustained and powerful thing I've done so far. On the tapes you can see that I'm sort of deteriorating. I've got a bloated, permanently sweaty look to me, and I have the distant expression that junkies often have – be they a *Big Issue* seller or a corporate lawyer – just the appearance of being absent.

Yet somehow all the madness is being channelled towards some higher goal. Some of those programmes are literally unbelievable – there's some jaw-dropping stuff in them, which I'm still proud of now, even despite the embarrassment it causes me to see myself in such a state of obvious disarray (I'm still trying to think of a way of releasing them on DVD which wouldn't get me disowned by everyone I know). They weren't much reviewed at the time, though Dominik Diamond from the *Daily Star* said RE:*Brand* was the best thing he'd ever seen on TV.

People used to come up to me in the street and tell me they loved it. Obviously it was only ever seen by tiny audiences, because it was on a ridiculous satellite channel that, almost as soon as RE:*Brand* had been broadcast for the first time, went out of business. They pulled the satellite out of the heavens, and broadcast no more. ☞

27

Call Me Ishmael. Or Isimir. Or Something . . .

While *RE:Brand* was the zenith of my pre-emptive 'Vegas Elvis' period (do the decline into bloated egotism before anyone knows who the hell you are, then it can be a secret), 'Cruise of the Gods', a one-off BBC comedy special, would go down as the nadir.

I'd convinced the agent Conor McCaughan, whose clients include Paddy Considine and David Walliams, to represent me for acting work. He came and saw me do stand-up a couple of times in Edinburgh – when I was being all mad and reckless and injuring myself – and really liked it, as well as on that nightmarish evening at 93 Feet East.

My friend Karl Theobald had wisely advised me to be wary of those who give me approval when I'm in a self-destructive mode. This is how he characterised the ensuing dynamic: 'Oh yeah, look at him go. Wow! He's like a runaway train. Go on Russell, wooh! Tear it up. He's wild he's dangerous! He's unstoppable! . . . He's done what? Sorry Russell you're fired.'

And so to the 2002 Baby Cow production *Cruise of the Gods*, starring Rob Brydon, David Walliams, Steve Coogan and me – in a much much, much, much smaller role, but nonetheless present on the boat throughout the trip.

Cruise of the Gods was filmed on a ship sailing the Aegean sea for three weeks, visiting Greek islands and the Turkish port of

Istanbul. I was in no fucking state to be going anywhere on my own, but it was a great job and an amazing opportunity. Coogan was huge at that time, Rob Brydon wasn't doing badly either, and while David was not that famous yet – he'd done *Rock Profile* on the telly – I was really looking forward to working with him.

The story concerned a TV science-fiction convention, held on a cruise ship, where obsessive fans of a *Star Trek*-type show would get to meet the heroes of the programme they had watched in its heyday, ten to fifteen years before. The central theme was the interaction between these aged and jaded stars. I can't remember the exact intricacies of the plot; I didn't read the script.

But it should not be assumed that I embarked on this cruise ship with a bad attitude: quite the reverse. I put myself through a mild heroin withdrawal before going on board (falling back on whisky and grass), as I thought it would be stupid to take hard drugs on the boat. I said to Martino, who demonstrated his limitless compassion by remaining my friend after the carnage of *RE:Brand*, 'I don't want to get in any trouble on this job. I want to be known as the bookish actor who just kept himself to himself.'

Martino encouraged this. 'That is a good ambition to have, Russell. If you can achieve it, you will have done well.' So off I went with that goal in mind. Within a week, I had been fired and sent home in disgrace.

Part of the problem was that I was so busy congratulating myself on not doing hard drugs that I just got pissed and stoned all the time instead, but that was not all there was to it. Some of the details of what happened on that boat are sketchy, but one thing I do remember is that the cruise ship wasn't exclusively for the use of the production. There were passengers on that ship, and some of them had daughters, with whom I could pursue romantic entanglements.

Not a 'daughter' in a terrifying way. She was eighteen – old enough by two long years to have sex with. I was safely above the legal age and under my drug-brella – the device that protects me from all condemnation. Beneath its shelter I cannot be damned, nor can judgements affect me; they are deflected like the rain, as I skip off into the decadent night. One drunken evening up on the deck, off the coast of some bejewelled isle, I was trying to make the daughter love me by shouting into the Aegean night, 'Let's kiss, with the moon as our witness and the ocean as our priest.' She was against it, saying things like 'I hardly know you' and 'you're drunk'.

A quest such as this was beyond the realm that language could conquer: the daughter was German. I was prepared. I leapt over the railings that ringed the boat, and I hung off the edge, chivalrously proclaiming, 'This is how badly I want you!', dangling over the sea, switching hands and doing it one-handedly – just dicking around, really. This was one of the most unsuccessful seduction strategies that I have ever employed. The daughter started crying. 'Sorry about that,' I said, getting back on deck. 'A kiss may cheer you up.' It did a bit, but not enough for sex to happen. I pointed out some stars, did a bit of Shelley and Taylor Coleridge, *The Ancient Mariner*, but there was definitely to be no sex so I cleared off.

Later that night, there was a cabaret. It was a drab affair. There were a few people scattered around the room. And Poseidon, saddened by my earlier plight, provided dancers. I lured one back to my cabin by saying things to her. The quickness of it was brilliant, actually. One minute she was on the stage, the next minute I was talking to her, and then we were having sex. She was one of those rare women who recognised that life is finite and saw orgasms as a wonderful distraction.

A few stolen moments from this encounter linger in my memory – the hint of a leotard, the glint of a blue eye, the smell of her hair, the touch of a woman, momentarily comforting me amid all the confusion that swirled around me. I got sad at sea and missed my drugs and comforts – other drugs. Sure I'd brought some drugs, but not proper ones that smash down on thoughts like Thor. I felt shy with the others, Rob, Dave and James Cordon, out of *The History Boys*. Coogan was off somewhere, I didn't meet him till years later.

It's not that the professionals weren't interested in talking to me. Rob Brydon seemed fascinated by me and said, 'It wouldn't surprise me, Russell, if you took to the air and flew away off the back of this ship [sadly, this was a pretty accurate prophesy of what did happen] . . . You're like Peter Pan,' he enthused. 'You're gonna be a massive star.' Although I secretly believed this, and yearned for it to happen, it didn't seem very likely at the time, 'cos I was in a right state.

The idea that I would one day share a yoga class with David Walliams would have appeared even more improbable at this juncture. I didn't particularly like David at first (and he later revealed that he fucking hated me). He had a certain charm, but there was inevitably something of a clash between his effete head-boy and my subversive truant.

I found the idea of making conversation with them nerve-wracking. Yet there was Rob, who's such a socially skilful man, constantly playing the piano and bursting into his impeccable Tom Jones, and Walliams with his high-camp Kenneth Williams routine. Everyone just seemed so at ease and comfortable, and I didn't know what to do with myself. So when we got to Istanbul, I said, 'I'm gonna go out tonight.'

The boat was in the harbour, and when the suggestion was made at about eight in the evening, everyone agreed to come – I remember Rob and Walliams saying, 'Let's all go.' By the time it got to midnight, of course, they'd all changed their minds. (People do this a lot. They don't seem to realise that the future is just like now, but in a little while, so they say they're going to do things in anticipation of some kind of seismic shift in their worldview that never actually materialises. But everything's not going to be made of leather, the world won't stink of sherbet. Tomorrow is not some mythical kingdom where you'll grow butterfly wings and be able to talk to the animals – you'll basically feel pretty much the same way you do at the moment.)

At midnight, I swaggered drunkenly down the gangplank and got into a cab, on my own. 'Alright, mate,' I said to the cab-driver, 'I'm looking for birds.' He was Turkish, so he didn't understand; he looked at me in the rear-view mirror, perplexed. I did the internationally recognised mime for a woman – the silhouette of a Coke bottle, or Marilyn Monroe, or an hourglass. He said 'Ah, lay-dees!' I went 'Yeah!' And off we sped. (In my imagination, smoke flew out of the back of the taxi, and there was a wheel-spin and a skid noise as well.)

We made our way at breakneck speed through the streets of Istanbul, and eventually arrived outside a brothel – miles away from the boat, so I was already thinking through my drunkenness 'this is a bit mad'. Outside this place was what I can only describe as a snaggle-toothed crone. In fact, if you're ever looking to use a 'snaggle-toothed crone' in a film, and this one turns up to audition, book her. Don't go, 'No, there might be a better one round the corner', because there won't be.

She was wearing a black shawl over her head, which she pulled in at the chin with one hand, while the other stretched out begging. She had two or three teeth, and one of her eyes was all milky and upward, while the other stared at you. She was looking for a tip for not doing anything, which I suppose is what begging is.

That brothel was more of a lap-dancing club really, but sex was never far away. It was like the set of an old-fashioned Saturday night ITV gameshow – *You Bet*, or maybe *Family Fortunes* – but produced on a budget of about thirty-five quid. There were four or five women in C&A frocks, hobbling about on this floor that would light up like in the 'Billie Jean' video, but not so well coordinated.

I didn't really fancy any of them, and the atmosphere was quite depressing. There were a lot of burly great Turkish men, sat around in drab suits, the same way those who operated beyond the fringes of legality in London in the old days would dress in suits to lacquer over the criminality. I sat down in the corner, and a bloke came over with some suspicious looking bar-snacks. 'See anything you like?' he asked. 'No, not really,' came my response.

At this point, he introduced himself – I've still got him in one of my phones somewhere – I think he was called Ishmael or Isimir or something like that. 'Why don't you like these women that we've got here?' he demanded, with a grandiose sweep of the arm across his dreary kingdom, gesturing towards the broken-faced marionette women doing a stringless dance of death on the Billie-Jean floor. 'They're just not my cup of tea,' I maintained. When he asked what I was after I replied, 'Oh, probably someone in their twenties, with massive boobs,' and he said inevitably – 'Come with me, I have the perfect thing.'

She was not a thing but a person, with feelings, but there are two ways this tale can be told. The first is from the perspective of someone who is a connoisseur of sex in general but also prostitution. The second is through the eyes of a man who has since awoken from the amoral dream of commodified sex.

You'll probably enjoy the whole thing more if I take the former option, so I shall write from the perspective of a man who is unaware that the suffragette movement ever happened. I shall adopt the stance of a man who, if he'd seen Emily Pankhurst chained to some railings, would probably have thought, 'Hello, she looks vulnerable – get your bloomers off.'

So Ishmael made a phone-call, and the girl then arrived at the club, announcing herself with some ridiculous name for a Turkish woman: Bev. The issue of payment was raised. He said 800 euros or something; it was quite a lot and I didn't have enough cash on me. I don't know much about exchange rates and global finances; except for a fierce pride in the strength of the pound – COME ON YOU POUND! – I have no interest in it, and suspect the whole silly business is a ploy to keep us bewitched by numbers.

Ishmael looked at my Solo card – this preposterous debit card I had that only seemed to work inside the confines of my house – and said, 'Well, this is problem.'

Me, Ishmael and this girl – who looked alright, actually – set off through the streets of Istanbul in search of a cash-point. Eventually, I managed to get the money out. We arrived at the hotel and I discreetly handed over my 800 euros to Ishmael (who paid the guy an hour's fee – they obviously had an arrangement). Then he slipped off, and me and Bev went upstairs.

As we were going up to the room, she kept taking calls on her mobile. When we got there, I suggested she undress, and she came back from the bathroom completely naked, meaning I missed the Christmas moments of bra and knicker removal, so I asked her if she could put her underwear back on, and she looked at me like I'd asked her to plough a field. Her phone kept ringing every couple of minutes. She just carried on living her life, without really acknowledging that she was working as a prostitute.

'Look,' I said, and bear in mind that a substantial sum of money has been paid, 'can I have some oral sex on my privates please?' And she said, 'Yuk! I don't do that.'

I tried to be resourceful, racking my brain for things I'd done or even read about. 'Felching?' 'Bagpiping?' 'Donkeybiting?' There was barely anything she would do. And mine were pretty standard requirements. Frankly, this girl was a sorry, fair-weather excuse for a prostitute.

Eventually she agreed to have sex, but a kind of weary, half-hearted, semi-erect, bored, disappointing bit of sex, for which I'd paid a lot of money. During this act of tawdry friction her phone rang again.

'Could you turn that phone off?' I asked. 'I can't relax.' She took the call. I began to wish I hadn't left the boat. 'Brydon's probably doing "Delilah" by now,' I mused, which actually helped my erection.

Another twenty seconds of boring rubbish goes past, then the phone rings again, and I, and this is the worst act of misogyny I've committed since the spitting debacle, took the phone out of her hand and threw it at the wall. Slow motion. It hits the wall and smashes, and she looks at me, the sex stops, and we separate. Silence. Then I say, realising my position is compromised, 'For fuck's sake, you kept answering the phone.' And she looks at me again, suddenly mortified, and the scene becomes real and awful, and she just starts crying.

And now we're two human beings in a room on earth. Our previous roles, a prostitute, and customer, a tourist, a drunk – that's all gone now; the shards of that illusion lie shattered amid the pieces of her phone. We're just people, one of whom has behaved atrociously towards the other. I apologise: 'Look, I'm really sorry, I didn't mean to do that, but the phone kept ringing, and I was frustrated.' And she just says, 'It's OK, I'm going to go now.'

She went back into the bathroom and starting getting dressed and came out wearing her underwear, and I thought, 'Bloody hell she looks nice. I wonder if there's anything I could say to . . .' But there isn't. As we picked up the bits of her phone, this atmosphere of faint possibility dissipated all too quickly, and by the time we were going downstairs I was thinking, 'This is not looking good – I'm going to have to walk past reception in a minute, five paces behind a crying prostitute.'

We both head out into the street, and she goes her way and I go mine. Momentarily I feel full of pity and regret for myself and the poor girl stranded in the world. I fight back compassionate tears when I think of her situation: young, beautiful, perhaps in love; maybe it was her boyfriend on the phone. Or her mother; she does have a mother. I think of my own mother and the times I've let her down and am rinsed with pain at the thought of the son I could've been, the son she deserved.

Then I decided to go back to that brothel and get my fucking money back. Tension, it gets a bit loud and argumentative with Ishmael, all those Turkish blokes in suits start gathering round and I'm thinking, 'Fucking hell, I'm on my own here.' But at this point I call upon the – soon to be patented – 'Oh yeah, sexy Turkish boys, you want me to tap my cock on your curly slipper' technique, and this, quite miraculously, secures me a fifty per cent rebate.

Honour satisfied, I got into a cab and went back to the boat, and went to bed, then woke up terrified in the middle of what was left of the night, just thinking, 'You did that thing: you smashed the prostitute's phone, you risked getting into that fight at the brothel – what if they find out? You're meant to be here doing this fucking job, you idiot. These are not the actions of a quiet bookish man who keeps himself to himself . . . OK, well you seem to have got away with it. Just don't do it again.'

The next day, I woke up feeling so bad and guilty about the whole thing that the only option was to get drunk and pick up where I'd left off. Athens was our next stop, and we disembarked. But I soon got bored in the hotel. I remember Walliams was always in the pool (and this was before he became the world's best swimmer – swimming himself away from his presumed homo-sexuality).

As luck would have it, there was a lap-dancing club just down the road. I didn't have loads of money, so I walked. Once you got inside, it was an amazing place – a despicable sexist hell, really. Architecturally, it had the feel of a World of Leather or PC World – there was a vast low ceiling, but the place was full of swirling smoke and dense music and cheap liquor. I got myself properly pissed (I'd always have a bottle of spirits that I'd carry about with me and not so surreptitiously swig from).

You know those kind of laser key-rings that shine a red dot? The men that worked there had those. You'd identify a girl who you'd like to do a lap dance for you, and the male staff would shine that pen into their face and eyes – really startle them – and then lead them to you. If they were stood in the northwest quadrant of that giant warehouse of debauchery and you were in the southeast, they'd have to go, 'Ooh, I'm being shined at' and then trace the laser back towards you.

A more misogynistic den of iniquity it would be hard to conceive of. But in one respect this establishment was special. It turns out that the 'no touching' rule that applies in most British lap-dancing clubs does not apply in Athens.

This reckless deregulation enabled me to lose my mind in there with those women; I was wanking and drinking and touching, it was disgusting. I came about three times in there. Mental. The evening rendered by the brush of Hieronymus Bosch.

Of course, I went back straight away and told the others – 'You won't believe this fucking joint, you've got to get down there.' That's why I got in trouble really – because I couldn't keep my mouth shut. I kept telling everyone all the terrible stuff I'd done, in the hope of entertaining people and making them laugh (as a way of compensating for my pitiful inadequacies in more conventional arenas of social interaction).

Walliams refused to go back there with me, but I jostled Rob Brydon and a few of the others into giving it a go. None of them liked it, though – they all went home straight away. Everyone was nice, that was the problem, really. I was living a different lifestyle – I was a petty criminal, drug-user, who was hardened to the minor skirmishes such misdemeanours invariably entail.

I went back to the hotel with them to get some more money, and that was the moment Coogan finally arrived. I felt a frisson, seeing him go into the hotel. And then I made my way back to the retail park of debauchery for my third and final visit.

I'd gone in there hoping to get one of the girls I'd had before, but this time she didn't want me to touch her. I said in that case I didn't want a lap dance, and she said I'd still have to pay, and went off and got some management bloke. I thought, 'Oh, here we go.' So off I went out of the club's main entrance. There were two big geezers and one tiny bloke on the door. 'Night gents,' I said and walked up the road towards the hotel.

I'd gone about a hundred yards when I heard a full-throated cry of rage coming up behind me. I think it was 'WAAAN-KEEEER!' I turned round – even though I've learned in this life that if you ever hear anything like 'Oi!' or 'Wanker!' the best thing to do is keep going – run if anything –'cos it's never going to be good news, is it?

No one ever goes 'Wanker! You may already have won a million pounds in our cash prize draw.' Or 'Wanker – would you like to go out with my sister?' It's always 'Wanker . . .' SMACK! In this case, when I turned round it was the little one of the doormen who was racing towards me. He punched me in the mouth, really hard.

A brief tussle followed. He was a knotted, sinewy little man, beaten hard by ultra-violet rays – a kind of sun-dried Greek feller. My jaw were put out of alignment by the blow – it was uncomfortable for ages afterwards. I staggered back to the hotel and – this is how out of control I was at the time, I was literally fucking sex-mad – I think I had a wank.

Next day, I went upstairs. Walliams was in the swimming pool on the roof again. There he was, swimming about again, like a pristine amphibian. It was funny, because it did strike me at the time that he could be a proper swimmer. I remember thinking 'there he is, in his white trunks.'

At this moment, one of the production staff interrupted my Walliams-based reverie by asking if he could have a word with me. 'Alright,' he said, 'we're giving you a week's shore-leave, better go and get your stuff together.' I went back to my room and packed my stuff up with a faint suspicion that perhaps this was not good. But when you live in the psychological space that I did, life is not about confronting reality, it's about ignoring it.

So when someone says, 'You're getting a week's shore-leave', you don't think, 'Hang on a minute, I'm not a sailor,' you just go, 'Oh alright.' I got a lift to Athens airport off Brendan Coogan – Steve Coogan's brother, who was also working on the production. What was slightly tragic in retrospect was me going, 'Do you want me to bring any newspapers or baked beans or English things when I come back?' He was like, 'No, that's alright mate.'

When I told Matt this story later he said, 'You were like a dog being taken to the vet's to be put to sleep that thought it was going to the park to have a run – all excited, with your head out of the window.'

I got back home, and almost as soon as I arrived, Conor called me up from ICM. 'Russell,' he asked, in an ominously sombre tone, 'what did you do on that boat?'

'Oh, nothing,' I muttered, 'just the usual . . . I can't really remember.' 'Well,' he said, 'they've sacked you. I've never had a client sacked before, and the people down there, the producer and the casting director, say they've never in all their careers experienced anything like it: they just think you're an animal.'

Before I could blurt out, 'But I just tried my hardest to fit in – I thought I was this bookish sort of feller,' Conor said, 'I'm going to have to talk to you face to face.' I realised this was bad, so I went out and bought a load of heroin.

I knew I'd really ballsed things up. It should have been a fucking amazing job, that 'Cruise of the Gods'. There we were, stopping off at all these gorgeous islands – going to Athens and Istanbul – and look how I, as usual, converted these beautiful experiences into a grimly picaresque ordeal. My mate Jimmy Black said to me when I got back from that holiday to Bali and Thailand with my dad:

'Fucking hell, Russell, you've been to all these amazing places and all you do is come back after three weeks and go, "Oh, I fucked some prostitutes." What else have you done?' 'I saw a mongoose fighting a snake . . . I rode on the back of an elephant . . . I saw these monks that don't ever talk, walking through the city, guided by a child.' 'Well then, why are you only talking about the fucking prostitutes? What's wrong with you?'

I've always been drawn to the seamier side of life. Those are the kind of characters I'm attracted to, there's an energy I get from them that drives a lot of the work I do. At this stage, though, my predilection for decadence and abuse of drink and drugs was threatening to bring my career to an end before it had even properly started.

On my way to meet Conor, I saw Johnny Vegas in the back of a cab. 'Oh dear God,' I thought, and smoked some more smack (by this stage I was able to use more or less anything as an excuse, even a sighting of another comedian). I finally met Conor in a café in Soho Square. It was raining. He said, 'I'm sorry Russell, but I've got to let you go.'

I was all too familiar with the feeling that overtook me at this juncture ('I've had a lot of sobering thoughts in my life' – as Lennard Pearce said to Del Boy – 'it was them that started me drinking'). I'd felt it when I couldn't go back for a second year at Italia Conti, when I was thrown out of Drama Centre, when I was sacked from MTV and XFM, and on numerous other occasions when I'd been sacked from jobs.

Up until those particular instants of helplessness and despair, I felt myself to be an invincible blur, impervious to any kind of judgement – 'Your bullets can't harm me, my wings are like shields of steel!' – but then suddenly, like Icarus, I'd clatter back to earth. The difference was, on this occasion, I had no idea how I was ever going to get back up in the sky again. ☞

PART IV

'The insatiable thirst for everything which lies beyond, and which life reveals, is the most living proof of our immortality'

Charles Baudelaire

'Forwards ever, backwards never'

Mr Gee

28

Mustafa Skagfix

The aim of heroin use is to get to the point where your eyes roll back, your head lolls forward, your mouth drops open and drool hangs from your lip. 'Gouching out' is the technical term for it. During the period after I got the sack from *Cruise of the Gods*, Matt would often come round to my flat and find me in that state. At other times, the evening would start off with me chatting fairly normally, but as it wore on I'd slowly descend into a kind of vegetative stupor, a waking anaesthesia. And if we ended up sleeping in the same room or even the same bed together, Matt would often wake up in the night to find me hunched 'like Gollum' (this was the image he always used, and when I eventually saw the film, I understood why) over the tin foil. He also coined a new nickname for me, based on my newly acquired predilection for wearing Arabic robes. 'Here he comes,' Matt would greet me cheerfully, 'Mustafa Skagfix.'

When Conor McCaughan finished with me, I realised – with the last vestige of survival instinct that remained to me – that my other agents, KBJ, would be next. So I phoned up John Noel.

I'd first met John maybe a year or so earlier, when I had a round of meetings with different agents. I went to his office in

Chalk Farm (just round the corner from Drama Centre) with lovely Martino. I had a little tennis-ball-sized rubber globe, and I was throwing it up against the wall and catching it. When John gave me and Tino the tour of his offices, pausing to marvel at Brian the pervert accountant, he gave me a beachball-sized globe. 'Ere are. Have that son.'

I recognised this as a good metaphor – that I had a little world, and he gave me a bigger one. I liked him, he was very complimentary about my work, and lots of people said he was the right agent for me because he was strong and I needed controlling. But I didn't sign with him then, because I wanted to go with this woman Joanna Kay at KBJ, which is the presenters' wing of PBJ (this huge agency which has Eddie Izzard, The League of Gentlemen, Reeves and Mortimer – all the people I adored – as well as lots of the comedians I grew up with, like Rowan Atkinson and Lenny Henry). When I'd turned John down he'd been quite disappointed.

John Noel, for those that don't know him – and I've got to assume that's the majority of you don't, although he's become increasingly notorious – is a gruff, Northern, working-class, alpha male: fists and fangs and fury and 'fook off's are the things that characterise him. He has cold, steely eyes, but a warm passionate heart, and the temperament of an Andalusian widow. He's quick to temper, yet fiercely loyal: a loving, generous man who runs on anger and bullishness but is hugely compassionate to people that are vulnerable. A quick look around his offices reveals that the place is cluttered with waifs and strays – John's projects . . . among whose number I was soon to count myself.

When I went in to see him for the second time, I was a very different – visibly bruised – figure from the cocky young man who'd bounced the world off his office wall. I told him everything that'd happened, all the people who had sacked me, and that while I was still formally with KBJ, things there weren't looking good. He just said, 'I think yer great, I'll sign you.' He didn't play any games, or oblige me to take any time to think about it, which was a good job, because a few days later, sitting alone in my empty Spitalfields flat, I received a letter releasing me from my contract with KBJ.

If you're living in a fifty quid-a-week bedsit, you'll be lucky to get a month's leeway before they threaten to throw you out, because they know you're dirt poor. But if you live somewhere that costs ten times that much, they assume you're rich, so if you just don't pay the rent, no one notices. Aware of this, I hadn't paid rent for a year.

My professional relationship with John began with him giving me money. Not to pay my rent, because he didn't realise how bad things had got in that department, but he used to say, 'What ideas have you got – what do you want to do?' I told him I wanted to make a documentary. There was a vibrant arts and crafts market in Spitalfields over the road from my flat. Several multinational companies were lobbying to close it down for redevelopment, and I wanted to make a film about the campaign to stop that happening. He just said, 'Go on then – I'll give you whatever you need.'

A substantial portion of that limited budget was allocated to the crack-houses of Bethnal Green, but the remainder we spent wisely – I remember the ever idealistic John Rogers and Mark Pinheiro toiled for expenses – and the result was GADAFFI, an acronym for something that started with Global Action and had Faction near the end of it; I can't remember exactly how it fitted together, but it worked and we were all quite proud of it. It wasn't flawless, but it was a noble attempt, given the state I was in at the time.

We spoke to the local council and various protest groups, and I turned up at the offices of Balfour Beatty, dressed as my old staple, the Elephant Man, and claiming to be the spirit of Victorian London. There was some funny footage of me getting thrown out on the street by a security guard, still with my sack over my head.

And after he'd seen it, John kept on giving me these odd bits of money – £500 here and there – to go on these little quests, often with no end in sight other than keeping me out of trouble. Me and Matt made this short film called 'Littl'uns', with all these toys and dead animals. The two of us walked up the ceramic stairwells of my Spitalfields apartment block, naked except for white masks that looked like the walls. Then we reversed the film so it looked like we were walking backwards, let these locusts loose in the corridors, and told the story of this Victorian man in a top hat called 'Jack Scratch', who had to lie in bed all the time, because he had chicken's feet. There was a good bit with Matt in a clown's wig in a Perspex disabled lift, and I ended up calling all these toys to follow me, going 'Littl'uns, Littl'uns' in a really scary voice. It was mad.

My troubled state of mind meant that I was much better suited to this kind of experimental endeavour than anything that might conventionally have been considered entertainment. Metres away from me as I write this, Nik Linnen, John's eldest son, is here watching and ensuring that I don't drift off and do something naughty as the book goes to print within weeks and this deadline, its umpteen predecessors lying dead from negligence, must be observed. When I met him this ridiculously handsome and generous soul was still young and dwelt in the enormous shadow of his powerful father. He has emerged as together we have forged a working relationship that has taken me from digital TV to Hollywood films in three years. We do not yet know if the film I've made for producer and director Judd Apatow (*The 40-Year-Old Virgin, Knocked Up, Superbad*) will be any good, but Universal have commissioned a further project – and whatever happens it's better than signing on. Nik, who is a partner in Vanity Projects with me, John and Matt, has been invaluable in keeping me well.

The first time Nik came to see me do stand-up I'd been at the agency for a week. Gunther von Hagens was on the TV that night. The Comedy Café was the venue for a performance that made Gunther's cadaver-bothering look like jaunty high-jinks. I opened doing Elephant Man impressions, determined still that he was funny. A hen party were sitting near the front, so I took this woman's handbag and did an autopsy on its contents, to be topical, and scattered her knickers, lipstick and phone around the room. Then I jumped on a table in front of this group of office workers, kicked over all their booze, and ended up pulling down a lighting rig that I'd been swinging on. Ta da!

The gig had to stop for about half an hour while everything I'd broken was put back together. During this hiatus, I walked over to someone at the venue and magnanimously told them not to worry about the twenty quid I was meant to be getting paid, as it could go towards the damages. They said, 'Not only are we not going to pay you – we don't want you to come here ever again.'

I cheerfully asked Nik afterwards 'That was alright, wasn't it?'

Nik scrambled around for a bright side. 'No one died.' He had a look of what I now realise was horror etched on his face, as the magnitude of the challenge he and his dad had taken on hit home.

The overall tenor of my life at this point was really rather bleak; most of my friends reported an air of doom around me.

The true extent of my disarray was finally about to become apparent to people with the strength of personality to help me actually do something about it.

I realise that my whole life had been leading up to this moment. People say that when they win an Olympic medal – 'My life has been leading up to this moment,' they say. But that's true of every moment. Even if you're only doing the washing up, your whole life's still been building up to that moment. Just because something's insignificant you can't immediately relegate it to the past, it has to be in the present for a moment. That is the nature of a chronological existence. Even if at birth I'd splintered into a thousand clones and each of these existed in a parallel world, they'd still have to live their lives in some sort of order. And, eventually, they'd all end up at John Noel's Christmas party in 2002.

I'd only been with John a couple of months by then and didn't know him that well, yet. All I really knew was that at our first meeting he'd farted in a very loud and unapologetic way, and I'd asked Nik, 'Fucking hell – who's this character?'

I can discern a clear progression in my agents – from those tragic avuncular whoopsies running extras agencies with thinly veiled homoerotic names, through slightly more savvy, wideboy-esque characters like Nigel Klarfeld, to charming middle-class ex-presenter women like Joanna Kay. Until eventually I came across the patriarch I'd always required in John Noel: this sort of heavy-fisted, surly but gentle Northern brute of a man, who has come from a difficult background and overcome his own demons and thereby has an eye for a misfit, and was willing to take me on when I had all but destroyed my own career.

John's parties are notorious, because he often behaves abysmally in public. Twice to my knowledge he's been thrown out of his own social functions, but that was not to happen on this occasion. The venue was some place above an Irish pub in Kilburn. John's not ever really succumbed to the glitz and glamour of showbiz – he's always stayed true to his roots. (Frankly, I find that a little disappointing, because I personally like the glitz and glamour – that's why I got into this damned industry in the first place. Well, that and my cursed talent.)

Low-rent location notwithstanding, the 2002 John Noel Management Christmas Party was attended by such luminaries as Davina McCall, Tess Daly and Dermot O'Leary. My escort for the evening was a homeless gentleman called Harmonica Matt, who couldn't speak without stammering, but could sing the blues perfectly when he picked up his harmonica. He told me once that he'd taken a load of acid some years before, and had 'never come back'.

Making that 'Homeless James' episode of *RE:Brand* had done nothing to diminish my interest in down-and-outs. I just used to get fascinated by them. I know that's the sort of thing people say, and I really hate it when people say the sort of things people say. I always think, 'You don't mean that. You just think it sounds good'. Like *Big Brother* contestants insisting they want people 'to get to know the real them' before they've even been on the show. 'But I don't know the un-real you. I don't know any aspect of your personality. I have no opinion of you at all. I don't want to see the real you, or an artificial you, or some you that you've made out of Twiglets – give us further oblivion, you nit.' But, aware as I am of the contrivances of compassionate language, I do tend to identify with those who watch life from the periphery. Harmonica Matt. I can't remember exactly where I found him – he'd have been at the bottom of some escalator somewhere, playing his mouth organ. He used to haunt the central line at Liverpool Street, singing a haunting melody to a baby doll in a pram he pushed: 'There's something wrong with my baby, there's something wrong with me.' There was; he was eccentric. 'Even Nostradamus couldn't've predicted that' was another of his hits. I befriended him, and in the spirit of 'Hey, yeah man, it's the sixties', invited him to John Noel's party.

I'd always found Harmonica Matt to be a charming fella, and I was aware of many of his idiosyncrasies, but one that had escaped my attention until the night of that party was that he had something of an eye for the ladies. I always tend to feel a bit on edge in those kind of supposedly convivial situations, and the sight of Harmonica Matt looming over assorted permatanned digital TV starlets, breathing his vomity-Wotsit breath over 'em ('I like him,' I used to tell people, 'he smells of Wotsits': 'That's not Wotsits,' Matt would reply, 'it's his own sick') did nothing to put me at ease.

The resulting social anxiety prompted my customary response. I disappeared off to the lavatory to see if my brain was so committed to thinking its thoughts that it would be prepared to do battle with its nemesis and saviour, Auntie Heroin. I drizzled some in and it were, like, real horror show. Nik ambled in.

'Fookin' hell mate,' he exclaimed, 'is that heroin?' I admitted that it was (I had mentioned to John before that I had a drugs problem, but I think he just took this to mean that I smoked a bit too much grass). 'You need to do something about that, mate,' Nik insisted, with a sense of urgency that I had not yet learnt to recognise. 'Yeah, yeah, I know, I really should,' I said, distractedly, not expecting anything to come of it. But before I knew it, I found myself embroiled in a series of brief but life-changing meetings.

Meeting One was in the Lansdowne pub and involved John Noel buying me and my mum pizzas and saying, 'Russell's got a problem; we need to sort it out.' My mum had the same air that she's had at countless previous meetings with headmasters and counsellors and policemen – that kind of bruised and battered love for me. On this occasion though, she seemed a little more confident – perhaps because there was an alpha male offering to help.

As he spoke John was characteristically and confidently interfering with the fireplace. John could never leave an open grate alone. Nik's the same – they have to put wood on it, or stir up the ashes with a poker. I'm not like that. I might play with a fire if I'm on my own, but not in a pub – it's not my job. But John's straight in there, meddling with the fire, that's how primal he is: it wouldn't surprise me if one day he fashioned a wheel out of granite.

John said that he was going to introduce me to a man called Chip Somers, who it turned out had been instrumental in Davina McCall's recovery from addiction. Intrigued though I was, I broke off from the conversation at this point to go and meet Gritty and score some heroin – just to get through the rest of the meeting about how I had to give it up. It was easier to have that discussion once I'd taken some (in fact, the impact of that specific inhalation still gives me a nostalgic pang of comfort, the sort of warm glow one might get from remembering a beloved Christmas gift – Batman costume aged seven). Once you've had some heroin, the idea of stopping taking it is bearable; it's when you've not had any that it becomes fucking terrifying.

Meeting Two, the next day, was with Chip Somers, at John Noel's offices. In the blink of an eye I'd gone from scoring drugs from Gritty – 'Oh Gritty!' – to applying for salvation via the ridiculously joyfully named Chip Somers: a man who sounded like a Mommas and Poppas song title.

Chip turned out to be a distinguished, bespectacled gent, warm and forceful, like good sodomy; he'd been to Radley College, so perhaps that's where he got it from. He carries himself with dignity and has incredible insight. You wouldn't know that he's served four years in prison for armed robbery and was an intravenous junkie five times longer than that if I hadn't just blithely told you. He wouldn't mind because now he is a living monument to the possibility of redemption and change. He founded and runs a treatment centre in Bury St Edmunds called Focus 12.

He sat me down and asked about the extent of my drug use. I took him through how it developed, and told him that for the last four years I'd been taking heroin and crack every day, but for a few failed 'clucks', and now had a £50–£100 a day habit. He told me that I was a 'complete garbage-head' and needed to come into treatment straight away. While he was talking I was doing something I often do; I just watch a conversation happening – the real me sat away all snug, thinking, 'This will have no consequences: none of these proposals will be implemented.'

Then we went back into John's office across the corridor, with all its gifts and photographs and newspaper stories concerning his notorious clients, and he said, 'Right, so what's the fookin' situation?' Chip explained swiftly that if I didn't stop taking drugs straight away, I'd be in prison, a mental asylum, or a coffin within six months. He said it was vital I came into Focus 12 within the week, and that an integral part of the process would be that I made this decision myself. 'There's no point making him if he doesn't want to,' Chip counselled gently.

There was a pause while Chip eyed me encouragingly and waited for me to do the right thing. He would've had a long wait but for John. 'Fook that,' said John, 'he's going.' And that was the end of the matter.

In my case, flying in the face of rehab convention by not giving me any choice probably was the only way forward. Especially as the best reason I could come up with for not going into treatment straight away was that I was due to start making a programme called *Five Go Dating,* an E4 reality show that would chart the relationships of five 'celebrities'. Not even as the host of it, just as one of the five twerps that was taking part.

Chip left and I stood up and looked out of the office window. It was a winter day, crisp and clear and bright, and sharp naked trees scarred the sky. The eager moon prematurely looked down. John said, 'I only want what's best for you, Russell.' He was standing by the window, all big and solid, and me all empty. I stood there and silently cried. Only my eyes though, the rest of me was frozen. John formed a protective barrier around me, with his arms, and the edifice of his character, and told me everything was going to be alright.

When I went outside, I looked up. 'I suppose you don't have to take drugs every day,' I thought. Since the age of sixteen this had never occurred to me. I was a child, then a drug addict, and then this. Now.

I learned later that a girl I'd been at drama school with – on hearing that I'd stopped drinking and taking drugs – said, 'Well, what does he do then?' Like there was literally nothing else to me: I was just this thing that drank and took drugs. For the next two days, I didn't use hard drugs at all, only drank and smoked weed. Then, on the night before I went into treatment, I had a smack and crack wake. I called Gritty for the last time and gave him everything I had, and told him I was off; he was supportive, he's a nice bloke. I called my mate Gee, who I'd got close to after John Rogers's poetry nights and told him I was fucked and that I was going away. He said he'd visit. I went to see Karl and spent most of the night in his toilet dosing myself up. Then I went to my flat and spent my last few hours with heroin, just the two of us like lovers. I took everything I could from heroin and it took everything it could from me; then we fell asleep together. I woke up fucked for the last time on Friday 13 December 2002. I'd missed my train. ☞

29

A Gentleman with a Bike

I got the next train from Liverpool Street Station on Friday 13 December 2002. This was the beginning of my life in recovery.

For all the damage it had enabled me to do to myself and my career, heroin had also provided a degree of sanctuary. Marianne Faithfull once said that heroin had saved her, because she was suicidal and it kept her alive.

In Twelve Step recovery programmes the personification of drugs and addiction is common. I thought of heroin as a companion. Like 'Footprints in the Sand' – that bloody poem that goes on about footprints in the sand. It's about a person dreaming that one set of footprints is theirs and the other is the Lord's. And then noticing that at the times in their life that have been the most difficult, there was only one set of footprints. They ask: 'God, why did you desert me?' And he goes: 'That is when I carried you.'

When I hear that, I think, 'Come on God, don't fuck me around. That's convenient – how come the footprints aren't deeper then? 'Cos you'd have been carrying my weight. And they're not deeper, are they? How come one of those footprints has only got three toes? It's a dinosaur footprint. And that one next to it is a cat's paw. What's been going on on this beach? Why is God at the beach anyway? With all the chaos? And war? What the fuck is God doing on holiday at a time like this?'

Perhaps heroin had, similarly, held me in times of trouble. The prospect of relinquishing it was terrifying. The only reason I did so was because I was more afraid of what was going to happen to me if I didn't.

I'd been forced to go to an AA meeting once, while I was at Drama Centre. There was a tramp getting a cake for not having drunk for twenty years. I thought, 'What's the fucking point of that? One of the few benefits of being a tramp is that you can be pissed all the time.' A couple of years later, a comedian who'd been clean for a few years took me to Narcotics Anonymous a few times.

I sat in a meeting in Notting Hill, just off Portobello Road, and cried. I didn't know why. They really get to you. While I was tearfully applauding people being given their commemorative key-rings for eighteen months, or ninety days, or multiple years of clean time, the idea of not taking drugs for a whole day seemed impossible. I took the one-day key-ring anyway, but I knew I wasn't going to give up until the day came where it was imposed upon me. Chip and John impressed upon me that that day was now day.

Chip had specified that the whole treatment process would take about seven weeks, which seemed an insanely long time.

On the train they called me and did an assessment of what drugs I'd been taking (they'd rather rushed me through the induction process, because of the charity work John Noel had done for Focus, and Chip's association with Davina). And when I arrived in Stowmarket, Chip picked me up in his red car and gave me a lift to the Focus offices in Bury St Edmunds.

Chip embraced me; I thought, 'That's a bit weird.' But of course in NA land and rehab world, hand-shaking is eschewed in favour of the culture of the hug. It's lovely really, I suppose, because the whole thing is built on solidarity and shared experience, so there's no reason not to have a bit of a cuddle.

When I got to Focus, everyone was coming back from a trip, which is how I know it was a Friday, because Friday is trip day – where you learn how to readjust to society by going on the kind of jaunt a divorced dad would take you on: bowling, the zoo, the cinema.

The building was two terraced houses that they'd knocked through, with a garden area and rooms for group and general counselling. It felt a bit like a doctor's waiting room, but wasn't madly institutional.

I was feeling very fragile and didn't really know what was going on, but they took a urine test and prescribed a drug called Subutex, which mildly sedates you and is also an opiate blocker, so if you take any heroin you won't get a buzz off it. They also gave me some sleeping pills, which were meant to be taken an hour before going to bed.

If I hadn't already known I was a drug addict, the way I approached this latter medication would have given me all the evidence I needed. I took them the first night at ten so I could go to bed at eleven, the next night at nine, the next night at eight, then the next at six, 'cos I realised you get a buzz off it. Well, not exactly a buzz. But if you're trying to stay awake and you're on a sleeping pill, it at least feels like you're a bit drugged.

At that stage, Focus was a day centre. Now they've got two or three flats where residents, patients or clients – they generally they call 'em clients – can stay overnight, but at that stage you had to find your own accommodation, the logic being that if you were out there in the community, having to walk past normal people in pubs, your recovery would have a better chance of enduring than if you'd spent the whole time ensconced in some treatment centre.

Initially I had to lodge in a little garrety den in this ramshackle bed and breakfast run by some Quakers. I can still remember the

IDENTA SM — CHAIN of CUSTODY FORM

Customer No: FALR

CUSTOMER

Name: FOCUS

Address: 82 RISBYGATE STREET
BURY ST EDMUNDS SUFFOLK

Contact Name/Number: CHIP SOMERS (01284 761702

DONOR

Donor Surname: Evans   Forenames: Vashti

Date of Birth: 04/06/75   Male [✓]   Female [ ]   Donor ID No:

I certify that I have provided my oral fluid sample(s) to the collector, that I have not adulterated it in any manner, that I have observed the sample(s) being placed and sealed in the transport vial(s) and that the information on this form and on the sample labels is correct. I also understand that my results will include the name of any drugs found and its significance, and I consent to this.

Donors Signature: [signature]   Date: 27/02/02

SAMPLE

COLLECTION

Date: 27/12/02   Time: 15.45 p.m

Declared substances used within the last 7 days

PHARMACEUTICAL

Drug Name	Days used in Last 7	Last Day Used	AM / PM	Amount	Units
Methadone					
Dihydrocodeine					
Codeine					
Dextropropoxyphene					
Buprenorphine	2	23/12/02	PM	0.2mg	
Benzodiazepines					
Amphetamine					
Morphine					
Diamorphine					
Other					

Declared substances used within the last 7 days

NON-PHARMA

Drug Name	Days used in Last 7	Last Day Used	AM / PM	Amount	Units
Heroin					
Crack/Cocaine					
Speed					
Cannabis					
Ecstasy					
Other					

Laboratory Analysis

TESTING

Please Tick	Confirmation (Please sign and PRINT NAME)	Additional Test(s) Requested	Confirmation (Please sign and PRINT NAME)
Amphetamines [✓]	[ ]	Cannabinoids [✓]	[ ]
Benzodiazepines [✓]	[ ]	Buprenorphine [✓]	[ ]
Cocaine [✓]	[ ]	Methamphetamine [✓]	[ ]
Methadone [✓]	[ ]		
Opiates [✓]	[ ]		

CHAIN OF CUSTODY

	Name	Signature	Date	
Collector	SAMMY MARLARI	[signature] Marjoram	27/12/02	I confirm that the sample(s) identified on this form is the sample(s) presented to me by the donor and that I have followed the accepted sample(s) collection procedure.
Laboratory Receipt				I confirm that the sample(s) identified on this form was received at the laboratory in a sealed condition.

Donor's Copy

DTT0/2000

smell of the bathmats – it was a like a nan's house. And as for those whey-faced Quakers, it is beyond my recollection as to whether either of them actually wore half-moon spectacles, but they seemed to be peering at me over the top of something. Bury St Edmunds is a very old-fashioned, provincial sort of place (I was surprised to find out that Nick Cave had once briefly lived – and written poetry – there). It has a beautiful monastery, and there's a cathedral as well, so the atmosphere of the whole place has a religious tinge.

The centre of town is cobbled. There was a comedy venue called Fat Cat Comedy Club in The Corn Exchange which I'd played a couple of times when I was off my head. And a Caffè Uno and a Café Rouge, where I would lurk – all bamboozled – between group therapy sessions, intermittently chatting up innocent eighteen-year-olds – quite successfully, I might add. I still had that extra gear, though I'm not sure how pleased their parents were to meet a bruised and raw twenty-seven-year-old recovering heroin addict when I came back to stay the night.

It snowed that Christmas, and I bought a bike to ride around town on, and did my best to establish a newly sober and contemplative identity. It was a mark of how much I changed in that initial period that on one occasion Matt rang up the Quakers and asked to speak to me. There was some confusion about my identity, so he described me as a wild, Dean Moriarty crazy man, an octopus-limbed loon, a human Catherine wheel of vibrancy and excitement. There was a pause, and a Quaker offered, 'We do have a gentleman with a bicycle.'

One night – it was Christmas night actually – my mum came to visit. There was a tribute to Peter Cook on the telly and Jimmy Carr did a turn. He'd been in the same heat as me at Hackney Empire New Act of the Year, and I'd gone through to the final. (He's a lovely fella actually, Jimmy.) And there he was on the TV, successful, and here I was watching it on a little portable in a B&B room, not two weeks clean, with my mum sat on the end of the bed, looking wounded and fragile. 'This is it,' I thought. 'Me and my mum the same as when I was born, I've achieved nothing. I've made things worse.'

I couldn't go on living like this. I had to become successful. 'I want to change the world, and do something valuable and beautiful. I want people to remember me before I'm dead, and then more afterwards.' And at this juncture I was finally willing to do whatever it was going to take to bring that about – up to and including giving up drugs. From that moment on, I really did take things, in the textbook rehab fashion, one day at a time.

An awful lot of what went on at Focus was incredibly humdrum and utterly without glamour. It wasn't like what I imagine going to The Priory would be – I think of that as being incredibly stark and white, with all these crisp, clean sheets and orderlies shuffling about with an air of hushed reverence. Focus was a very drab kind of experience. It's cold, it's in Suffolk, and all these drug addicts and alcoholics are sitting around, raking over the past.

It was in these sessions that I first came across the 'To my shame' technique. This is a secret generally only known to those who have been in AA, or NA, or pretty much any other kind of rehabilitation treatment, which I have impulsively and perhaps somewhat recklessly opted to 'share'. That's what we say, 'share': it just means 'say' that you don't even feel embarrassed about it any more. Here's the 'to my shame' technique, it'll blow your socks off. OK. Here it is. Tell no one, just do half, ride the snake . . . You can get away with any admission, however appalling, so long as it's preceded by the words 'to my shame'. That's it. If I've learned one thing from months of intensive therapy, and I haven't, it's that. 'TO MY SHAME.'

SHORT TERM GOALS

AREA OF CONCERN: RELATIONSHIPS

OVERALL PLAN: Find astonishing / beautiful
intellectually equal / powerfull - sexy
woman Have children.
keep good friends I have. Make recovery
friends

3 MONTHS PLAN OF ACTION
- Socialise with people from AA/NA
- Do Yoga / Kick boxing / Acupunture with friends
- stop sleeping with prostitutes
- Control casual sex
- Spend time getting to know people
- Maybe contact Amanda
- Contact Sophie

6 MONTHS PLAN OF ACTION
- keep up friendships
- look for partner

SHORT TERM GOALS

AREA OF CONCERN: WORK / CAREER.

OVERALL PLAN: To become as successfull as
possible. To use my success positively
- to help others. keep control of my
Ego and lust for power.

3 MONTHS PLAN OF ACTION
- Put one hour stand up show together
  and perform it
- Write synopsis / pilot for sitcom / drama
- write / make O.V.C - short film
- Make Pilot for radio show. Start it.
- Make pilot with So tv / Sort out mtv
- make pilot for comedy lab
- Read as much as possible (at least book a week)
- Work on Script for feature film
- Push Gadapi. develope it.

6 MONTHS PLAN OF ACTION
- Establish self as stand up.
- get Gadafi on t v
- get show on terrestrial
- Make sit com pilot
- look into making films
- keep radio show;
- Don't fuck up bits I have

SHORT TERM GOALS

AREA OF CONCERN: ACCOMODATION

OVERALL PLAN: To find an affordable, pleasant dwelling in which to reside with my at yet imaginary dog.

3 MONTHS PLAN OF ACTION

- Move out of Shoreditch
- Stay at Lucy's until I find somewhere?
- look for place where I'll be safe and happy
- get papers / loot
- register with estate agents

6 MONTHS PLAN OF ACTION

- Move into affordable home
- look into getting mortgage

SHORT TERM GOALS

AREA OF CONCERN: RECOVERY

OVERALL PLAN:
To remain clean and sober, one day at a time, for the rest of my life.

3 MONTHS PLAN OF ACTION

- Stay in touch with positive people I've met through peers
- Attend as many meetings as possible (minimum of 3 per week) • Acupuncture
- Make some recovery friends in London
- Continue with diet • Find Counsellor
- continue exercise find own gym
- find Yoga class / Join it
- Find kickboxing • Come to aftercare sessions
- work out boundaries

6 MONTHS PLAN OF ACTION

- Settle into meetings get commitments
- Maintain recovery friendships
- Find New benefits to being clean, new activities
- Establish / explore routines that I consistently use - eg meetings diet, Yoga, kickboxing
- Continue counselling

E.g. 'To my shame, I used to, in my darkest times, steal money from my mum's purse.'

That brave confession would have a very different impact without its first three words. The self-accusatory prefix robs the listener of the right to disapprove.

E.g. (ii) To my shame, when I was drinking, I used to often forget to pick up my kids from school.

CORRECT RESPONSE: Aahh, you poor thing, it must've been hell.

Compare this to:

SANS 'TO MY SHAME'.

I used to exploit women because I couldn't cope with being alone . . .

CORRECT RESPONSE: He didn't say 'to my shame'! You bastard! You vicious selfish bastard.

It's like 'Simon Says' for junkies.

The sessions would be eight to fifteen people sat in a room together, talking through all their worst addiction experiences with a counsellor. Many of the staff of Focus had – like Chip – been junkies themselves in the past, but this fact in itself was quite hard to deal with, because they just seemed so straight and normal compared to the rest of us, bruised and (emotionally) naked as we were. Don't get me wrong, they were really good people – I suppose they'd just calmed down a lot – but at first I found the whole process quite difficult to get to grips with. Gradually, though, you start to hear everyone's stories, and the whole thing becomes quite tragic and beautiful.

I was astonished by the array of humanity that I encountered in that group, and quickly became fond of them. There was a woman called Lisa who I took quite a shine to, a couple of sort of pepper-pot alcoholics – tiny, brittle people – and a housewifey woman, who was addicted to cough medicine. Then there was this guy called Mark, who was like a giant toddler. He was quite a tragic character. About five years previously, he'd been on a fireman's training course and failed the exam at the end, but he was still obsessed with being a fireman and used to wear fireman t-shirts and had a fireman pencil case.

There were some hardened junkies as well – one quite clever bloke, who I was a bit threatened by.

And Steve, who became one of my best friends in rehab. He was a big skinhead, about forty-odd, who had the demeanour of Roy Keane – that kind of steely masculinity. For some reason I got on really well with him.

He'd lived quite a dark life and was, I think, a Satanist; at least he had all these satanic tattoos up and down his arms and quite high up his neck (he'd obviously thought, 'Well, I'm not fitting in anyway, so I might as well write all over my body, as there's no point trying to get a job'). He was a nice bloke though, and he used to pick me up in his van from the B&B and take me to Focus. 'Alright, Russell, how's it going?' he'd ask, all psycho-pathically slow, surveying the terrain for constant invisible threats.

I was always glad to see the back of the Quakers in the morning, with their titchy eating area full of sub-Constable landscape prints and horse-brasses, and all the polished accou-trements to tend a fireplace, but never once a fucking fire. I decided to eat fruit and nuts, and live like a monkey. After some minutes of struggling to get the attention of the Jesus-loving real-people-hating Quakers, I put my head round the door of the kitchen and said, 'Ooh hello, could I just get some fruit, please, instead of the normal fried breakfast?'

I noticed this huge mound of fruit on the sideboard, like one of Carmen Miranda's hats. Of course it was crap fruit that you have to peel – great big oranges and bananas and stuff – not nice posh fruit like I'd have now: strawberries, grapes, blueberries, little soft round fruit that you can stuff in your gob straight away. The woman looked at me, and said, in a June Brown sort of voice – this really did happen, and I thought at the time, 'It is funny that she has said this thing' – 'we don't have any fruit here.'

'But what about that big mound of fruit by your elbow?' I countered. She looked down at it with a sort of curled, peeping letterbox mouth and spat, 'Well, I suppose you could have a lemon.' I said, 'Won't that be rather sour?' Adding, just as a joke so I could write it down one day, 'Though compared to this conversation, 't'would be as sweet as candy.' I giggled to myself at how splendid I'd been and she gave me an orange.

Steve, who used to come and rescue me from that breakfast room, is dead now, so I suppose there's nothing to prevent me from telling you the story he once told in the treatment centre. It put my life in perspective at the time and perhaps can do so again. As a lad of eleven or twelve, he'd worked at The Cut market in Waterloo, helping his brother on the fruit-stand. They'd always detested the mean, brown-fingered fishmonger, and one day, when they were playing football up by the lock-up garages where the market traders kept their stock, Steve accidentally kicked the ball against his garage.

Steve told us this story in a group session, staring impassively ahead as he did so. His brother just ran off, but the fishmonger – fat, stinking and in a leather apron – caught Steve, and dragged him into his lock-up. He had a rusty old tin bath in there, full of cold, grey water, and the heads and eyes and innards of the fish he'd gutted for the stall. He bent Steve over the edge of the bath, plunged his head into the filthy water and raped him.

'Too much fuckin' perspective.' Because you're so busy taking everything one day at a time, one of the things they try to do for you at Focus is build some idea of a future, so you don't just get trapped in the present. This technique might come in handy if you know someone who's dead depressed. If that person tells you they don't think there's any point in living any more, just say, 'OK, well, I'm off now, but remember, we're going to see *Shrek 2* on Wednesday [or *Shrek 3* or *Shrek 4*]. It's important to plant that idea in their heads, because later on they might be about to put a bag over their head and tie it shut with an elastic band, or run the bath full and hot so they can die like a Roman general, razor blade on the forearm. And at the exact moment when they're about to end their grim life by taking that final journey into dark sweet relief, they'll think, 'Oh no, I can't do this, I've got to go and see *Shrek 2/3/4* with Russell.'

Because what they're dealing with is a room full of people who have just got through life by being off their heads, they try to create some sort of structure for you to arrange your day around, and then hammer it home via endless repetition. They make you write a daily diary in the morning, and at night you have to reiterate what your plans are for the next day.

I felt pleased to have had an effect on Steve eleven or twelve days in. One by one, they went round the room, asking everyone what their upcoming projects for the next day were. The standard response would be something like 'might go for a burger'. But Steve said, 'I imagine I shall probably go for a spot of lunch' – an uncharacteristically grandiloquent phrase, which I took to be evidence that I had infiltrated his mind.

Unfortunately, Steve was one of a group of three who got chucked out of Focus for relapsing. This was a terrible shock, because we'd seen a couple of people graduate, but prior to that, no one had been forced to leave for any other reason, and it felt as if we'd all found sanctuary. I'd really got into the ethos of the place by then, having resisted it initially. When that unhappy trio were thrown out, I felt betrayed. They'd got together to drink some wine and smoke a joint. They'd not taken any of what I'd call 'men's drugs', but they'd nonetheless breached the strict rules of Focus. Individually they were summonsed before the counsellors. I thought: 'They'll be alright. They'll just be told off.' One by one they emerged, and said, 'Yeah, I've been thrown out.'

I found it difficult to accept and groped around for a way to assuage my impotence. I remembered the speech from *Antigone* I'd performed at Drama Centre, in which Haemon convinces his powerful father, Creon, to show clemency. I acquired a copy of Sophocles' masterpiece and delivered it with renewed authenticity. Chip agreed to give Lisa a further opportunity, but drew the line at that adorable necromancer Steve. In explaining why, Chip outlined the principle of common good. He said, 'What's important is the process, and those people can't stay within it once they've relapsed, as there's a danger they'll fuck it up for everyone else.'

When I eventually graduated from Focus, I occasionally received text messages from Steve. I'd responded while I was still there, but when you're in early recovery it's deemed unwise to stay in contact with junkies, so we lost touch. He addressed me with an eerie Native American name, 'Once Were Friends'. He'd start a message, 'Hello Once Were Friends', which was poignant. Six months after I left Focus, I heard that Steve had been found dead, with a needle in his arm. 🖝

30

Out of the Game

I was cheesed off with the evictions from Focus. Then the Quakers threw me out of their B&B (it was something to do with women or noise, or a combination of the two). I thought this was going to be a blessing in disguise, as I moved into this amazing health spa which didn't cost much more but had a swimming pool, a gym and a sauna.

I only lasted two nights there, because the nightwatchman (whose previous job had been in a funeral parlour – he kept telling me and my mate Gee, who'd come to see me, about the bodies coughing at night; I bet he diddled with those corpses) got me thrown out for trying to let Gee stay in my room – adding racism to the already worrying charge of necrophilia – when I was off with some girl. I was gutted to have to leave that place, even more so when the next place I ended up in turned out to be a Travel Tavern.

For the next two months I lived a life as close to Alan Partridge as one could without infringing Steve Coogan's copyright. I kept my bicycle in my room and cycled into treatment every day, where the message, 'Don't take drugs 'cos you'll ruin your life . . . right, now, look – here is an alternative way of living' was endlessly drummed into my selfish little mind-hole.

Among the visitors were my dad, Karl Theobald, my darling stylist Sharon Smith, and John Noel – who drove the wrong way round the Bury St Edmunds one-way system, and brought me an ounce of weed to help me cope with getting off drugs. (I had to tell him, 'Thanks very much, John, but I'm in a drug rehabilitation centre' – I don't think he realised it was a drug.)

Matt came up just after I'd had to write my life story as an exercise. He went through the whole thing taking the piss out of it (God knows what he'll make of this – especially the bit in the next chapter, where I out him as a pervert and a casual drug-user). He detected a somewhat self-aggrandising tendency within the narrative. He kept reading out bits where I emphasised successes in my career, saying, 'This is meant to be a therapeutic exercise, not an opportunity for you to show off.'

For me, though, a therapeutic exercise that did not involve an opportunity to show off would be a contradiction in terms, as the next anecdote will clearly illustrate. The best thing about drug rehab I think are the day trips they take you on, to try and get you used to civilisation again. It is my personal belief that you cannot consider your life complete until you've been indoor go-kart racing with twenty junkies.

The place we went to was supervised by the most humourless, joyless sixteen-year-old boys I've ever encountered in my life. They knew we were all smack-heads, but they treated us with absolutely no empathy whatsoever. The worst one was the kid who did the induction, telling us how to safely operate the go-kart: a relatively simple task which he approached in the following fashion.

'OK,' he proclaimed sternly, 'when you are riding in these karts, there will be no overtaking on the inside . . . or you'll be out of the game. During the race, you will not remove your crash helmet . . . or you're out of the game. You will also not crash your car into the central chicanery . . .'

You know when people are so utterly dull that you feel yourself severing the cord that connects you to their reality and floating away from their tedium like helium?

I remember thinking, 'This kid is sixteen years old. When some of us were sixteen years old, we were down by the disused railway track with an empty Hovis bread-bag filled up with solvents, inhaling deeply – you're wasting your life, son.'

There was this (much nicer) eighteen-year-old boy called Gavin, who was actually in treatment with me and recognised me from MTV and thought I was all cool. He looked up to me. 'Russell [and I can't swear that these were his actual words, but this was definitely what he was thinking], you're so cool and mad and dangerous, and we're going go-kart racing together. It's gonna be such fun, because you're so crazy and wild.' I thought, 'This kid thinks I'm crazy and wild! I can't let him down, with his little face all full of hope.'

So we get into the karts and set off, and pretty soon, not long after the race begins, I overtake Gavin on the inside. A klaxon sounds, and the sixteen-year-old comes charging over, waving a flag. 'OK,' he admonishes, 'any more of that monkey business and you're out of the game.'

We set off again, and this time Gavin overtakes me on the inside. I quickly reciprocate, and swing my car right into the central chicane which is made of all these tyres. As the kart makes its impact, I feel like a cattle rustler or an animal rights activist. Tyres – cartwheeling, silly, giddy tyres – are flying in all directions: 'Free, free, free, my pretties . . .'

What happens next is actually ridiculous. Lights flash, people are running around with flags, a widow wipes a single tear from her cheek, black-shirted youth look nobly towards a racially pure future. It's like fucking Nuremberg in there. The boy's reaction is apoplectic. He comes over to me and demands to know my name. I tell him, and he says, 'Well, Russell, because of what you've done today, you're out of the game. Not only that, but all your friends . . . they're out of the game too. All of them. You're all out of the game! Out of the game!' Hysterically.

I feel a show of unity might have been a more appropriate response but Tim, who I was in treatment with, went, 'Oh well done Russell.' 'Bloody hell Tim,' I said, 'I've not breached the Geneva Convention; this is just an arbitrary rule plucked from the brain of a boy.' I wouldn't have minded, but Tim had been addicted to crack-cocaine about two weeks earlier. Could we get some perspective on this maybe? On the one hand, the go-kart trip has been cut short, and that is bad, but on the other, you're not dependent on crack-cocaine any more, so it's swings and roundabouts really.

That was one of my favourite days in treatment, but there were others that I really loved. And fortunately, they're all recorded in my daily diaries. The idea behind these is that you write a log of everything that's happened, then you hand it to your counsellor, and that one person reads it to check you're not going to kill yourself or relapse or go mad or something. But I'm such an inveterate show-off that I wrote mine in the sort of style which suggests I knew that a couple of years later I'd be reading it out in front of a live audience (which I did when I did a stand-up show called 'Better Now') and a couple of years after that transcribing it into my autobiography.

Here is a sample daily diary to show you what they looked like, then I'll transcribe a few, so you can just read them without having to decipher my expressionistic penmanship.

Oh amoré, love, romance
let cupids arrows rain, Salutations
Eros — lets bathe in Casanovas
Sperm (he was impotent — the
pedants cry) How many Cards?
Ooh, let me count... a big
fat zero. Still, you don't get

bitter, do you? You've got to
laugh at life. Look at all
the cruelty, injustice, propaganda
and terror and laugh. HA
HA . HA . HA, HA HA.

I will find her...

21/12/02

I have decided to overthrow the government. I feel right proper chipper – like Dick Van Dyke

01/01/03

I am a slithering knot of neurosis, a tumour of tumult. Incapable of the merest social encounter, my days are a series of embarrassing ordeals, strung together with miserable intro-spection. The grim weather, but for its potency, reflects my maudlin soul

07/01/03

Got in adventures on my way home: was threatened with anal rape with a broomstick by an enraged jeweller. Feel a bit nauseous . . .

15/01/03

I am my own higher power. God of Yoga. High Commander of Destiny and the Fates. I feel quite cheerful

29/01/03

In my dreams last night I was in the garden of my childhood and I thought I could see burrowing moles. On further inspection they appeared to be giant bald donkeys writhing in the earth. Still, not to worry

13/02/03

A beautiful 'pheasant thing' ran across my path as I cycled here today with almost phosphorescent colours about its neck, quite marvellous. Being a simple man I took this to herald some mystic event or magical era. Or perhaps it's a load of Mephistopheles and we're all damned . . .

14/02/03

[In honour of the special significance of the date, this entry is decorated with hearts]

Oh amoré, love, romance . . . Let cupid's arrows rain. Salutations Eros – let's bathe in Casanova's sperm (he was impotent – the pedants cry). How many cards? Ooh, let me count . . . a big fat zero. Still, you don't get bitter, do you? You've got to laugh at life. Look at all the cruelty, injustice, propaganda and terror and laugh. HA HA HA HA HA HA.

[four more hearts follow]

I will find her . . .

Terrifying.

Jackie, a very astute counsellor woman who was a nice version of Nurse Ratched in *One Flew Over the Cuckoo's Nest* (I'm being R.P. McMurphy) once said to me, 'Russell, I think you're really not taking this seriously: in your mind, you're just taking notes for your stand-up comedy.' This is something they said at the KeyStone place as well . . . 'cos I fucking was, and always have been, because that's all life is to me – raw material for comedy. People tell you 'Life's not a rehearsal'. Well, mine is – it's a rehearsal for when I get onstage and do the real performance.

My whole time in rehab is a bit of a blur really, 'cos I was just getting my brain back, but quite a lot of rubbish did go on with the locals. I remember going to visit Chip once – who kindly gave me a lot of personal attention, and is now my sponsor in Narcotics Anonymous. Chip lived above this jeweller's, and for some reason I had to climb over an iron gate to get in. The second I started to do that, the jeweller came out with a rubber glove on one hand and clutching some sort of mop as a makeshift weapon, and we had this ridiculous exchange where I said, 'What are you going to do with that – stick it up my arse?'

I am still immensely grateful to that Focus place, though (I've subsequently gone back for reunions and become a patron), and I do feel that between them John Noel and Chip Somers saved my life. Had I not gone into treatment, I do honestly feel that I would either be dead now, or living a life so close to death that it would be difficult not to take the final step. I don't think that's melodramatic, that's just the way I was going. But John wouldn't let it happen, and Chip had the ability to see me through the process till I came out the other side.

I cried when I left Focus. When you graduate, they go round the room and people say what they think of you, and it's lovely. Chip came to mine. I'd written something I wanted to read out, but when the time came to do it, I couldn't speak. Everyone was dead proud of me.

I was determined not to relapse, but there were powerful forces pulling me back. My whole identity was built around being this kind of crazed, swashbuckling, intoxicated man. I remember Karen – my first girlfriend after going in treatment – saying that when she spoke to people who'd known me before, 'They talked about you like you were a monster.'

It wasn't just me who had to adjust to a new idea of the kind of person I was; everyone else did as well. Not long after John had brought me that dope as a present, when I was still in Focus, I got a couple of days off and went back to Essex for a little break, where I soon found myself chopping out lines of coke for people while they said, 'Go on, Russell, have a bit of a toke – it's just heroin that's the problem.'

I was very nervous about the idea of sobriety. Again, quite early on in my time in rehab, they took us to this huge New Year's Eve show that Eric Clapton was playing at Guildford Leisure Centre. The idea was that the gig was completely dry, and I fucking detested it. I suppose it was probably one of the first

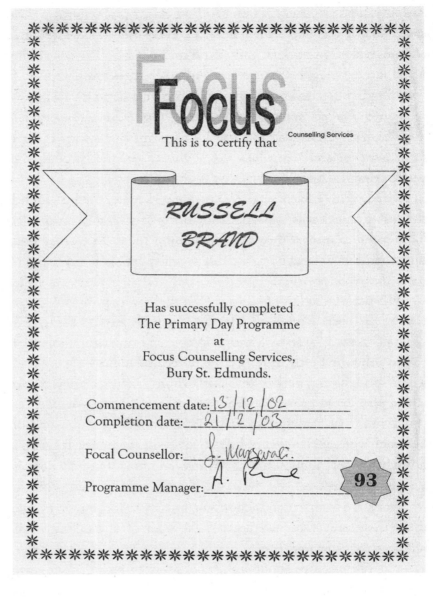

Focus

Counselling Services

This is to certify that

RUSSELL BRAND

Has successfully completed
The Primary Day Programme
at
Focus Counselling Services,
Bury St. Edmunds.

Commencement date: 13 / 12 / 02

Completion date: 21 / 2 / 03

Focal Counsellor: _____

Programme Manager: _____

93

social functions I'd ever been to as an adult where I wasn't on drugs, and it was like being in hell. I was wearing this jacket with all these zips on it, that still had loads of tin foil left in the pockets, which made feel really strange, and I said to the girl I was with, 'This ain't for me. If this is what it means to be saved or redeemed, I ain't gonna be a happy ending.'

In order to distance themselves from temptation, and draw a line under their previous misdemeanours, a lot of people become very puritanical once they've been through the rehab process. But in contrast with a lot of recovering addicts, I've never felt the need to gloss over what it was about drinking or taking drugs that I liked so much. Apart from anything else, I think doing that puts up a barrier between you and those people who have had the self-restraint to keep their indulgence in those pleasures within socially acceptable limits.

The fact that I had a drug problem meant that wherever I went in the world, from Havana to Ibiza to the mean streets of the Edinburgh Festival, I always had to seek out the poor and the dispossessed, as they are the people who generally know where the drugs are. The thing about being an addict is – as you'll find from the poetry of Charles Bukowski or the novels of William Burroughs or Henry Miller – it forces you into unusual places: 'Down among the have-nots', as Lucky Ricky's accomplice put it.

George Orwell, in *Homage to Catalonia*, wrote (on the first page, thank God, otherwise I wouldn't know about it) of the immediate recognition of shared humanity.

When he was signing up for POUM – the rebel socialist army fighting against Franco in the Spanish Civil War – there was a red-haired Italian soldier who was just in front of him in the queue where you signed up to fight. Orwell said he instantly liked him, and could tell he would get on with him and could love him, though he was only in his company for a minute, and barely any words were spoken.

Down among the have-nots, the drunks and the junkies, fleeting moments of mutual connection happen quite frequently. With Barry, fine brown hair, concave chest, sad, sad eyes, the Queens Arms pub; "'Ello me old mucker, put one in the pipe for us, I'm brassick.' With his handler Pats, who looked like Mike Reid crossed with an ox; they did house clearances – taking all the stuff out of old people's homes after they'd died. Pats told me that the first thing Barry would do was go straight to the medicine cabinet, rifle through all the pill packets and bottles, and neck the lot. It made no difference what they were for – rheumatism, athlete's foot, piles.

Barry, perpetually upbeat, had never got over the death of his father, who was a boxer. I once went round to the place where he'd lived with his dad. It was quite a big terraced house – and there was hardly any furniture in it. I sat in there with just this electric bar heater for comfort, smoking dope and taking daft prescription drugs.

We'd induced a comfortable silence and I glanced at Barry; orange in the three-bar glow, he just looked lost and sad, like my nan when I recognised that she was ready to die, but he was in his twenties – just a man in an empty house, lit by a bar-fire, on drugs he'd found in a dead man's cupboard. A beautiful soul who fell through life.

Once in Soho, drunk and alone, coping with the spiteful light of an Old Compton Street off-licence, I tumbled into the nocturnal camaraderie that only penniless drunks can purchase. My fleeting companion, my soul-mate for that moment, was a Scottish lad, young and reeking. I told him how I missed Amanda, he told me how he missed his home. 'My love is like a red, red rose,' he said, all wistful about Burns. 'That's newly sprung in June,' I said knowingly, thinking about her. Then together: 'My love is like a melody, that's sweetly played in tune.' We defiantly recited Rabbie Burns's poem, entangled arms kept us from falling. 'Till a' the seas gang dry, my dear, And the rocks melt wi' the sun.' Just two more drunks serenading an indifferent world. The poem and our Brotherhood ended simultaneously and we carried on alone into the night. 'And I will love thee still, my dear, While the sands of life shall run.' ☞

31

Hare Krishna Morrissey

I graduated from Focus in the early spring of 2003 and moved into a small flat on the fringes of Hampstead in North London, where I lived for the next four years. In the early stages of recovery, I lived a quiet life of AA and NA meetings and seeing friends, as I struggled to adjust to a drug-free existence. I'd taken up yoga, and for eight weeks I didn't have sex or masturbate as an experiment. My life was held together by my beautiful friends, my lovely mum and my cat Morrissey, who was an irresponsible Christmas gift from a girl I was seeing for about a week. Morrissey remains my constant companion, sauntering and judging, eating and attacking life with a sense of entitlement that makes the Duchess of Kent look like Saint Francis of Assisi.

I became enchanted by the Hare Krishna devotees; I went to the mansion in Watford that George Harrison bought them. I met a swami who radiated the truth from his eyes, he was clearly living by principles that, though I can understand, I find it difficult to apply. He understood that life is transient and that material attachments bring suffering. Not the way I understand it, which is by sagely nodding when it's brought up in conversation then sneaking home to marvel at my glorious skull-emblazoned boots. Radanat swami would not politely greet me, wisely discuss the *Bhagavad-Gita*, then after I'd left frantically buttonhole some luckless assistant yawping, 'you better get me some of those fucking cowboy boots,' before collapsing into desperate tears. He knows the boots are a temporary distraction from mortality and lives his life accordingly. Looking at the boots now in all their holy glory, it's difficult not to write to him saying, 'Come on mate, you must want these boots really.' If I did he'd just laugh; he had a terrific sense of fun.

The first year or so after I came out of rehab was mainly flavoured by continuing John Noel-funded escapades into the world of TV. Graham Norton's company SO television agreed to make a Comedy Lab, a broadcast pilot for Channel 4, with us, so we thought we'd get some footage to show them what we were into. Me and Matt said, 'Let's make a film about them adult baby perverts.' We found one on the Internet – this woman who looked a bit like the housekeeper out of *Tom & Jerry* – I know you don't ever see her face, but if you close your eyes and imagine it you get the face of this adult baby woman which is stored in a Jungian brain library we all have access to.

We went to Folkestone to meet her. That woman was no more a provider of an 'adult baby service' than I am of trouble-free holidays. What she was can only be described with the words 'vicious dominatrix'. Having got hopelessly drunk, she thrashed me with a carpet-beater, a shoe and a belt before stripping me naked and attaching clothes pegs to my nipples and prize-winning genitals. I don't know of a baby the world over that would require that service. Then she gleefully poured piping hot wax onto my penis and looked at me as if I was a killjoy Calvinist when I refused to let her repeat the trick up my anus.

While I received this agonising treatment, all in the hope that 'it'll be funny', I caught sight of my beloved Matt, who was the entire crew that day, in the mirrored wardrobes that flanked the floral fleapit where goolies came to die. Far from diligently observing another soon to be 'smash-hit TV show' with compassion and concern, he was pointing the camera with one hand while with the other he was boredly texting a chum – utterly desensitised to the constant mayhem that our work comprised. I've dragged that lad through brothels and hellholes across the globe and he's never once said 'thank you': is that too much to ask?

I'd never before seen the attraction in sadomasochism – 'I don't want to pay money to get sexually tortured, I get enough of that at home' – but after that woman had administered her painful medicine I had to diddle her just to set the record straight. Kindly she agreed to let us spend the night in her 'work flat' while she cleared off home with her husband, whose mind must be so broad that John Merrick's cap would perch on his head like a thimble. Matt has always been obsessed with hygiene and microscopic viruses and such, so was rather anxious about dossing down in a bed where a prostitute tortured perverts. I assured him that he was being insufferable and nimbly leapt between the stiff sheets while he neurotically swathed himself in towels like an Egyptian Rain Man.

When we proudly showed the film to John Noel he said, 'We're not giving that to Channel 4 – it should be impounded by the fucking police.'

Nik concurred. 'Yeah, it's true mate, you've lost sight of what's normal.' The fools. Me and Matt insisted that we were ahead of our time and began to wait for conventional morality to catch up with our depraved pilot. I used this time to relearn my craft as a stand-up comedian – tentatively doing material into Dictaphones, going back to The Enterprise pub, then taking on five- and ten-minute open spots in the same sort of places I'd started off in when I left Drama Centre.

Some of the stand-ups, among my contemporaries, who I particularly admire are Daniel Kitson, Ross Noble and Paul Foot (who I did a double act with for about six months), and Andrew Maxwell, he's very good too. Simon Munnery and Stewart Lee I like because they both slip you information like Rohypnol then touch you up with the chuckles. On telly I love *The Mighty Boosh*: Noel Fielding is an angelic dream weaver and Julian Barratt a world-weary connoisseur. And Garth Marenghi.

Billy Connolly was the first stand-up I really got into, as a teenager – particularly that special he did on LWT. I love his enthusiasm and spontaneity. He and Richard Pryor (alongside Bill Hicks, of course) were probably the two stand-ups I was keenest to emulate at this stage in my career. Pryor has that anecdotal element too, and I'd always loved the way he acted out different parts to bring the whole thing to life. But the most important thing about him, for me, was the way you could tell so many of the things he talked about were back-breakingly painful – real traumas from his life – that he somehow alchemised into comedy.

Throughout this period, as I was gradually feeling my way towards a stand-up persona that would work for me, John Noel was not just a patriarch, but a kind of staunch, ever-present, dominating figure in my life. For the first eighteen months after I came out of rehab, he paid my rent and gave me a generous allowance of about a thousand pounds a month, so I could write some new stuff without having to get a job. He nagged me about paying my bills, though.

One morning I was just in my flat, lazing around in my pants, when the doorbell rang. I went and opened it, and there stood a burly bailiff character in a woolly hat, and some kind of smartly dressed handler; they claimed they were there due to non-payment of council tax, and they'd have to take either £500, or goods of equivalent value. I nodded politely before slamming the door in their faces; I dislike bailiffs as I remember them turning up when I was busy being a toddler, troubling my mum for money. I called John, who was the barrier between me and problems of this nature. He said, 'I fookin' told you to pay your bills.' Then there was another moment when the one who was there for carrying and fighting put his foot in the door and was quite pugnacious when I tried to shut it. John told me to let him speak to them. I was relieved because he uses willpower to change facts as part of his job.

'You're gonna have to let them take your TV.' 'Oh no, I love that telly, my programmes, my precious programmes.' They oafed their way in and yobbishly unplugged it from the Sky Box, the PlayStation and the video, knocking loads of things over in the process. I called the council and haughtily said, 'I'm sure I've paid my council tax, I don't know what's going on.'

After they louted out with my TV set, I fought back the tears and rage and went to John Noel's offices. I phoned the council incessantly, each time more puffed up with rage. 'I've paid my tax, you better resolve this, I play golf with the mayor.' I waited while they found my file and, when I told them about the company the bailiffs were from – 'Camden Reclaim' – they said they'd never heard of it.

I unleashed a decade of distilled fury, desperately trying to get my TV back. Then John called me and Nik into his office, sat me down in front of a portable TV, pressed play on his VCR and, to my astonishment, the image that appeared first was my face – opening the blue front door of my flat in my underpants – then the boorish hateful TV-stealing bastard bailiffs.

'Well this doesn't make sense,' I thought, trying frantically to reconfigure my understanding ontology. Then, looking at the smirking Northern faces of John and Nik, the pointless truth began to dawn. Not only had John employed these two actors to come round my house and wind me up, he had also hired three cameras, so he could capture my humiliation from a number of different angles. There was one concealed in the bailiff's woolly hat, one in their van, and one in the house opposite. He had done this for two reasons: first and foremost for a laugh. He does stuff for a laugh all the time. Nik is a sensitive man and I later learned he'd been against this vindictive, and unnecessarily expensive prank, which had employed, in addition to the actors, a producer, a researcher, a runner and several of my neighbours. And a distant second to remind me to control my finances.

I didn't take this lesson well, my surly response prompting, 'Fookin' hell Russell, where's your sense of humour? You're supposed to be a fookin' comedian.' I swore revenge. 'I'll get you John, I'll use my cunning and my talent and I'll avenge this affront.' John got onto his hindquarters like a bear would. 'I'll use all my resources and power to destroy you.' ''Ere you two, pack it in.' Nik, the voice of reason. I've yet to get revenge and, since then, John has tried to get that tape broadcast as part of every TV show I've done – 'Russell, you could put that on *Big Mouth*, it'd be fookin' hilarious.'

One of the reasons I've found it easy to forgive him for this is that I wouldn't have been doing that show without him. Because John Noel also looked after Davina McCall and Dermot O'Leary, he was quite powerful in the *Big Brother* set-up. When he found out they were planning a new debate show to accompany it – *Efourum*, it was called – he put me forward for it. The people making the programme knew of my work and my reputation, and were therefore cynical.

I had to go for an audition where they showed me a bit of footage from a previous *Big Brother* and I just had to say what I thought about it and muck about with researchers pretending to be guests or audience members. That went really well, but they were seeing lots of people for the job – I think the excellent brown-eyed chum of mine Simon Amstell was one of the final few – and before they would finally offer it to me, John had to sign a personal contract guaranteeing that I'd be no trouble.

John says he always has to convince people that I'm not mad. This is because I am. A bit. I was first diagnosed as depressive when I was still at Grays school, and our GP said I ought to take some kind of mood-stabilising drug. When I got arrested and cut myself in the course of that cannabis-farming episode, the police made me see a psychologist – as they always do when you're self-harming – and he said, 'Yeah, you've obviously got some form of mental illness.' Then I saw some kind of counsellor at drama school and he said I was manic depressive.

I've never had a sustained period of medication for mental illness when I've not been on other drugs as well. It's just not something that I particularly feel I need. I know that I have dramatically changing moods, and I know sometimes I feel really depressed, but I think that's just life. I don't think of it as, 'Ah, this is mental illness,' more as, 'Today, life makes me feel very sad.' I know I also get unnaturally high levels of energy and quickness of thought, but I'm able to utilise that.

I think that's one of the reasons I adore Tony Hancock so much – not just for his hubris and self-involvement – but because there's something so truthful about the melancholy of him. There's an episode of *Hancock's Half Hour* where he's talking to Sid James (who I also really love, but not in the same way – just as I've always favoured Peter Cook over lovely Dudley Moore, who was born at roughly the same time as my dad, and came from the same place. I suppose I must be more strongly drawn to the romantic Don Quixote archetype than the Sancho Panza realist), and Hancock says, 'Oh I might as well do myself in – I might as well just hang myself' – and, in the end, he did.

When he's talking about how depressed he is with that hangdog expression and those beautiful glassy eyes – 'Oh, stone me' – that is so English and so beautiful to me. I've always had the analogy that people who are depressed are often funny in the same way that England is a seafaring nation because we're an island; because you adapt to your circumstances, and if you're miserable you've got to become funny to fucking keep afloat.

I took Ritalin (the stuff they use to calm down hyperactive kids) for a while when I was still using other drugs, and that was awful. The analogy I generally employ for the way it slowed my mind down is that instead of the right word being readily to hand, I'd have to go up in the attic to look for it, but in fact it was more dramatic than that. What it was really like was severing the tendrils from the heavens that connect me to creativity. When I'm onstage or on TV, and everything's going well, I feel like there are these electric, celestial tentacles dangling from on high and I can swing on them, like Tarzan on his creepers. But Ritalin severed those tentacles – just lopped them off.

So when I'd finally got myself all clean and free of drugs of all kinds and I finally got that *Big Brother* job, it looked like a chance to prove myself. It was four shows a week for nearly three months, and it was quite a lot of exposure, not to mention money.

Nik and John filmed me when they told me the news; they'd created such a lovely nurturing environment for me – taking me on daft skiing and snowboarding holidays, even though I can't do either and bloody hate the cold. They had a camera set up to record the moment, because they thought I'd start whooping and yelping and leaping about. They were so proud and excited for me, and I just went, 'Oh, that's good.'

When I started doing that *Efourum*, I always thought I was going to say something mad on air. This anxiety was born of a long history of saying ridiculous things in public. Like that time at the Edinburgh Festival where I'd gone onstage and said odd things about child abuse, expressing complicated views about societal as opposed to individual responsibility: views which when I was on heroin I tended not to express very succinctly, so it came out all aggressive and ill-conceived.

Happily, the first series of *Efourum* was relatively uneventful, except for when Kitten came on, who was a supposedly radical lesbian anarchist character in the house. Kitten had been thrown out in the first week, and people had told me I needed to watch her. When she came on the show she was being all boisterous and sulky, but I really controlled her, and when she got in a bit of a strop and stood up and walked off the show, I just made a joke about it and carried on.

One thing that's been a great advantage to me in doing live TV is that after all those years when everything was so heightened and berserk, and I was always getting into fights and sticking Barbie dolls up my arse, there's not much that can go on in a studio that is really going to shock me. I have this feeling when I'm on TV that I'm resting. I'm not having to operate at maximum capacity, so if something mad happens, like someone being rude or walking off, then I actually quite like it.

I did get told off by the programme's makers on that occasion, though, and I had to apologise. Oddly, given what happens to a lot of housemates, they do have a sort of paternal attitude towards them. Phil Edgar-Jones, who's the overall boss of *Big Brother*, said, 'You've got to be a bit respectful because they've given so much to the programme.'

When I went to go and say sorry to Kitten, she was in her dressing room eating a McDonald's – even though she was meant to be an anarchist. I said, 'Look, I'm sorry about that, I didn't mean to upset you,' and she goes, 'Oh no, it's all cool.' Then there was a pause, which I felt duty bound to interrupt with the words, 'I see you're eating a McDonald's there,' and she goes, 'Yeah, they got that for me,' as if she had no choice.

There'd been a kind of fallow period for a while, but as work began to pick up, I started seeing different women again, quickly acquiring a harem of about ten, whom I would rotate in addition to one-night stands and random casual encounters. When I first came into the public eye, I wasn't quite as guarded as I ought to have been about these activities, but the things I've said have always been quite general. Once I started to feel a bit more confident, and realised there was now a great gaping hole in my life that wasn't filled by drugs and booze any more, my tendency to pursue women – which had always been quite rapacious – somehow became enhanced further. Because so much of my previous behaviour was now prohibited, I pursued the one thing that was still allowed especially relentlessly.

As I got better at stand-up, I started to have loads of encounters after gigs. As my sexual appetite grew, I found myself engaged in an increasingly desperate quest to satisfy it. I became so open to suggestion that when someone asked me if I'd like to go to an orgy, I didn't think twice before accepting this invitation.

The word 'orgy' is undeniably an evocative one. It conjures up sumptuous images of delicate muslin drapes being teased by a breeze, Turkish music playing everywhere (in fact my whole orgy scenario seems to have been lifted pretty much wholesale from a Turkish Delight advert), nubile Nubian women entwined about each other like a Henry Moore statue, people decadently devouring grapes. I thought there'd probably be a sort of Swiss bloke with no irises or pupils in his eyes as well, just kind of staring. But that ain't what I got in a tower block in Hackney.

The demolition of my fantasy was achieved in stages, but was ultimately no less complete than the more explosive end that seems to await so many of that hard-pressed borough's high-rise buildings.

When I arrived and got into the lift, there were already two blokes inside it, and I thought, 'Oh fuck, I hope they're not going to the same orgy I'm going to – I don't feel that comfortable in a lift with them, and would be positively alarmed at the prospect of a cuddle.' Fortunately they got off – and I'm talking about alighting – at an earlier floor.

So I continued my journey upwards physically, downwards spiritually, till eventually I was disgorged into this endless, long anonymous, Kubrickian corridor. It may well have been home to twin girls in floral frocks. And perhaps a little boy on a trike whistled by. Had there been a tidal wave of blood, I would have turned back.

Either way, I did not have the confidence to swagger into that orgy like a Viking narcissist – 'OK, meet the boys . . . let's orge.' My innate nervousness caused me to project more of a delicate Alan Bennett sensibility (at this point, readers are advised to call upon their very best Alan Bennett internal monologue): 'Oh I don't think you should be going in there, Russell, look at the curtains.'

So I'm standing at this door, kind of half knocking and half not-knocking – my own recalcitrant hand unwilling to do my bidding, like a disgruntled Rod Hull tribute act. Eventually I take the plunge, and wait in silence – or what was that? Did I hear squelching?

At last, the door was opened by this . . . well, woman I s'pose you'd call her. She filled the frame of the door, and I had to crane round her to check the orgy didn't consist of only her. 'Well, dear, there will be oral in the crook of me arm, watersports in the nape of me neck, and you don't want to know what's going on round the back.'

She told me that her name was Coral [I would imagine to evoke the exoticism and beauty of a coral reef, as opposed to the sheer fucking scale of one]. 'Do you wanna come in, love?' she asked in a friendly voice, and I stepped inside. As soon as I was over the threshold, I landed in this world of livid, lurid sexual conjunctions. It weren't like them nubile, Nubian Henry Moore women I'd imagined earlier. People who looked like they were made out of Ready Brek, swathed in Clingfilm, were waddling back and forth with towels about their waists.

The thing is, I went to that orgy to escape from humanity and mundanity, but you can't escape humanity if you're human – it's everywhere. And mundanity's just the same. So all that filth was going on in the foreground, but out of the window I could see a motorway flyover, and trundling over it was a Sunblest bread-van, making deliveries.

There was too much pathos at that orgy. I don't want pathos at an orgy – I get enough of that at home. And this was like an orgy directed by Mike Leigh. Everywhere there was this intangible sadness. I remember this woman came bustling out of a doorway when I first got there – she reminded me of my mum, which didn't help – and said, 'Just done my second . . . better go and rinse my mouth out,' a visible halo of sperm around her face.

Another thing which happened at that orgy that shouldn't is a washing-machine repair man turned up – not as a guest, but to repair the washing-machine. That's bad scheduling, isn't it? 'Are you busy between nine and twelve on Wednesday?' 'No, not really, well . . . I was planning to have an orgy.' People were being ushered into doorways, and I have an uncomfortable memory of some bloke brushing against my thigh.

Apart from anything else, I don't like the idea of being at an orgy where the washing-machine ain't working. It seems a bit grimy. Most of the people there had a kind of guilty air about them – features dripping down their faces like candle wax, as they dragged their shame behind them like Jacob Marley's chains. There was one bloke, though, who really seemed quite cheerful, and because he didn't appear to have any pangs of conscience about the whole thing, it kind of made what he was doing seem more palatable. He was behaving as if he was at a Pontin's table-tennis rally. In the hour and a half I was there (which was the minimum amount of time to do the necessary research) he fucked every woman there. And he did it in such a lovely way that there were times when I could have given him a high five.

For those of a slightly more bashful temperament, there was the odd awkward moment. I did find myself at something of a loose end at one stage, and I'd like to offer that you don't truly know loneliness until you've spent ten minutes in not-so-glorious isolation at an orgy – that's when you'll really start to feel the pinch of solitude. But I think the most tragic of the thousand tiny tragedies that occurred at that orgy was this one:

Here and there about the room, someone – the woman who opened the door, I presume – had placed little bowls of nibbles. That just made me feel sad inside. They were on paper plates. Not standard white ones, but the colourful kind with pictures of balloons and streamers on that I should imagine might be marketed as 'Party Plates'. I couldn't help imagine the woman at Woolworth's earlier that day thinking, 'I could get the plain white plates. I know the Party Plates are 45p dearer . . . but little touches like that can really make or break an orgy.'

The particular plate I remember was adorned with a forlorn selection of Minstrels. Apparently 'they melt in your mouth, not in your hand', but I did not want to test that theory on this occasion.

I did not enjoy that orgy, and I shan't be going again, but at least it temporarily satisfied my spiralling appetite for distraction, which was evidently getting a bit out of control.

It was to rescue me from these kinds of grisly scenarios that John Noel sent me to KeyStone. The Chinese have a phrase, 'regulation of the affairs of the bedroom': this means, 'Watch it with the winky water', which was mooted as an alternative title to this book for a while, by me; suddenly the publishers finally began to look favourably on 'My Booky Wook'. While I was at Focus, counsellors had concerns about the 'hows yer father'; the phrase that got bandied around was 'blindingly obvious cross-addiction'. Knowing that Focus 12 had been fundamental in my recovery from substance abuse, John sought the advice of Chip. 'He needs to go into a specialist treatment centre,' said Chip, 'but, the important thing is, he's got to want to go.' I interjected: 'I'm not going into a sex addiction centre . . .'

Can you guess what John said? ☞

32

And Then Three Come at Once

Here is an excerpt from one of a series of letters I was asked to
write at KeyStone:

Russell,

You have fucked up every professional opportunity you have
ever been given. Now that you've been given yet another last
chance and are finally free from drugs and alcohol, you have
already begun to tarnish your reputation at *Big Brother*. All the
things you profess to want – the absent dreams that constantly
stoke your inadequacy – could already be yours, but for your
slavish dedication to addiction . . .

Do you see how you are beginning to destroy once again the
reputation that you and John have worked so hard to
resurrect? . . . He forced you to go to KeyStone because he
knows you are an inveterate self-saboteur, and that without
serious help and work on your part, you could once again be
unemployable . . .

I was a bit browned off about being sent to KeyStone, not only
because I knew it would mean no diddling, not even by my own
porcelain hand, but also because of the unanticipated high
number of paedophiles there. I don't like to be judgmental; after

the life I've lived and the tolerance I've been shown it would be unfair. It just seems to me that my problem, really fancying adult, human females, is distinct from the difficulties facing a paedophile. As is outlined in the first chapter of this booky wook, once I realised that I was expected to live the next month of my life sharing a room with a chap who'd run off with his thirteen-year-old foster daughter, I was on the old blower pretty pronto. 'I'm living with paedophiles,' I told anyone who'd listen. In this case that was John Noel's answerphone and Chip Somer's earhole, and I didn't get much change out of either.

'Come on,' I reasoned, 'I know I've been a bit excessive with the threesomes and the orgies, and by Jove, I'm prepared to change, but can I come home now please? I look unusually young for my years and I don't want any R. White's secret lemonade drinker-style creaky floorboards as I lie quivering in my wretched institutional bed.'

But Chip said I should stay. So I stayed. And I'm glad I did, because if the purpose of the trip was to give me a new-found compassion for people with a terrible illness, it succeeded, and if it was to furnish me with some jaw-dropping anecdotes, it was also a triumph. Additionally it made me think 'enough's enough' on the old obscurity front, and the moment I was released from perv prison I focused on becoming successful and it took hardly any time at all. Here are some of the funnier diary entries from my month in that Philadelphian treatment centre for sexual addiction:

31/03/05
So here I am in this hospice for perverts . . .

The 'naked woman', whose presence in my copy of the *Guardian* necessitated its confiscation, is actually made of marble. My sexual addiction hasn't yet involved the molestation of sculptures. I don't – on seeing the Venus de Milo – think 'Phwooar! I wouldn't mind a go in her armpit.'

Why am I always being sent to these places? I just want to make people laugh

01/04/05
The joke's on me – I'm in a sex addict's hospital. April Fool.

Initially what I'm finding difficult is the culture of aphorisms, platitudes and – beyond that I suppose – the whole American celebratory/therapeutic culture. I suppose all therapy is American in a way – it was here, after all, that Freud became all-encompassing . . . I just feel so English amidst all this homespun backslapping and animal-impersonating (they actually miaow like cats on hearing the word 'love')

02/04/05
Old Popeychops is dead . . . wonder if the *Sun*'ll do a pun?

Freaked out and threatened to leave. Changed my flight to tomorrow night, then had a few pleasant chats and a game of Boggle and felt better. Boggle with sex addicts is up there with go-kart racing with junkies. Words included 'orgy', 'tits', 'rape', 'teat' and 'teen'.

Spoke to Sarah – she was fabulous. I love her. She was strong and said I should try

03/04/05
Still here. Intense day. Went to Philadelphia art museum where the potency of my sexual appetite came crashing back into my life

04/04/05
A few funny things . . .

At an SLA (sex and love addicts) meeting last night one bloke candidly spoke about how he can now masturbate healthily and safely – 'I'm practising healthy self-touch and masturbation' like it had some spiritual value, like his wanking was an ode to God or some charming natural phenomenon like birds nesting or squirrels hiding nuts. He was all earnest and American I thought – it don't matter if there was a joss stick burning and Enya playing, you were still just laying on your back having a wank like a filthy Bonobo. A Bonobo in a smoking jacket grinning and strumming his cock is not evidence of spiritual evolution.

Someone in my group, Lee, mid-forties Californicator who speaks fluent new age but is quite cool, was proselytising and I said, 'Lee, you have the soul of a poet.' He said, 'I am a poet – I've written over a hundred poems,' which, I think, is about the least poetic thing I've ever heard.

I miss Sarah and feel jealous and resentful of her continuing life. I imagine her to by now have adjusted to my absence and be frolicking in springtime ecstasy with a series of dashing suitors.

I have practised yoga for the few days I've been here and watched the clock with the hollow fervour that only the incarcerated know.

The KeyStone building is a grey stone house surrounded by crossroads and traffic lights, perpetually amber. They never say 'Go'. I am in Chester near Philadelphia. The sister institution for junkies and drunks is across the street, many of its graduates on discovering that they're colossal perverts make the short trip to the E.C.U. (extended care unit), heads rattling with jargon. There is an interesting cross-section of deviants here. My roommate Arthur who molested his foster daughter now spends his time groping for words in puzzle books or Boggle, which he plays with Peter – a well groomed, silver bearded Christopher Lee figure smiling, clean toothed and chummy. Peter had sex with his wife's sister when she was twelve. They are both nice blokes.

I hope I can continue to journal long enough to inform you of the menagerie in its entirety. But you know me . . .

The chief problems I confront are integrating and missing Sarah. I've not had an orgasm since early on the morning of the 31st. Sarah and I had a lovely meal at Ravel's unpretentious bistro, down the road in Hampstead, dear sweet beautiful Hampstead. I'm not nearly as unpretentious as Ravel's where I've twice seen Michael Palin and his wife.

We ate well, Sarah and I, in an alcove – which is now our table, and I must strike from my memory the previous meals I've eaten there with previous 'victims', as Philip Salon calls them. Sarah is the first girl I've given the best seat – back against the wall – I usually sit there.

We then quarrelled because I made some joke during one of her anecdotes from adolescence, which in her case is not particularly distant. She is, after all, nineteen.

She sulkily picked spots in the bathroom. I lost my temper; feeling unable to contact her I smashed a glass, and to demonstrate the depth of my angst I gestured self-destructively to my wrists. There was some screaming and hollering, blood coagulated on the toilet seat – she went all Florence Nightingale. We cleared up together.

The cut was a minor one on the fourth finger of my right hand which impacts the way I write and reopens each time Lee sincerely shakes my hand.

It's difficult to maintain dignity when you're travelling in a group of more than eight people, especially in a van. You feel like a spastic . . .

05/04/05
Met Dr Kauffman yesterday who, from behind his spectacles, laptop and moustache, told me I have bipolar disorder – manic

depression – and recommended I take Abilofiar, some mood-stabilising drug.

Tomorrow I am the 'bus driver'. That means the group leader. It isn't an honour I've earned, it is issued on a rotational basis, and means I will be responsible not only for giving fifteen-, ten-, five-, and one-minute warnings before each group leaves, but also for making sure there's a good 'miaowing' atmosphere.

Tonight's trip to the shops was good fun. People are starting to show an interest in my comedy and stuff. I've made people laugh, and they keep saying 'that'll be good material'. In our 'Goodnight Share' last night I said, 'I feel better now I've been integrated and accepted, although I am being accepted by a bunch of perverts – is that the only place I'll fit in?' . . .

Miss Sarah and have been informed that the postie is an irresponsible drunkard who should be a resident at KeyStone, not collecting letters and dropping off parcels – but in fact Al (always on about being raped as a kid, looks like a hybrid of Colin Farrell's 'Bullseye' character in *Daredevil* and Bill Sykes's dog in *Oliver Twist*) said he never received any of his expected mail containing cash and that he'd seen the postie swigging booze on his bike: 'why do you think he's always chewing gum?' Al asked.

Al is a bit nuts. However I saw the postie with my own eyes and placed Sarah's letter adorned with a plethora of Yank-Stamps, which I got off Paul H (a gynaecologist who had an affair with a patient – inevitable). He did look a bit indifferent and all too hasty . . .

N.B. Not keen on taking the old Persian rugs, although happy to get further confirmation of the glamorous bipolar disorder

06/04/05

This 'bus driver' lark's going alright – mostly it entails bellowing up the stairs and a bit of mucking about and rabble rousing . . .

Today it is bright and sunny – I hung my washing on a tree in the grounds and climbed it

Alice Phenis and Deborah Kuntz join the list of improbably named staff, alongside baby-faced doctor Travis Flowers. This rubbish writes itself

07/04/05

The day ended with a 'Good Evening' group in which the group wanted to install me as permanent bus driver and chanted 'Four More Years!' This led to me getting a bit overexcited and showing off too much in the final group session

08/04/05

We did a shame confession exercise where people admitted shameful acts from their past – cue tales of child molestation, public wanking and group sodomy from anxious catamites. This has made my mind feel heavy, and the air is a thick noxious treacle that clogs and burns my weary lungs. I yearn for some clean, bright expanse – a Shangri-La in which to sit, away from all this

Obviously, I have developed an intoxicating crush on my female counsellor, Erika. She's twenty-six and has quite big tits (36DD/E). I spend our sessions doing nought but posturing. Starved of female company as I am, she is – to me – a glacier of unattainable beauty

Watched *Malcolm X* – great story but overlong and indulgent film-making

09/04/05

I dedicated a song to each member of the group and we listened to them in the grounds. It was very sweet

Eventful day including Paul H (gynaecologist who fucked patient) punching out his aggression on a punch-bag in the gym downstairs

Just watched *Invasion of the Bodysnatchers* – tosh

Tomorrow morning I awake at seven to call Sarah – my phone embargo is at an end – I already feel like I'm picking a fight . . .

10/04/05

Spoke to her – she's really missed me and was all teary and emotional. It made me feel secure. I know time will continue to pass and that I'll soon be with her

11/04/05

I suppose it's an indication of my further integration that my diary entries are growing shorter and less frequent. John called yesterday – got straight into badgering him about my career . . . Apparently things look good with *Efourum* . . . was tortured by mad hard-on all night – the puppet of my own desire. I fought not to wank. I feel like I'm at war with biology, battling millions of years of evolution

14/04/05

A few crazy days of contact with London – quarrelling with John about going on holiday – the dates clashed with work. Sarah spoke to him, this made me adore her

I'm now in the grounds watching frolicking squirrels who seemingly have no idea that they are at a centre for sexual addiction. They come only for the vim of spring

In the spazz bus the whole group sang 'The Star-Spangled Banner' – fifteen perverts in unison. They all knew it. American sex crooks are still patriots

We went to an NA meeting. I enjoyed being among proper junkies

16/04/05

Over halfway now. Did an exercise where we had to write letters to our parents as if we were children. We used our non-dominant hands and childish language. I struggle with the mawkish implications and tenor of these practices, but they are evocative

18/04/05

Had to write a victims' list – a litany of the women I've wronged as a result of my sexual addiction. I feel like Saddam Hussein trying to pick out individual Kurds . . .

12.20 p.m.

Bill has just been thrown out. Apparently he was flirting with the (hideous, old) cleaner and groped her arse. So he's gone . . .

There was very little spirit of mutual consolation among the men afterwards – seems it's every perv for himself

I leave in eleven days. I want to try and remember funny stuff like – Lee saying 'I lived a double life for ten years – I think I can manage a game of Balderdash'

That bloke Phil's healthy wanking story

Fitting in – with a flock of perverts

Transforming lust energy into healthy 'walk in the park' energy

19/04/05

Big cultural shift in the group after Bill's well-deserved banishment. The scriptural prophesy, 'The meek shall inherit the earth', came to a limited fruition when the ever-increasing contingent of squares wanted a change to end spontaneity and fun . . .

The conflict centres around the bizarre repertoire of slogans, yelps and squeals that make up our morning and evening groups. Despite my initial disdain for this culture of mawkish clichés and primitive bonding rituals, I came to identify with it as necessary and even charming. But the changing balance of power in our deviant menagerie now decrees an end to such practices

There have been a series of notable departures. They were replaced by Greg, an octogenarian, leather-faced, hang-dog, disgraced gunslinger-looking bloke from New Mexico. He is a psychologist long and aloof, held tall by a scaffold of pomposity bent by his years and trade. Carlos an immigrant from the Dominican Republic, brown with lazy, heavy-lidded eyes that for the first week streamed with constant salty rivers of regret. Typical of the new arrivals is Eric, a gap-toothed, gargoyle-faced Tweedledum, addicted to naught but rules. He is either a big midget or a tiny big-headed regular person. In groups he announces, 'I'm an alcoholic sex addict drug addict codependent compulsive overeater.' I doubt he's smoked more than an eighth of grass in his entire life

20/04/05
Set the alarm because I am bus driver today. Awoken at 7 a.m. by Robert Palmer's 'Addicted to Love'

21/04/05
Jacob, whom I liken to a well-intentioned, freckled *Thunder Bird* puppet – has just informed me of his recommendation that I stay another week. Ha, Ha, Ha. I imagine him in a silver space suit. Home spun 'aw shucks!' earnest kind nods and platitudes before groovin off in his H.P. metallic gleam mobile.

The church opposite chimes out its prerecorded religious melodies seemingly on a whim. Currently it's belting out 'Ave Maria' like there's no tomorrow. But of course there is a tomorrow, and I shall be spending it here whilst spring explodes around me, the trees drool voluptuous blooming squirrels, and this pair of red-breasted starlings eye each other up like strangers in the night exchanging glances. Amidst this fecundity I reside, sedentary, glum, and taut with raging celibacy.

John just informed me that *Efourum* – now renamed *Big Brother's Big Mouth* – will be screened on Channel 4. What do you want from me? Use me for your ends, or for pity's sake let me know the snug embrace of the grave

23/04/05

What a day the 22nd was. I've noticed the Americans are inherently consumers. They always want to pop pills for mental or physical ailments. I hurt my wrist yesterday, 'have an Ibuprofen', and, later when I hurt it again, 'take some more stabilisers.'

I took one of Arthur's completed crosswords out of the bin today. It was gibberish

Ah, a lovely stroll down memory pain . . .

After KeyStone I did continue to have sex with adult human females, but I made sure it didn't interfere with my work. This is the point that my life changed, the point that you may have become aware of me. *Efourum* became *Big Brother's Big Mouth*, a change suggested by Mark Lucey who, when he began to work on the show along with Iain 'Coyley' Coyle, transformed it from a parasite show into an independent piece of comic television of which I am proud. Coyley, a big slab of humanity with a Teddy boy-looking bonce, thought of the 'wand' microphone, and the inclusion of the viewers' recorded messages; also he did the voice of 'Little Paul Scholes' and hid inside the whale costume and horse's head to inhabit 'Rosebud', to provide characters and items that were, as far as I can work out, fuck all to do with *Big Brother*. Mark Lucey, a twinkle-eyed, soulful, QPR fan, was forever saying things like, 'Nice to be working on a *Big Brother* spin-off show . . .

if anything,' and ''Citing,' which formed part of the lexicon of the show. More importantly, the two of them – as well as being excellent producers – are comedy aficionados and approached making that lovely little TV show as if there were no consideration other than having a laugh.

We used to watch footage from the main *Big Brother* show in hysterics, particularly the racism, THAT WAS A JOKE; but in fact it illustrates rather well the mentality we had: it was, how far can we push this show and it still fulfil its remit to the channel. 'Ballbags', 'Pulled down my trousers and pants', and 'the swine!' Juvenile, silly catchphrases, all born of us lot just larking about. We also used to fuse those daft outbursts with irrelevant, esoteric references to art and literature. It made the show funnier and more popular than it had any right to be.

More people started to come and see me do stand-up, a craft that I had been practising for eight years, with material that had been written over a lifetime. I became employable, 6 Music gave me a little show that I did with Matt and Trevor Lock, the *NME* asked me to host their awards. Opportunities began to arise and I was prepared. More importantly, I was surrounded by people who love me, who made it their business not to let me self-destruct. The most rewarding aspect of writing this book has been to record the kindnesses I have been shown by all the wonderful people I've been privileged enough to know. John, Nik, Matt, Karl, Gee, John Rogers, Martino, Chip – all these strong, intelligent men. And women: girlfriends that have saved me from poverty and insanity, absorbing my madness, demands and indiscretions, and Sharon, my stylist, who I adore and who is like a sister to me. Hers is the only female friendship I've maintained. Since I was first at MTV, I've been stuck with her – she comes from an estate in South London, but really likes horses, where'd she get that habit? and speaks as fast as I do, faster sometimes. Lynne, who looks after my house and makes me and the cat eat food and ignores my indiscretions as resolutely as I imagine she did Steve Coogan's, who she looked after before me.

And Nicola, who does my make-up. Who reminds me a little bit of my beloved nan, the way she rolls her eyes at me with weary acceptance and affection. At the times when I've been bilious with self-pity and self-loathing, I've thought 'look at these people that love you,' all these amazing people. I can't be that bad. I'll write another book one day about how it feels to become famous – it's beserk, amazing; but to the people who know me I've been famous for ages. Nothing really changes, now I'm just a rich poor person.

There's loads more I could harp on about, famous people who've helped me and said stuff that'll look funny written down: Jonathan Ross, Noel Gallagher, Courtney Love – but all that rhubarb you kind of know. The Brits, Radio 2, *Ponderland*, tours and now a couple of films, I'll tell you all about it next time. I have done some terrible things over the course of this booky wook – not while writing it, I've been the model of restraint – no, I mean over my life. In the Twelve Steps you're taught to make amends rather than just apologising but, by way of mitigation, I felt a tremendous compulsion to express myself, not in a smutty fashion, artistically. From the first school performance in Grays, I've been in pursuit of a destiny that always felt beyond my reach.

The most insightful thing I ever heard, was overheard. I was waiting for a rail replacement bus service in Hackney Wick. These two old women weren't even talking to me – not because I'd offended them, I hadn't, I'd been angelic at that bus stop, except for the eavesdropping. Rail replacement buses take an eternity, because they think they're doing you a favour by covering for the absent train, you've no recourse. Eventually, the bus appeared on the distant horizon, and one of the women, with the relief and disbelief that often accompanies the arrival of public transport said, 'Oh look, the bus is coming.' The other woman – a wise woman, seemingly aware that her words and attitude were potent and poetic enough to form the final sentence in a stranger's book – paused, then said, 'The bus was always coming.' ☞

Acknowledgements

Suzi Aplin
Gareth Roy
Jack Bayles
Nick Davies
Paul McKenna
Nik Linnen
Lynne Penrose
Lesley Douglas
John Noel
Nic Philps
Ron Brand
Matt Morgan
John Rogers
Chip Somers
Tony/Sam and all at Focus 12
Jackie
Joe Star-twin
Malcolm Hay
Tony Arthur Hay
Ben Miller
Dr Abood
Dr Gormley

Sam Crooks
Moira Bellas
Barbara Charone
Mark Stone RIP
The Macleans
Dennis Noonan
Ian Coburn
Alfie Hitchcock
Brian Cox
All my secret fellows
Kevin Lygo
Meredith Church
David Marshall
Christopher Fettes
Yat Malgren RIP
Reuven Adiv RIP
Mark Lucey
Iain Coyle
Andrew Newman
Andrew Antonio
Lindsey Hughes
Heidi La Paine
Janet and Jimmy
Joan and Rex
Leela Miller
Jamie Hodder-Williams
Daisy Poppets
Ben Dunn
Mr Gee

Photographic Acknowledgements

Plate sections, pages 1-16.

All photographs are courtesy of the author with the exception of 16 above: Mirrorpix; 16 below: Rex Features.

Every reasonable effort has been made to contact the copyright holders, but if there are any errors or omissions, Hodder & Stoughton will be pleased to insert the appropriate acknowledgement in any subsequent printing of this publication.